> *Let us not forget that the cultivation of the earth is the most important labor of man. When tillage begins, other arts will follow. Farmers, therefore, are the founders of civilization.*
>
> —Daniel Webster

Cover Illustration by Alyssa Kosmer

Book designed and typeset by
Pogostick Studios in Troy, NY.
www.pogostickstudios.com

Savor New York acknowledges The National Baseball Hall of Fame and Museum,
Otsego 2000, and CADE for permission to use graphics under their control.

Printed and bound in Canada by Webcom, Inc.

ISBN: 0-9796802-0-4
ISBN-13: 978-0-9796802-0-5

Editorial Sales Rights and Permission Inquiries should be addressed to:
Savor New York
Rights & Permissions
6 Westridge Road
Cooperstown, NY 13326

Substaintial discounts on bulk quantities are available to corporations, professional
associations, and other organizations. If you are in the USA or Canada, contact:
Savor New York
Sales Department
6 Westridge Road
Cooperstown, NY 13326
Phone or fax: 607-547-1870
E-mail: sales@savorny.org
www.savorny.org

10 9 8 7 6 5 4 3 2 1

# HOME PLATE
## *The Culinary Road Trip of*
# COOPERSTOWN

## *Brenda Berstler*

*A dear friend, Dominic Visconsi,*
*once taught me that to adore someone*
*was more powerful than merely to love them,*
*because adoration encompasses not only*
*love, but also admiration and respect.*

*To my daughter, Elizabeth,*
*whom I adore utterly.*

## The Mission of Savor New York

Savor New York books and products celebrate New York's distinct regions, promoting family farming and local products, determined small businesses and outstanding visitor attractions. Savor New York illuminates the remarkable people and unparalleled spirit that makes New York State extraordinary.

***Savor New York invites you to Savor Cooperstown.***

*Home Plate: The Culinary Road Trip of Cooperstown*
is an illuminating handbook of the Cooperstown vicinity,
offering three-dimensional insights to restaurants, accommodations,
attractions, baseball celebrities, local farmers and food purveyors.
All are paired with a favorite recipe using New York ingredients,
often reflecting the contributor's personality. With great recipes,
generous dashes of food lore, enjoyable anecdotes, and a sprinkling
of humor throughout, *Home Plate* is designed to satisfy the traveler's
and newcomer's appetite and curiosity. Get to know the character
of Cooperstown and the Leatherstocking Region,
from baseball to beekeepers and the arts to artisan breads;
from music to maple syrup and opera to orchards.

# Acknowledgements

While there is only one name on the cover, *Home Plate: The Culinary Road Trip of Cooperstown* was born of a considerable collective effort. Good intentions, great ideas, and even individual talent are hardly enough to make the journey from a single blank page to a professional book. The words usually attributed to those behind the pages, such as support, encouragement and back-up, barely begin to cover the contributions of the following people. I frequently quote Mark Twain, "The difference between the right word and nearly the right word is the difference between lightning and lightning bug." In this case, "Thank you" is only a lightning bug of my gratitude:

The Savor New York Team: Marketing director Melissa Manikas (M1,) whose industry is inspiring and perpetual optimism is priceless. Book designer Melissa Batalin (M2) of Pogostick Studios; Major League Baseball itself couldn't have provided a better relief pitcher. Public Relations specialist Elise Schiellack, whose constantly even temperament I view with equal parts admiration and bafflement. Alyssa Kosmer, for once again gracing *Home Plate* with her artistic gifts, and for her persistence in making sure we used them. Photographer Richard Duncan for sharing the products of his keen eye and perceptive soul. Graphic designer Sara Terrano, whose discerning pen strokes capture Savor New York's personality. Attorney and business counsel Jim Konstanty, for going another round with us, doing the heavy lifting and pitching in with on-target editorial advice.

"Breakfasts with Bud" Ballard, for his reminiscences of more than eight decades in Cooperstown.

The National Baseball Hall of Fame and Museum. To Pat Kelly, of their photo archives department, for her efficiency, good humor and wise choices, and to Tim Wiles, the Hall's Director of Research and his baseball-brilliant crew, for answering the most obscure questions.

Marcella Steinman, for still listening to me with a mother's rapt attention.

My husband, John, and my daughter, Elizabeth: for myriad errands, bits of research, invaluable suggestions, calming rationality, cups of coffee and glasses of wine. Your patience is boundless, as is my appreciation of it. You are what love means to me.

—Brenda Berstler

# Table of Contents

# Points of Interest Alphabetically

# Recipes Alphabetically by Category

# Introduction

Savor New York invites you to Savor Cooperstown. Explore and discover this influential village, and the rolling green splendor that surrounds it, with the unhurried appreciation that the word "savor" denotes. Enjoy your stay, love New York, make wonderful memories, but above all savor the rich experience that is Cooperstown.

Savor New York was established to celebrate the resolute spirit of Upstate New York's unique regions. In the first of a series of *Culinary Road Trip* books, we showcase the character and industry of the farmers, the entrepreneurs, the artists, and the stewards of culture who make the Cooperstown area extraordinary.

The Savor New York team carefully evaluated and selected those profiled on these pages. They are chosen using several criteria, including: standards of excellence, diversity, historical significance, and community contributions. We have included a representative variety from this region. Selections are the subjective opinion of Savor New York. No remunerations are exchanged for inclusion in any Savor New York book.

Eating is to dining, as touring is to experiencing, and the difference between them is a matter of approach. You can plow through whatever is put in front of you in a matter of minutes – and forget it just as quickly – or you can enjoy every taste, texture and aroma that creates a lifelong memory.

Savor New York invites you to revel in every leisurely, considered bite of Cooperstown.

# *The Main Course*

## Cooperstown and Vicinity
### Including Fly Creek, Springfield Center, Route 28

# Cooperstown and Vicinity
## An Introduction

They have a little baseball in Cooperstown, did ya know that? Undoubtedly, you do. Practically *everybody* knows that. Cooperstown and The National Baseball Hall of Fame are completely, beneficently entwined, with one term freely exchanged for the other. Since "The Hall" was established in 1939, Cooperstown has become a metonym for baseball. In linguistics, a "metonym" is a single word that identifies a more complex entity. For millions, the three syllables of "Cooperstown" represent the legacy, the passion and dreams, and the decades of heartfelt pride that is baseball.

Cooperstown is like one of those people who has it all – looks, talent, resources and infinite charm. Most villages would count themselves fortunate with only one of the jewels that gleam in Cooperstown's mesmerizing crown. Not only does the heart of baseball thrive in William Cooper's town, but also the Bassett Healthcare complex, here and throughout this region; the world-respected Glimmerglass Opera, the New York State Historical Association, Fenimore Art Museum, The Farmers' Museum, and Otsego Lake – James Fenimore Cooper's "Glimmerglass" – are all enticing reasons to visit and, for many, compelling reasons to stay.

The Village of Cooperstown is just a bit more than a mile square, so in practical terms the Cooperstown area generally refers to adjacent villages as well. Springfield Center is at the north end of Otsego Lake and next door to the Glimmerglass Opera, Glimmerglass State Park and Hyde Hall. Just three miles north of Cooperstown on Route 28/80 is Fly Creek, the hamlet originally named by Dutch settlers for its marshy or "vlie" area, and the home of writer Jim Atwell. Route 28 South is the much-traveled road between Cooperstown and Oneonta, and the location of many *Home Plate* entries.

Welcome to this haven of natural beauty, literature, music, history, and America's Game.
Welcome to Cooperstown.

# Bassett Healthcare

By far one of the finest assets of the Cooperstown area is the state-of-the-art health facility that is Bassett Healthcare. From their main campus in Cooperstown and satellite facilities in towns and villages throughout the region, Bassett serves the health needs of their rural patients with metropolitan expertise, including their Heart Care Institute, Regional Cancer Program and Women's and Children's Services.

Founded in 1922, Bassett Healthcare is named in honor of Dr. Mary Imogene Bassett, a compassionate and skillful physician who devoted herself to the sick and underprivileged people of Cooperstown and the surrounding area. Since then, Bassett has made major contributions in the field of medicine, primarily by establishing new methods of providing high quality, affordable healthcare to rural populations.

Bassett continues to invest in and expand its services and programs, and remains dedicated to its threefold mission of excellence in patient care, medical education, and medical research. Affiliated with Columbia University, Bassett provides a unique environment to educate new physicians – creating sophisticated "big city" healthcare in a rural setting.

One Atwell Road
Cooperstown, NY 13326
1-800-BASSETT
1-607-547-3456
bassett.org

# Vegetable Pasta Salad
## Bassett Healthcare

Get out the cutting board and sharpen your chef's knife. This colorful, fresh, and flavorful salad is perfect after a trek to the farmers' market. An easy and versatile side dish, or main course with some added protein, you can eat this salad all summer long. It's heart healthy, of course.

1 cup cooked orzo pasta
1 cup lightly steamed asparagus, cut small
½ cup chopped carrots
½ cup sliced green onions
½ cup chopped yellow summer squash
1 cup chopped fresh spinach
1 cup small cherry tomatoes
¼ cup low-fat vinaigrette dressing
2 tablespoons grated Parmesan cheese
¼ teaspoon salt

Combine all ingredients in a large bowl. Toss to coat pasta and vegetables evenly with the dressing and cheese. Serve with grilled chicken or fish at a barbecue or picnic.

*Thin asparagus spears aren't necessarily more tender than thick ones. Size is just an indicator of gender; female spears are plumper than male ones. In general, steam the skinny spears, and grill or sauté the fat ones.*

# Bear Pond Winery

**N**ew York State produces *a lot* of grapes. Its burgeoning wine industry is third nationally and centers of viniculture are found statewide, from the Niagara Region to the eastern end of Long Island. Bear Pond Winery is the heart of New York's fine winemaking traditions in the Cooperstown area.

Named after the Bear Pond where the original vines were grown, Bear Pond Winery is handily located on Route 28 on Goodyear Lake, between Cooperstown and Oneonta. Their diverse selections incorporate their own grapes, as well as varietals from small vineyards throughout the state.

Take a stroll through the Bear Pond gift shop, tasting as you browse. Find wine accessories, glassware, food, and, interestingly, remarkable bird kites. So remarkable, in fact, that their Dove Kites flew at the 2007 Super Bowl.

Bear Pond's home wine parties create an unforgettable gathering! Their ingenious service invites you to get together with friends and learn about terrific New York vintages. Tasting is just part of the pleasure of these personal events. You'll learn about wine heritage, grape growing and food pairing, and take home great bottles to remember the night.

Mark and Brenda Lebo
Michael Bordinger
2515 State Highway 28
Oneonta, NY 13820
607-643-0294
bearpondwines.com

> *"Wine makes daily living easier, less hurried, with fewer tensions and more tolerance."*
> –Benjamin Franklin

# Oak Bear Chardonnay Salmon Salad
## Bear Pond Winery

This flavorful dinner salad is perfect during summer, when farmers' markets spill over with fresh produce and cooking is taken outdoors. Get a couple of bottles of Oak Bear Chardonnay – one for preparation and one to enjoy with dinner and friends.

### Grilled Salmon
Salmon filet (with or without skin)
1 bag Chardonnay Oak Chips
1 bottle Oak Bear Chardonnay
Olive oil, salt and pepper

### Salad Components
Salad greens of your choice, i.e. baby spinach, arugula, endive, etc.

Feta cheese crumbles

Sweet red onion, thinly sliced

Black olives

Tomatoes, cut into wedges

Anchovies (optional)

Sunflower seeds

Fresh green beans

*Dressing* – Your choice of favorites, such as poppy seed, sweet onion or ginger mushroom. Drew's Sesame Orange (Cooperstown Natural Foods) is very good.

Early in the morning or the evening before, place oak chips and enough Chardonnay to cover them in a zippered plastic bag. Shake and turn occasionally to soak all chips.

Heat grill to medium high. Wash salmon and pat dry. Drizzle with olive oil and sprinkle with salt and pepper. Place the wine-soaked chips evenly on the grill. Place the salmon, skin side down, on top of the chips. Close lid and grill salmon 10 minutes for each inch of thickness, until center reaches 135 degrees. While salmon cooks, steam or blanch green beans until just cooked and colorful.

To serve, fill plates with salad greens and components, top with green beans and finish with salmon and dressing. Pour glasses of Oak Bear Chardonnay and enjoy!

*Recipe courtesy of Michael Bordinger*

# BlueStone Farms

Delicious granola from their original recipe, organic vegetables, blueberry-scented candles, baked goods, and gift bags full of treasures are all part of the BlueStone Farm repertoire.

Find BlueStone Farm's friendly proprietor, Marty Bernardo (or his sister, Jodie) every Saturday of the season at the Cooperstown Farmers' Market. Sample their fabulous granola, or one of Charlie's Famous Granola Cookies (Marty's brother-in-law). Fresh, natural vegetables fill the table, changing depending on the season. Take home a beautiful gift bag overflowing with tempting goodies – it makes a perfectly delicious present for any occasion.

The family-run BlueStone Farm embodies the importance of local, natural farming. They invest lots of time and care in their products, instead of taking chemicals or using additives. As a result they produce a better crop and protect the quality of their soil and water. BlueStone Farm represents New York agriculture at its best.

Be sure to find more Granola recipes on the BlueStone Farm Web site. Add their marvelous concoction of whole grains, seeds, local Johnson's Honey, and dried fruit to enliven muffins, cookies, pancakes, even pie crust!

Find BlueStone Farm Granola and fine products online and locally at Cooperstown General Store, Cooperstown Natural Foods, Fly Creek General Store, Stagecoach Coffee, and Bassett Healthcare.

Marty Bernardo
Bissell Road
Cooperstown, NY 1326
(607) 547-8227
bluestonefarm.org

*Marty Bernardo is active in dog rescue*

# Granola Pancakes
## BlueStone Farms

The mélange of nuts and dried fruits in BlueStone Farms Granola gives these steadfast breakfast favorites a wholesome texture and a delicious array of flavors. All marry well with New York State maple syrup or farmers' market jams.

1 egg, beaten
¾ cup buttermilk
2 tablespoons vegetable oil
½ cup all purpose flour

1 tablespoon brown sugar
1 teaspoon baking powder
½ teaspoon baking soda
½ teaspoon salt
1 cup BlueStone Farm Granola

Combine beaten egg, buttermilk, and oil in small bowl. In a separate bowl stir together the dry ingredients except granola. Add the liquid mixture to the dry ingredients and stir well. Fold in the granola until well-blended mixture.

Heat griddle over medium-low heat. Put ¼ cup of batter (look for ladles in this volume) onto hot griddle. Makes 9 four-inch pancakes.

*Pancakes are one of the oldest forms of bread in the culinary history. As flapjacks, blinis, johnnycakes, or crepes they are used in sweet and savory meals in almost every cuisine.*

# Boppa's Berries

**B**ob Snyder's soft fruit farm is the outcome of family heritage and inspiration. The wines and jellies of his youth had their source in the wild grapes and berries he and his parents gathered from the fields around Rochester, NY. Building on the experience of tending his father's raspberry patch, Bob has expanded his operations to include marvelous gourmet berries, more familiar in the British Isles than Upstate New York.

Raspberries, currants (black, red and white,) elderberries, blackberries, and tongue tantalizingly tart gooseberries grow in their designated beds on Bob's hillside farm. Their names are as gorgeous as the summer fruit itself, and as alluring as shades of designer lipstick: Consort Black, Red Lake, and Pink Champagne currants, Triple Crown blackberries, and the uncommon Jostaberry, a cross between a gooseberry and black currant.

Look for Boppa's Berries for sale seasonally at Cooperstown Natural Foods served at Cooperstown bed and breakfast Bryn Brooke Manor, and at fine area restaurants. Direct purchases can be made by calling Boppa's Berries and arranging a delivery. Availability depends on demand, yield, and, like any crop, sun and rain.

Granddaughters Sadie and Bryn have continued the Snyder family fruit tradition by endearingly dubbing Grandpa Bob's enterprise, "Boppa's Berries."

Bob and Barbara Snyder
607-286-7252

# Triple Berry Jelly
## Boppa's Berries

While all are favorite condiments, jellies, jams, preserves, and conserves are defined separately. *Jelly* is made with sugar, pectin and juice only, and is usually smooth and clear. *Jams* are smooth, but made with fruit pulp and are opaque. *Preserves* have chunks of fruit suspended in the sugar base, and *conserves* are a thick mixture of usually multiple fruits with the addition of raisins and nuts. *Marmalades* are citrus-based, with bits of fruit and strips of bitter rind offsetting the sweet jelly.

When traveling in British countries, if you order "jelly", you will be served, not a sweet spread for your toast, but gelatin.

1½ cups elderberry juice
1½ cups currant juice
2 cups raspberry juice
1 tablespoon butter (to reduce foaming)
Juice of half a lemon
2 pouches of liquid pectin
7½ cups sugar

Put juices and pectin in a large (six-quart) pot. Add butter and bring to a full, rolling boil, stirring occasionally. Stir in sugar and return to a full boil, stirring constantly. Boil and stir for exactly 2 minutes.

Ladle jelly into clean jars, leaving a quarter-inch of headroom. Wipe jar rims clean, if necessary, and cover with lids. <u>The jelly must be refrigerated</u>.

If making jelly to keep, use a canner and process in a hot water bath. The simple instructions come with any canner or canning jars. Both are available locally at Haggerty Ace Hardware.

*Fruits are used to make prized liqueurs. Black currants are the basis of Cassis and distilled raspberry juice makes Chambord.*

# Brewery Ommegang

**B**rewery Ommegang (literally "a walk in the meadow") brings a heady Belgian flair to Cooperstown's significant beer-making history. Their full-bodied ales and the many events celebrating them are terrific reasons to visit the area.

This aptly-named farmhouse style brewery is set on 136 acres, appropriately once the site of a hops farm. Brewery Ommegang's picturesque setting, just four miles outside of Cooperstown, provides the perfect venue for the only Belgian style brewery in the United States. Marrying substance to style, each of Ommegang's five distinctive bottle-conditioned ales is handcrafted and intriguingly complex, appealing to both the connoisseur and the casual consumer.

Take a tasting tour and find your own favorite. Choose their first brew, the Trappist-style Ommegang Abbey Ale, beautifully dark, and emanating fruit and spice. Try the golden Hennepin, refreshing and perfect with spicy cuisines, or their "witbier" (white beer), Witte, brewed for summer sipping and available in draft. The classic amber Rare Vos blends notes of spicy orange with smooth caramel, and Three Philosophers is a special quadruple, so intricate with flavors of cherry, chocolate and malt that it commands your full attention.

Make a point to visit the Brewery Ommegang website at www.ommegang.com and mark the dates for their lively events, including Belgium Comes to Cooperstown, the White Nights Ultimate Frisbee Tournament, and the holiday cheer of Sint Niklaas's visit.

656 County Highway 33
Cooperstown, NY 13326
607-544-1800
ommegang.com

*"The more I drink, the better I sing."*

# Ommegang Onion Soup
## Brewery Ommegang

The simplest recipes require the best quality ingredients. This delicious twist on French onion soup uses a chicken base instead of beef and it has a fascinating kick from the reduced ale. Slicing all those onions is the biggest challenge.

### Soup

½ cup butter

6 pounds yellow onions, thinly sliced

3 quarts chicken broth

One 12-oz bottle Ommegang ale
  or Three Philosophers Ale

1 tablespoon brown sugar

Salt and pepper

Parsley

Thyme

2 bay leaves

Melt butter in a stock pot and sauté onions over medium-high heat, for about a half-hour until they start to caramelize. Add the sugar and stir occasionally. Add ½ cup chicken broth every few minutes, allowing the onions to absorb the flavor. Use 2 ½ cups broth during this step.

Stir in remaining broth with two pinches of parsley, two pinches of thyme and two bay leaves.

Let simmer and add salt and pepper to taste.

In another small pot, boil and reduce Ommegang Ale to about a cup. Add to soup.

### Cheese Toast

Good French or Italian bread, sliced and toasted (a baguette from Danny's is perfect)
Gruyere cheese, grated

Sprinkle toast slices with grated Gruyere, and salt and pepper, if desired. Broil briefly under medium heat, until cheese is melted and browned. Ladle onion soup into individual bowls and float one or two slices of cheese toast on top.

*Based on a recipe provided by Maia Fong*

# Brookwood Garden

Quiet and picturesque, Brookwood Garden is a Cooperstown treasure. Its idyllic setting is perfect for weddings, receptions, afternoon picnics, romantic strolls, or quiet reflection. The lovely lakeside location, thriving plants, softly flowing fountains, and graceful blooms inspire contentment.

Brookwood Garden is located just two miles outside of Cooperstown on Route 80, elegantly positioned on the shores of Otsego Lake. Its volunteer caretakers invite you to explore the grounds and appreciate this beautifully tended and carefully preserved property. Admission is free; donations are welcomed.

A part of Cooperstown history since the early nineteenth century, Brookwood Garden and Garden House were built from 1915-1920 by landscape architect Frederick dePeyster Townsend, and his wife, Kathryn Jermain. The Cook family purchased this scenic property in 1944 and its heir, Robert Wiles Cook, created the Cook Foundation in 1985 to maintain Brookwood Gardens' pristine presence on Otsego Lake.

Brookwood Gardens is the site of many events throughout the year, including their own fundraising plant sales and the annual Art and Antique Auction. A highpoint of the season, you can choose from exceptional auction items, surrounded by spectacular summer flora in this splendid setting.

Brookwood Garden is funded through grants and private donations. It is maintained and managed entirely by dedicated volunteers, lead by the indefatigable Pat Thorpe.

Pat Thorpe
6000 Route 80
Cooperstown, NY 13326
607-547-2170
brookwoodgarden.com

# Garden Herbs and Soap
## Brookwood Garden

**H**erbs are so easy to grow. A little good dirt, light, water, and care produces fabulous enhancements to simple cooking. Schedule a tour of Brookwood Garden and learn more about the possibilities. Whether you live on acres or in an apartment, you can have an herb garden. Almost any container will do, and strawberry jars – those big terracotta urns with holes in the sides – are great for small areas or patio gardens.

### Herb Garden

**Sage** – great with poultry and winter squashes

**Peppermint and Spearmint** – these fragrant herbs are useful for recipes from tabbouleh to Kentucky Derby juleps. They spread prolifically, so consider putting them in their own containers.

**Lemon Balm** – see the refreshing tea recipe from the Perennial Field.

**Oregano** – terrific with anything Italian

**Rosemary** – wonderful with pork and lamb

**Chives** – these oniony shoots top scrambled eggs, baked potatoes, soups, and much more with flavor and color.

**Thyme** – common in French cooking. There are a number of varieties.

**Marjoram** – widely used in Mediterranean cooking.

### Herbal Soap

1 tablespoon dried herbs, pulverized. Mint, thyme, rosemary, sage, or a combination, are good choices. Lavender flowers or chamomile can be added, too. Experiment!

Pour ¼ cup boiling water over herbs and let steep 15 minutes. Add a few drops of essential oil of your choice for a stronger scent.

Grate one personal size bar of Ivory soap. You should have 2 cups. Reheat herb water to boiling and pour over soap shreds. Mix well (use your hands) and let stand 15 minutes. Mix again and divide into 3 or 6 parts, shaping into balls or bars. Place on wax paper and let dry for 3 days.

> *"The air was fragrant with a thousand trodden aromatic herbs, with fields of lavender, and the brightest roses blushing in tufts all over the meadows..."*
> –William Cullen Bryant

# Bryn Brooke Manor

This elegant bed and breakfast sits gracefully on three hilltop acres ("bryn" means "hill" in Welsh) in the Village of Cooperstown, walking distance to restaurants and attractions. A rambling, shingle-style house filled with period antiques, warmth and welcome, Bryn Brooke is named for the owners' daughter, Elizabeth Brooke.

Bryn Brooke Manor offers four comfortable guest rooms with private baths, spacious common rooms, a full-sized swimming pool, and grand porches caressed by summer breezes.

The Bryn Brooke full breakfast features the best local products available. They serve farmers' market fruits and vegetables, local meats, homegrown herbs, Otsego County honey and maple syrup, and hormone-free dairy products, because they believe that cows, like baseball players, should be off the juice! Everything is made from scratch. Let them know what you like – they cook to order and don't mind if you sleep in a bit. Breakfast is available until 10:30AM.

Like so many enterprises in the Cooperstown area, Bryn Brooke is a family effort. Brenda does the cooking; John tends the pool and gardens, and Elizabeth sees to your room and can tell you the best ghost stories in the area. Be sure to ask one of them to show you their magnificent white oak, one of the largest hardwood trees in Otsego County.

Brenda, John, and Elizabeth Berstler
6 Westridge Road
Cooperstown, NY 13326
607-544-1885
brynbrookemanor.com

# Hot Milk Punch
## Bryn Brooke Manor

Upstate New York has an abundance of many things, including indomitable spirit, winter and dairy products. This chilly day warm-up makes the most of the resources available well north of the Mason Dixon line. After a day of cold weather activities, a hot milk punch quiets the soul and makes the blood run warmer.

**1½ ounces rum**
**1½ ounces brandy**
**Honey or genuine maple syrup to taste**
**Hot milk**
**Cinnamon or nutmeg**

Fill a good-sized stoneware mug with hot water to warm. Heat milk (any fat content) on the stove or in the microwave. Empty hot water from mug and replace with rum, brandy and honey. Fill mug with hot milk and sprinkle with nutmeg or cinnamon. Wrap up in a generous throw in front of a crackling fire. Add a good book and let it snow.

> *If wine tells truth — and do have said the wise — It makes me laugh to think how brandy lies!*
> —Oliver Wendell Holmes
> (1809-1894)

# Chutney Unlimited

Tanna Roten's chutneys just get better and better, and her Chutney Unlimited product line has expanded to tempt you with more surprising flavor combinations.

Chutney is a variable mélange of chopped, flavored, sweetened and spiced fruit and/or vegetables. Master chutney makers keep their long-practiced recipes secret for good reason. It takes countless experiments to perfect the right balance of texture, flavors and consistency. Creating superior chutney that teases taste buds and complements an assortment of foods is a remarkable accomplishment.

Tanna makes *the best* chutney. Versatile and delicious, her Ginger and Garlic and Lemon Fig varieties enhance eggs, poultry, couscous and grains, and are unbeatable on New York State cheddar. Try it with shrimp instead of cocktail sauce or on a peanut butter sandwich as a tantalizing change from jelly. It even makes a delicious topping on vanilla ice cream (*really*).

Just open a jar of Tanna's Garam Masala and slowly inhale its spicy complexity. "Culinary aromatherapy" is what Tanna calls it. This alluring blend of eleven spices is perfect for curries or stir-frys.

Tanna's chutneys are available online or locally at Cooperstown Natural Foods.

Tanna Roten
52 Pioneer Street
Cooperstown, NY 13326
607-547-7272
chutneyunlimited.com

# Tanna's Turkey Salad
## Chutney Unlimited

This flavorful salad is a natural after Thanksgiving, but is delicious anytime of the year using turkey, chicken or even pork. Tanna's Chutney Yogurt is handy to keep on hand and use for sandwiches.

*Tanna's Chutney Yogurt*
   ½ cup Greek yogurt
   ¼ cup Tanna's Chutney
   2 tablespoons fresh lemon juice
   1 tablespoon snipped fresh chives

In a small bowl, gently combine all ingredients. Keep refrigerated, if not using immediately.

*Turkey Salad*
   3 cups cooked bite-sized turkey, chicken or pork
   ¼ cups small dried fruit (cherries, blueberries, raisins, etc.)
   1 cup seedless grapes, halved
   ⅓ cup slivered almonds
   1 ripe avocado, peeled and thinly sliced
   Assorted salad greens

In a large bowl, combine the turkey, dried fruit and grapes. Fold in the chutney yogurt and thoroughly combine. Toast the almonds in a tablespoon of butter, if desired, and add to turkey mixture.

Make a bed of greens on plate. Place a mound of the turkey salad in the center and fan avocado slices around. Drizzle a dressing of your choice, if desired.

# Christmas Around the Corner

"*Christmas is not a time, nor a season, but a state of mind,*" President Calvin Coolidge accurately observed.

On sultry summer days, a browse of Christmas Around the Corner stirs memories of frosty temperatures, a child's gleeful anticipation, and warm remembrances of charitable hearts. Projections of future holiday gatherings surface while considering the perfect ornament or memento. Find nutcrackers, Santas, fabulous Kurt Adler designs, and special Cooperstown ornaments. Their themed Christmas trees make it easy to find the right decoration for the baseball fan, fisherman or pet lover. Celebrate Irish heritage, traditional Victorian pretties or the New York Yankees, all with a tinseled twist. Even during the dog days of August, at Christmas Around the Corner the edict is "Believe in the Magic of Winter."

Christmas Around the Corner offers those wonderful trappings of the only holiday described as "merry." Most celebrations are "happy," but the singular, joyous jubilation of the Yuletide deserves the heartfelt expression, "Merry Christmas!"

*In 1889, President Benjamin Harrison's family decorated the first indoor Christmas tree in White House history. This treasured White House tradition would not be repeated until the early 1920's, when First Lady Grace Coolidge revived the practice. First Lady Lou Henry Hoover began the official custom of the White House Christmas tree, overseeing its decoration. "Trimming the tree" has been the duty of every First Lady since.*

Richard Busse
46 Pioneer Street
Cooperstown, NY 13326
607-544-1075

*Visit Pioneer Patio behind the Christmas around the Corner for casual fare and libations.*

# Holiday Snuggles
## Christmas Around the Corner

Christmas and candy canes have a long and happy association. The scent of peppermint is as much a hallmark of the season as evergreens. And, in many households, Christmas just isn't Christmas without chocolate.

To make a grown-up version of this rich hot chocolate, add chocolate liqueur and/or peppermint schnapps to make a "Snuggle."

**4 cups milk**
**4 ounces good dark chocolate, chopped**
**4 peppermint candies, crushed**
**4 small candy canes**
**Whipped cream**

In a saucepan bring the milk to a simmer. Add the chopped chocolate and the crushed peppermint candies. Whisk, until both are melted and mixture is smooth. Pour into heated mugs, top with whipped cream and a dusting of cocoa. Serve with a small candy cane, hooked over the rim of the cup.

*The modern concept of the Christmas tree is of German origin. Its holiday use became popular in England under the influence of Queen Victoria's German consort, Prince Albert. Holiday trees have long been decorated with fruit, cookies and candies, including hard white sugar sticks that were eventually bent, hanging more easily on the tree. Red stripes were added to "candy canes" about 1900.*

*Peppermint Pigs of Saratoga Springs are an Upstate Christmas tradition. Look for the pink peppermint porkers at holiday time, sold in a velvet bag with a story card and individual hammer.*

# Clark Sports Center

Clark Sports Center is one of the many benefits of living in the Cooperstown area. This superior facility offers a wide range of activities including a walking track, bowling alley, basketball court, a top-notch workout center, soccer fields, tennis courts, Adventure Programs, and classes in everything from Aerobics to Yoga.

Daily or weekly passes are available for visitors. Keep up with regular workouts, climb the rock wall, enjoy a swim or a game of racquetball.

If there is a "magic pill" to good physical health and a positive sense of well-being, it is surely daily exercise. Keeping your body in motion provides a wealth of feel-good benefits, including living longer with fewer chronic illnesses and greater mental acuity. Active people are generally healthier and happier, experiencing far less depression. Exercise provides the necessary balance to enjoy the great recipes showcased in the Savor New York food travel guides.

The Clark Sports Center offers a full menu of activities sure to entice everyone from the most eager to the most reluctant participant.

124 County Highway 52
Cooperstown, NY 13326
(607) 547-2800
clarksportscenter.com

*Every pound of muscle on your body burns 40-120 calories per day to maintain itself. A pound of body fat burns a measly 1-3 calories each day.*

# Broccoli Dip
## The Clark Sports Center

Sporting events and tailgate parties are natural occasions for this tasty appetizer. Broccoli Dip was employee Dawn Mindurski's winning entry for the Clark Sports Center's recipe contest for *Home Plate*. Delectable and easy, it also has the added nutrition of broccoli.

Preheat oven to 350 degrees.

**One 10-ounce package frozen chopped broccoli**
**1 cup mayonnaise**
**1 cup sour cream**
**One envelope dry Ranch dressing mix**
**2 cups shredded sharp cheddar cheese, divided in half**

Mix all ingredients, reserving one cup of the cheddar cheese for topping. Spread in a 9" pie pan and top with reserved cup of cheese. Bake about 25 minutes, until hot and bubbly.

Serve hot with crackers, cocktail breads, or fresh vegetables. Also delicious served cold.

*Cheddar cheese is named for the English village, Cheddar, in the County of Somerset. The cheese is naturally white, just like the milk it is made from. It derives its yellow or orange hue with the addition of annatto coloring, from the seed of the tropical tree of the same name.*

# Clay Café

It's not an eatery, but you could create your own dinnerware at this cleverly named place. The Clay Café is a paint-you-own-pottery studio and a delightful diversion for all ages and genders. Paint and create not only plates and bowls, but choose from a wide selection of bisque blanks. Make a personalized coffee mug, a special dish for a favorite pet, or add to a salt and pepper shaker collection.

Express yourself on more than serving pieces. Paint a soap dish and toothbrush holder to accent bathroom décor or make one-of-a-kind switch plates to highlight a room. Fashion distinctive vases, napkin rings, piggy banks, trinket boxes, or make the perfect drawer pulls for a newly refinished chest.

Owner Nancy Angerer provides the tools to find your artist within. She offers paints, brushes, sponges, stencils, and lots of advice for you to make a very special gift or souvenir. Have fun – no special talent is required to make beautiful pieces and wonderful memories.

Make a terrific party! Stop by the Clay Café and fill one of their brightly colored washtubs with your chosen ceramic blanks, paints and all the accessories and take it home for a child's birthday party, family gathering, or girls' night in. Take the painted pieces back to the Clay Café for Nancy to fire. Your unique creations are ready in just three days; your event will be remembered much longer.

Nancy Angerer
Route 28 (in the Barnyard Swing Barn; next door to Dreams Park)
Cooperstown, NY 13326
607-435-3387

# Metta Telfer's Kahlua Cake
## Clay Café

Clay Café owner Nancy Angerer is the great-grand-daughter of Arthur "Putt-Putt" Telfer of the celebrated photography duo of Smith and Telfer. Washington Smith and Arthur Telfer captured priceless images of Cooperstown and vicinity for over a century. See many of them displayed at the Otesaga Hotel, Fenimore Museum and online at fenimoremuseum/collections/smith-telfer. You'll find a gorgeous photo of Metta Telfer, Nancy's grandmother among them. This recipe was handed down from Metta to Peggy Clark, Nancy's mother, and on to Nancy.

⅓ pound unsalted butter, softened
½ cup sugar
1-2 tablespoons egg substitute
(1 egg yolk was used in the
original recipe; but in these days
of salmonella awareness, the
pasteurized product is safer)

4 ounces finely chopped almonds
1 teaspoon vanilla
7 tablespoons Kahlua liqueur
1½ pints whipping cream
36 lady fingers
1 tablespoon confectioner's sugar

Combine butter, almonds, sugar, egg substitute, vanilla and 4 tablespoons Kahlua in a mixing bowl. Use an electric mixer and whip well. Set aside.

In shallow bowl combine 1½ pints whipping cream and 3 tablespoons Kahlua. Dip the ladyfingers in the cream/Kahlua mixture, allowing a few minutes to absorb.

Place 12 lady fingers in the bottom of a serving dish. Spread half of butter-almond mixture over them. Repeat with a second layer of ladyfingers and butter-almond. Top with remaining ladyfingers.

Beat leftover whipping cream and Kahlua until stiff, and spread on top of the ladyfingers. Position toothpicks evenly in the dessert, so the whipped cream frosting is undisturbed, and cover with plastic film. Refrigerate overnight. Dust with confectioner's sugar before serving.

*Metta Telfer, 1912. Photo from the Smith and Telfer Collection, Fenimore Museum*

# Cooley's Stonehouse Tavern

"Pub grub" is a unique culinary specialty in its own right, and Cooley's Stonehouse Tavern is in a category of its own. Bars and pubs have long inspired spicy, salty, yummy foods to encourage greater quaffs of ales and lagers. Worldwide favorite Buffalo wings (created at the Anchor Bar in Buffalo, NY), blooming onions and potato skins are just a few favorites.

Cooley's Stonehouse Tavern's best includes irresistibly succulent pulled pork, perfectly complemented with sweet potato fries, on its tempting bill of pub fare. Their Turkey Chili was a favorite in the first volume of *Home Plate*, and their Fish Fry Fridays are a great way to round out the week.

But a tavern is, after all, about the bar, and this one is a beauty. Large and well-stocked, Cooley's offers domestic, imported and local brews, spirits and wines.

Along with brewskis is Cooley's own "shotski," an antique wooden ski fitted with four shot glasses. Four of the willing fill the glasses with their favorite potable and, "CLANG!" down the hatch in unison, to the reverberation of the brass bell.

Stop by Cooley's, named for the headstone maker who did business at this address in 1872. Kick back and relax with a cold one. Be sure to look for the photos of major leaguers Phil and Joe Niekro and Bruce Sutter adorning the walls of this friendly neighborhood tavern.

Tim Gould
49 Pioneer Street
Cooperstown, NY 13326
607-544-1311
cooleystavern.com

# Cooley's Pulled Pork
## Cooley's Stonehouse Tavern

The word "succulent" should have been coined for Cooley's pulled pork. The long, slow, redolent cooking is key, and part of the complete enjoyment of preparation and devouring. Enjoy it at Cooley's with their Sweet Potato Fries. *Home Plate* thanks Chef Glenn Lane for parting with his recipe.

**One 5-6 pound pork butt**

*Dry Rub*

½ teaspoon salt

½ teaspoon cumin

1 teaspoon chili powder

¼ teaspoon cayenne pepper

*Cooking Liquid*

2 cups water

1 tablespoon Worcestershire sauce

1 cup cider vinegar

*The Sauce*

½ cup cider vinegar

¼ cup yellow mustard

¼ cup brown sugar

1 teaspoon crushed red pepper

¼ teaspoon white pepper

1½ cups ketchup

¼ cup barbeque sauce

2½ teaspoons salt

¼ teaspoon black pepper

Prepare the pork in a smoker, crock pot, or in the oven. If using a smoker, you will not need the cooking liquid.

Dry rub the meat and cover or wrap in foil or plastic. Refrigerate overnight. Place meat in preferred cooking apparatus. Cover with liquid if using a crock pot or oven. Cover with the lid or foil and cook for eight hours at 350 degrees, or on high in the crock pot. Heat may be reduced a few hours into the process. After a day's cooking, the meat pulls from the bone. Shred, cover with sauce and serve on a crusty roll with coleslaw.

# Cooperstown Baseball Bracelet

Women are an integral part of America's game. They play it, they cheer for it, they hit backyard pop-ups, and they attend countless Little League games. The Cooperstown Baseball Bracelet is a perfect gift to recognize their passion and their indispensable contributions.

Anne Hall's and Jennifer Stewart's sterling idea was born at Three Mile Point, on the shores of Otsego Lake. Inspired by the same tranquil waters that encouraged James Fenimore Cooper's creativity, the Cooperstown Baseball Bracelet attractively fits the baseball lover's sense of style. This classic, timeless piece is available with a sterling silver or 14-karat gold baseball. The bracelet's beauty is further accentuated with a finely polished tag, stamped with the Cooperstown Baseball Bracelet logo, as your assurance of authenticity.

Simple and stunning, this bracelet looks appropriate with casual dress at the game or gorgeously accenting formal wear at a gala. It is an original design, created in Cooperstown, by Cooperstown natives.

Gentleman, pay heed; you will not go wrong with a gift of a Cooperstown Baseball Bracelet. It is available for purchase online.

Anne Hall and Jennifer Stewart
Three Mile Design, LLC
51 Pioneer Street
Cooperstown, NY 13326
607-437-1492
cooperstownbaseballbracelet.com

# Ballpark Belles' Broccoli Salad
## Cooperstown Baseball Bracelet

*T*his versatile salad is a nutritional slugger. All-star broccoli teams up with other flavorful players that add color and texture. All together it makes a healthy and delicious combination to fuel players through the extra innings.

*Salad*
> 4 medium crowns or 2 heads of fresh NYS garden broccoli
> 3 strips of bacon, cooked and crumbled, or ½ cup diced ham
> ¼ cup chopped sweet or red onion
> ½ cup shredded mozzarella cheese
> ⅓ cup sliced almonds
> ¼ cup Craisins, currants, raisins, or other small dried fruit

*Dressing*
> 1 cup mayonnaise, regular or low fat
> 3 tablespoon, plus 1 teaspoon red wine vinegar
> 2-3 tablespoons granulated sugar
> ½ teaspoon poppy seeds

Wash and dry broccoli and cut into florets. Toss together with bacon, onion, shredded cheese, almonds, and Craisins. In a separate bowl, combine ingredients for dressing. Stir together until smooth. Pour over broccoli mixture and toss, coating evenly.

Experiment with this salad, substituting the players as you like or adding to the line-up. Sunflower seeds, sliced strawberries, walnuts, dried blueberries, etc. are all possible designated hitters. Adjust the amount of dressing accordingly.

# Cooperstown Book Nook

Few shops are as congenial and inviting, or add more to the character of a Main street, than a well-run bookstore. Karen Johannesen's Book Nook celebrates 10 years of offering well-chosen bestsellers and classics, new releases and book club choices, as well as a complete inventory of books of local interest.

The Book Nook's shelves boast local products and gifts, as well as books. Find handcrafted soaps and note cards among the many treasures. You'll surely discover something here to please everyone on your list. The Book Nook shares their space with F.R. Woods, one of the oldest sports shops in Cooperstown, so if your diverse tastes run from Willie Mays to Willie Shakespeare, this is the place.

Karen devotes a special section to children's treasures. She offers a large selection of children's books, puzzles, games, American Girl products, Legos, and other delights to keep the little ones amused. Look here for attention-diverting travel games, too.

Just two doors from the National Baseball Hall of Fame, the Book Nook is a convenient and entertaining stop for everyone in your party.

Karen Johannesen
61 Main Street
Cooperstown, NY 13326
607-547-2578

> *There have been only two geniuses in the world; Willie Mays and Willie Shakespeare. But, darling, I think you'd better put Shakespeare first.*
> —Tallulah Bankhead

# Pigs in a Blanket
## Cooperstown Book Nook

*T*his recipe is a simple and tasty version of stuffed cabbage, not the hot-dogs-baked in dough appetizer of the same name. It is a great use of leftover rice and for New York's abundant cabbage production.

Preheat oven to 375 degrees

1 large head of cabbage
1 pound ground beef
1 pound ground pork
1 egg
2 cups cooked rice
1 jar (32 ounce) spaghetti sauce

Separate cabbage into large leaves. Steam leaves until pliable and set aside to cool.

Mix beef and pork together with egg, then stir in rice. Form meat and rice mixture into flat patties.

Wrap each patty in a cabbage leaf and place in a baking pan. Pour spaghetti sauce over all. Cover pan with foil and bake for 30 minutes.

> *An idealist is one who, on noticing that a rose smells better than a cabbage, concludes that it will also make better soup.*
>
> —H. L. Mencken

# Cooperstown Brewing Company

Cooperstown Brewing Company interlocks two of Cooperstown's most dynamic historical elements – beer and baseball. Owner Stan Hall's family traces its brewing heritage to nineteenth century Cooperstown, when this area was essential to American beer-making and practically every acre was entangled in hop vines. Stan Hall's grandfather grew these prolific, high-climbing plants just three miles from the site where Cooperstown Brewing now stands. Every harvest time his grandmother housed and fed a dozen hop pickers "from the City."

Two English-style breweries flourished in Cooperstown in the nineteenth century. In recognition of that flavorsome tradition, Cooperstown Brewing draws on English brewing methods, carefully selecting from scores of hops varieties, to make their outstanding ports, ales, and stout. Each is labeled with a distinctly American name, honoring America's game: Nine Man Ale, Strikeout and Benchwarmer, to name a few.

Cooperstown Brewing still grows the distinctively flowered hops, survivors of the 1911 blight, and uses them to finish their Backyard India Pale Ale. Don't miss a tasting tour of this fascinating facility, just 10 minutes from the National Baseball Hall of Fame, including their handcrafted root beer for kids of any age. Be sure to take home a variety of gifts from The Cooperstown Brewing Company's shop. You'll find glassware, baseball bat tap handles, fabulous shirts and, of course, great beer!

Stan Hall
110 River Street
Milford, NY 13807
607-286-9330
1-877-FINE ALE
cooperstownbrewing.com

*Visit The Farmers' Museum! Peer into Cooperstown's mesmerizing past and learn more about the sweeping influence of hops.*

# Kielbasa in Beer
## Cooperstown Brewing Company

This easy recipe can hardly be made wrong. The ingredients and their amounts are flexible, depending on your preference and what's abundant in your refrigerator or at the market. It is a good use for flat beer, if you happen to have any.

1½ pounds kielbasa, cut in chunks or rounds
1 onion, coarsely chopped
½ pound mushrooms, halved or left whole, if small
4 medium potatoes, scrubbed and cubed
2 or 3 carrots, peeled and cut in chunks
½ pound green beans, trimmed and cut
1 six-pack of Cooperstown Brewing beer (one for the recipe,
  one to drink while cooking, four to serve)
1 cup chicken or vegetable broth

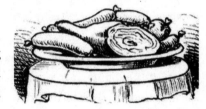

In a large pan with deep sides, sauté kielbasa, using a little oil if the sausage is very lean. Add onions (and garlic and celery, if you'd like) and sauté until onion begins to soften. Add mushrooms and stir to combine. Add potatoes and carrots (the root vegetables) and green beans. Cover with beer and chicken broth. Let cook 20-30 minutes, partially covered. Stir occasionally, adding more beer or broth as needed.

Cut cabbage, parsnips, garlic, celery, and summer fresh cut corn are also grand additions or substitutions to this one-pan supper. To be completely authentic, serve with dark rye bread.

*Author's note: This was our family's traditional lunch after Saturday morning outings to The West Side Market, when we lived near Cleveland, OH. That bounteous city market offers terrific Polish and Czech sausages, a plethora of fresh and international foods, and the best brats and falafel for many miles. The market is on West 25th Street, just across the Cuyahoga River from the Cleveland Indians' Jacob's Field. BB*

# Cooperstown Cheese Company

The building with the big red roof, across Route 28 from Wood Bull Antiques, represents small business dreams from all over New York, including those of the owners Sharon Tomaselli and Bob Sweitzer. Half of their building is dedicated to cheese making. This area's rich dairy farming once boasted dozens of individual creameries tucked into the country dales, and Sharon and Bob rekindle that fine tradition with their handcrafted curds and cheeses. Following the shortest distance between farm and table, the very cows that dot the pastures of Leatherstocking Country provide the milk that becomes the cheese that is called for in many recipes in *Home Plate*.

Great New York regional food specialties fill the other half of the Cooperstown Cheese Company's spacious building. They carry favorites grown or produced all over New York State, from Brooklyn to Buffalo. The scrumptious shopping includes many items local to the Cooperstown area. The creations of sole proprietors, whose tenacity took their products from the kitchen stove to store shelves, fill Cooperstown Cheese Company displays. Find ice cream, pasta, cookies, jams, cheese, barbeque sauces, pickles, maple syrup, honey, and more, made by New Yorkers employing New York products (and other New Yorkers!). Taste the pride and quality behind the producer's name on the label.

Sharon Tomaselli and Bob Sweitzer
Route 28 at Oxbow Road
Milford, NY 13807
607-286-7722
cooperstowncheesecompany.com

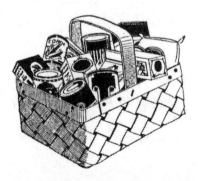

# New York Blue Pizzettes
## Cooperstown Cheese Company

*T*he dough is courtesy of Sharon Tomaselli's Grandma Fiorentina ("little flower"), and these "little pizzas" take an plucky detour from the familiar mozzarella, pepperoni, and oregano with pungent blue cheese, red grapes, and rosemary.

### Pizzette Dough
8 cups flour
1 tablespoon of salt
3 cups lukewarm water
1 cake of fresh yeast

### Pizzette Toppings
Seedless red grapes, halved
Old Chatham's Ewe's Blue Cheese, Gorgonzola or other blue cheese
Fresh rosemary

In a large bowl, dissolve the yeast cake in half of the warm water, along with the salt. When the yeast is dissolved, add the flour and the remaining water. Stir together, then turn out onto a floured board and knead well. Cover with a clean cloth, put in a warm place and let rise. When dough is doubled in size, punch down and form dough into 6-inch rounds. Place rounds on pizza sheet or stone, sprinkled with cornmeal, if you like. Cover and let rise again.

Preheat oven to 450 degrees. Top pizzette with halved red seedless grapes, sprinkle with Old Chatham's Ewe's Blue Cheese (available at Cooperstown Cheese Company), and a touch of rosemary.

Bake for 10 minutes, then reduce oven temperature to 350 degrees and bake another 15 minutes, or until crust in browned.

*Rosemary*

# Cooperstown Chamber of Commerce

*T*he Cooperstown Chamber of Commerce is, without a doubt, the single most effective source of information about this fascinating and multifaceted area. To help make your visit most memorable and satisfying, make your first stop their bright yellow house on Chestnut Street, across from the fire station and behind Doubleday Field. The friendly and well-informed staff disseminates advice on myriad diverse subjects from restaurants and accommodations, to wedding photographers and wine shops.

Roam the Chamber website, www.cooperstownchamber.org and immerse yourself in the history, the celebrations and attractions that make Cooperstown a preferred destination for thousands of new and returning visitors. When you get to the Village, chat with the congenial team for suggestions related to your interests. Like the water? They can recommend fishing excursions and canoe rentals. Does art make you smile? The staff will gladly list museums, galleries and current exhibitions. What to do with your six-year-old? Ask for the free and inexpensive child-friendly options.

The Cooperstown Chamber of Commerce represents more than 600 members of wide-ranging backgrounds, making it the key source for getting to know "America's Most Perfect Village" and the most appealing elements of the surrounding area.

31 Chestnut Street
Cooperstown, NY 13326
607-547-9983
cooperstownchamber.org

*Look for the pineapple, the Colonial American symbol of hospitality, on the Chamber's Welcome sign.*

# Chicken and Escarole
## Cooperstown Chamber of Commerce

Escarole is one of the green, leafy vegetables in the endive branch of the chicory family. A bunch resembles a head of romaine lettuce, but with frilly leaves and attitude. Escarole's pleasingly bitter flavor, sturdy leaves and deep color make a striking addition to entrées such as this one. The vitamin-packed green also enlivens soups and casseroles. Young or interior escarole leaves are especially good in fresh salads.

Colorful, delicious and healthy, this recipe is great with chicken cooked on the outdoor grill. It was provided by Janet L. Tamburrino, wife of Cooperstown Chamber Executive Director John Bullis.

| | |
|---|---|
| 4 chicken breasts, boneless and skinless | ½ teaspoon dried thyme, crushed |
| ¼ teaspoon salt | ¼ teaspoon black pepper |
| 5 cups roughly chopped escarole, loosely packed | 2 garlic cloves, minced |
| | 1 cup cherry tomatoes, halved |
| 2 teaspoons cornstarch | ½ cup fat-free chicken broth |
| 1 tablespoon lemon juice | ½ teaspoon grated lemon peel |
| | 1 tablespoon butter |

If not cooking the chicken outside, preheat the broiler. Season both sides of the chicken breasts with thyme, pepper and half of the salt. Coat the broiler pan with cooking spray, and place chicken on rack. Broil chicken 3" from the heat, about five minutes per side, until juices run clear. Place chicken on a platter and keep warm.

Coat a large skillet with cooking spray and place over medium heat. Cook the garlic briefly, until fragrant. Add the escarole and stir-fry about three minutes, until it begins to wilt. Add the tomatoes and remaining ¼ teaspoon of salt. Cook a bit longer, until tomatoes are soft and escarole is completely wilted. Place on platter with the chicken.

Put broth and cornstarch in a cup and stir until completely blended. Add to the cooking skillet, along with lemon peel and juice. Bring to a boil over high heat, stirring constantly, until sauce is slightly thickened. Add the butter and any juices from the platter and return to a gentle boil, cooking until the sauce is suitably thick. Pour over chicken and vegetables.

# Cooper Country Crafts

In the not-so-distant past, prior to the nineteenth-century Industrial Revolution that gave rise to speedy mass-produced sameness, whatever didn't grow was produced by human hands. Skill and patience placed an individual stamp on pottery, glassware, jewelry, clothing, metalwork, etc. Chandlers made candles, weavers made cloth, coopers made barrels, fabers were artisans; smiths worked in metal, potters in clay, and websters with fiber. A look at common surnames indicates how widespread and vital craftspeople were in human history.

Fortunately, the art of handcrafts survived the machine age and fine examples of local talent are on display at Cooper Country Crafts. Many one-of-a-kind items are available, including: hand-stitched quilts, yarn spun from local fibers, hand-tied fishing flies, to unique jewelry, hand-dipped candles and hand-knitted baby wear. Pottery, woodwork, all natural handmade soaps and more fill the shelves of this delightful cooperative shop.

Cooperstown counts numerous "craft-brothers" (and sisters), as practitioners were known in the era of craft guilds. Applying creativity, expertise and meticulous attention to detail, these artisans fashion ideal pieces with a lot of heart.

Cooperstown Country Crafts is located in Doubleday Court, across the parking lot from Doubleday Stadium and a few doors from Dog Wild Canine Supply.

Judy Curry
2 Doubleday Court
Cooperstown, NY 13326
607-547-9247

*The word "craft" derives from an Old English word "craeft," meaning "strength, power." The meaning evolved to mean a skill or art with the idea of "mental power."*

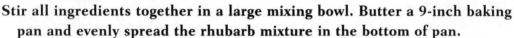

# Rhubarb Apple Crumble
## Cooper Country Crafts

*I*n England, a fruit crisp is known as a "crumble" and served swimming in Bird's Custard Sauce. The preparation takes the idea of "comfort food" to another dimension. Bird's Custard Powder is as common in British cupboards as peanut butter is in American pantries. Check the British food inventory at The Plaide Palette in Cherry Valley for its availability. In lieu of custard sauce, this crisp is excellent with ice cream.

Preheat oven to 375 degrees.

*Fruit*
   **3-4 cups diced rhubarb (1 pound)**
   **2 large New York cooking apples, diced**
   **3 tablespoons orange juice**
   **¾ cup granulated sugar**
   **½ teaspoon cinnamon**
   **Stir all ingredients together in a large mixing bowl. Butter a 9-inch baking**
      **pan and evenly spread the rhubarb mixture in the bottom of pan.**

*Crumble Topping*\*
   **¾ cup all-purpose flour**
   **½ cup light brown sugar**
   **¾ cup quick cooking oats**
   **¼ teaspoon baking soda**
   **½ teaspoon cinnamon (optional)**
   **6 tablespoons melted butter**

In a separate bowl, combine all ingredients thoroughly. Sprinkle over top of fruit mixture and bake for 40 minutes, until fruit is bubbly and topping is browned.

*\*Double or triple the ingredients of the topping and keep the remainder in the freezer for a quick topping for other fruit crisps, or as a streusel topping for muffins or coffee cakes.*

# Cooperstown General Store

The Cooperstown General Store is a mainspring of Village life and an absolute favorite of Cooperstown locals. Everyday necessities of every ilk are available right on Main Street, next door to the National Baseball Hall of Fame. Gifts, office supplies, art and craft needs, toys, pantry-filling foods, dry goods, hardware, pet food, greeting cards, and much more are all available under one roof.

Forget your toothbrush or socks? Need a fan on a hot summer day or an extra traveling bag to get home? Stop by the General Store. It's a good bet you'll find the perfect souvenir there, too.

In Cooperstown, there is a noticeable and pleasant absence of those "big box" behemoths that populate most areas. The Cooperstown General Store is the best evidence of why they are unnecessary. Manager Ron Jex and his experienced crew meet the locals' and visitors' needs at his well-stocked, well-run General Store. Prices are more than reasonable and the staff is informed and available.

Comfortingly reminiscent of the not-so-distant past when Main Street emporiums were a place of social greeting and a hub of small town life, the Cooperstown General Store keeps the village supplied with everyday goods and everyday good feelings.

Ron Jex
45 Main St.
Cooperstown, NY 13326
607-547-6196

*Practically everyone over a certain age in Cooperstown still refers to The General Store as "Newberrys".*

# Broccoli Salad
## Cooperstown General Store

There are so many reasons to eat broccoli, that simply not liking it is hardly an excuse for missing the nutritious punch of this striking vegetable. Potassium, iron, beta carotene, calcium, folic acid, and a boatload of Vitamin C are in just a few stalks of this Italian import.

This recipe should entice even the most reluctant vegetable eater.

### Salad
2 bunches of fresh broccoli, chopped
1 red onion, diced
1 pound bacon, fried crisp and crumbled
1 cup golden raisins
1 cup sunflower seed kernels

Fold all ingredients together.

Just prior to serving, toss with the following dressing:

### Dressing
1 cup Miracle Whip
½ cup sugar
2 tablespoons vinegar

The dressing may be tailored to personal tastes by choosing from a variety of vinegars, and/or substituting honey or real maple syrup for the sugar. Use within a day or two.

*Albert "Cubby" Broccoli, the famous producer of James Bond films from Dr. No to Goldeneye, is a descendent of the Italian family named Broccoli who crossed cauliflower (cavolfiore) with rabe, creating "broccoli."*

# Cooperstown Natural Foods

Cooperstown Natural Foods passionately embraces the concepts of "natural" and "organic." They stock great food, much of it local, and all of it reassuringly free of mystery and adulteration.

The dedicated Poulette family sees that the Cooperstown area is amply supplied with nurturing fare, free of "Frankenfood" chemical lab experimentation. This clean and bright shop boasts a tempting supply of organic produce and is a haven of great food, fascinating books, safe cleaning products, supplements, and pet supplies. Shop here and take home not only satisfying food, but a satisfying sense of well-being from supporting fair trade, responsible agriculture, and local farmers.

Cooperstown Natural Foods (CNF to the regulars) greets a steady stream of friends all day long. Established customers often call it simply "Ellen's Place," referring to owner Ellen Poulette. Husband Dave is usually on hand, as is sister Jeanne, sons Dan and Rob, and sometimes daughter Sarah, between her stints at college.

Among the high-quality goods you'll find on Ellen's shelves are the following homegrown and locally made products:

Tanna's Chutney
McGillicuddy's Soap
Stannard's Maple Products
Boppa's Berries (in season)
Hand's Honey
Dancing Veggie Farm Garlic
School House Farm Mustard

BlueStone Farm Granola
Heidelberg Bread
Lord's Honey
Acro-Spire Farm baked goods
Evans Dairy products
Goldpetals skin products
*Home Plate* books (of course!)

Ellen Poulette
61 Linden Avenue
Cooperstown, NY 13326
607-547-8613
cooperstownnaturalfoods@verizon.net

# Pumpkin Cookies
## Cooperstown Natural Foods

P umpkin is wonderfully versatile, colorful and exceptionally nutritious. It partners well with spices and sweetening for desserts and breakfast baking, and it is savory in soups, entrees and side dishes. Still, the vast majority of pumpkins are sold for decorative purposes only.

These hearty cookies, with nuts, raisins, and vitamin-rich pumpkin, make a great on-the-go breakfast food. As they say at CNF, *"as always, it's better organic!"*

Preheat oven to 350 degrees.

½ cup shortening (Spectrum makes organic shortening with zero trans fats)
1½ cups brown sugar, packed
2 eggs
2 cups cooked pumpkin, or one 15-ounce can

2¾ cups flour
1 tablespoon baking powder
1 teaspoon cinnamon
½ teaspoon nutmeg
¼ teaspoon ginger
½ teaspoon salt
1 cup raisins
1 cup nuts

Stir flour together with baking powder, spices and salt. Set aside.

Cream shortening with brown sugar, and add eggs and pumpkin, stirring until smooth. Add flour mixture, stirring only until ingredients are combined. Fold in raisins and nuts.

Drop by heaping tablespoons onto a prepared (greased or lined with parchment paper) baking sheet. Bake for 10 to 15 minutes, until the center springs back.

*Organic foods are one of the fastest-growing areas of the food industry. Since the early 1990s, the demand for organic foods has increased an average of 20 % each year.*

# Cooperstown Wine and Spirits

C ooperstown Wine and Spirits is stocked from floor to ceiling with fine vintages, lively spirits, and the latest offerings from new and familiar labels. You'll find Wine Spectator's best selections and fine gift boxes featuring your favorite liqueurs.

Owner Ed Landers and his knowledgeable staff are on hand to guide you through the array of potent elixirs neatly displayed on his shelves. Questions are welcomed! They can advise you on the best wine to accompany a new recipe or give great suggestions for the lucky bourbon or Scotch aficionado on your gift list.

Don't miss Ed's special case prices and his excellent selection of New York State wines.

To find Cooperstown Wine and Spirits, just look for Old Glory. The Village flagpole is situated literally in the center of the intersection of Main and Pioneer streets. The stately flag, surrounded with blooming flowers, keeps Main Street traffic calm and provides a wonderful reference point for directions. To the north is Otsego Lake, to the east is the Susquehanna River, to the west is Cooperstown's only traffic light and to the south, just a half a block up Pioneer Street, is Cooperstown Wine and Spirits.

Ed Landers
45 Pioneer St.
Cooperstown, NY 13326
607-547-8100

# Bourbon Slush
## Cooperstown Wine and Spirits

Keep this bourbon concoction in the freezer and a summer party is always at the ready. The sweet citrus juices play beautifully with the strong tea, and the bourbon packs a wallop. Sip it slowly and enjoy.

**7 cups water**
**3 cups bourbon**
**One 12-ounce can frozen lemonade concentrate, thawed**
**One 6-ounce can frozen orange juice, thawed**
**1 cup sugar, or to taste**
**2 cups strong tea**
**Club soda or Sprite**

Stir all ingredients except club soda in a large bowl or pitcher. Transfer to a covered plastic container and place in freezer. The bourbon slows the freezing considerably, so plan on making the slush 2-3 days before it's needed. To serve, place a scoop of bourbon slush in an old-fashioned glass and top with a splash of Sprite or club soda. Give it a quick stir and garnish with a mint sprig and a slice of orange or lemon.

Alternate version: A fruitier, sweeter Bourbon Slush can be made by replacing the water with a 46-ounce can of pineapple juice and increasing the tea to 3 cups.

*95% of all bourbon is produced in Kentucky*

# Cooperstown Village Bed and Breakfast Association (CVBABA)

Finding a place to stay in Cooperstown can be a confusing prospect – especially if you want to stay within the Village limits. The Village of Cooperstown is a just a little over a mile square, but a Cooperstown address may apply to properties that are a considerable distance from the enticing destinations of the Village proper. The members of the Cooperstown Village Bed and Breakfast Association are all located within the Village of Cooperstown limits. Stay with of them and enjoy the charm of being in town, and the time saving advantage of walking to attractions, one-of-a-kind shops and fine restaurants.

CVBABA members generally exceed industry standards for hospitality.

Cooperstown Village Bed and Breakfast Association
cvbaba.com

*The Purple Martin is the symbol of the CVBABA*

*You must come home with me and be my guest;*
*You will give joy to me, and I will do*
*All that is in my power to honour you.*
*–Percy Bysshe Shelley*

# Membership Listing
## Cooperstown Village Bed and Breakfast Association

2 Chestnut Street
Douglas Walker
2 Chestnut Street
Cooperstown, NY 13326
607-547-2307
2chestnut.com

Bryn Brooke Manor
Brenda, John, and Elizabeth Berstler
6 Westridge Road
Cooperstown, NY 13326
607-544-1885
brynbrookemanor.com

Cooperstown Bed and Breakfast
John and Linda Smirk
88 Chestnut Street
Cooperstown, NY 13326
607-547-2532
cooperstownbandb.com

Main Street Bed and Breakfast
Ron and Susan Streek
202 Main Street
Cooperstown, NY 13326
1-800-867-9755
cooperstownchamber.org/
mainstreetbb

Nelson Avenue Pines
Penny Gentile
20 Nelson Avenue
Cooperstown, NY 13326
607-547-7118
cooperstown.net/napines

Overlook Bed and Breakfast
Jack and Gail Smith
8 Pine Boulevard
Cooperstown, NY 13326
607-547-2019
overlookbb.com

Rose and Thistle Bed and Breakfast
Steve and Patti D'Esposito
132 Chestnut Street
Cooperstown, NY 13326
607-547-5345
rosenthistle.com

White House Inn
Edward and Marjorie Landers
46 Chestnut Street
Cooperstown, NY 13326
607-547-5054
thewhitehouseinn.com

# Dancing Veggie Farm

Every August at Dancing Veggie Farm, it's all about the garlic. Their annual Garlic Harvest Celebration celebrates these pungent bulbs with a delightful country festival. On the last weekend of August, their big post and beam barn (circa 1840) is festooned with garlic braids, wreaths and arrangements, hanging on the walls and from the rafters. Garlic and garlic accessories, cookbooks, locally-made pottery, soaps, candles, food, and music make for good fun at this aromatic jubilee.

The Ainslie-Hamblin family grows garlic, broom straw and natural vegetables on their farm, set in the pretty-as-a-picture gently rolling acreage between Otsego and Canadarago Lakes. Warren Ainslie puts all that straw to wonderful use in his handmade brooms. Using nineteenth century tools and methods, he creates a variety of practical and beautiful versions of these necessary household items. All of the Dancing Veggie Farm crops are grown using biodynamic methods, using natural fertilizers and crop rotation to maximize the health of the soil and the vitality of the yield.

One of the goals of *Savor New York* is to shine a light on area family farms. We believe that they are essential to a healthy food supply and a healthy America. These family endeavors embrace ecological land use and contribute valuable community involvement. In the Cooperstown region, Dancing Veggie Farm is a dandy.

Warren and Rachel Ainslie-Hamblin
246 Ainslie Road
Richfield Springs, NY 13439
315-858-0506

> *"There is no such thing as a little garlic."*
> —Arthur Baer

# Garlic Chicken with Peach Preserves

Dancing Veggie Farm

*T*his is a terrific recipe for a casual dinner party or a potluck. Easy to make in a slow cooker or in the oven, it blends the miraculous flavor of garlic with the succulent sweetness of peaches, and infuses all into the savory chicken.

### Chicken

3-4 pounds chicken pieces
1 whole bulb (about 6-10 cloves) garlic, peeled and minced
3-4 sprigs fresh thyme, rosemary, or sage
Salt and pepper to taste

### Peach Sauce

1 cup peach or apricot preserves
Juice of 2 large lemons

Place chicken pieces in a large slow cooker and sprinkle salt, pepper, garlic, and herbs liberally among them.

Thin the preserves with lemon juice to the consistency of barbeque sauce. Warm the preserves, if very thick. Pour over the chicken, coating evenly. Cook on low 5-6 hours.

Serve chicken of a bed of brown rice. Thicken cooking glaze on top of the stove, if necessary, and ladle over chicken.

Alternately, preheat oven to 325 degrees and bake chicken in a covered dish for about an hour.

> *Shallots are for babies; Onions are for men; Garlic is for heroes.*
> —Unknown

# Danny's Main Street Market

"*A loaf of bread,*" the Walrus said, "*is what we chiefly need.*" So wrote Lewis Carroll in his classic *Through the Looking Glass*. Had the Walrus and Carpenter been strolling Main Street Cooperstown, instead of that briny beach, they could do no better than Danny's Market to satisfy their desire for baguettes.

As if Sergio's freshly-baked artisanal breads weren't enticement enough (arrive early for the best selection), they are just an aromatic beginning. Coffee at Danny's is a morning ritual for many locals and regular visitors who anticipate steaming cups of java, outstanding scones and the morning news.

*Lewis Caroll's Walrus, Carpenter, and all those oysters*

Danny's bustles at lunch time; their impressive repertoire features deli–made soups, sides and legendary sandwiches made with lean meats, quality cheese and interesting, flavorful condiments. The bakery case is laden with cookies, muffins and inexcusably rich brownies, served with no apology whatsoever. If the seating is filled, not to worry; Danny's is an easy walk to Lakefront Park for pleasant lunching, *al fresco*.

As their name implies, Danny's is a market, as well as a fine deli. They carry specialty, local and gourmet items, beer, and prepared foods to go. They even have, as reads the next line of the Carroll poem, "*Pepper and vinegar besides, Are very good indeed.*"

Alice and Sergio Gaviria
92 Main Street
Cooperstown, NY 13326
607-547-4053

*Look for Danny's Market fare available at the concession at Glimmerglass State Park, at the north end of Otsego Lake.*

# Danny's Scones
## Danny's Main Street Market

Scones are such a pleasant way to start the day. Basically, they are a British version of an American biscuit and are pronounced "scon" (rhymes with "John") by the majority of Brits and Scots. British "biscuits" are American "cookies."

However they are pronounced, these scones, enriched with sour cream, are delicious either sweet or savory. The sweet version of Danny's day-brightener calls for dried fruit, but they are also delectable if you substitute diced ham (and/or cheese and herbs) for the currants and omit or reduce the sugar to a tablespoon or two.

Preheat oven to 300 degrees.

4¼ cups flour
⅓ cup sugar
2 teaspoons baking powder
½ teaspoon baking soda
Dash of salt
1½ sticks of cold butter, cubed
1 cup currants (or raisins, dried cherries, blueberries, cranberries, etc.)
2 cups sour cream
1 egg, beaten

Place all dry ingredients in a large mixing bowl and stir together. Using a pastry blender, cut in cold butter until incorporated, but not over mixed. Stir in sour cream, egg, and currants to make stiff dough.

On a floured board, turn out dough and roll to ¾" thickness. Cut into circles with a pastry cutter. Place on baking sheet and bake 15-20 minutes until golden brown.

*Some version of Danny's Market has been a fixture in Cooperstown for generations. It once stood on the site of the National Baseball Hall of Fame, where it offered bushel baskets full of goods and produce from the shop to the street.*

# Davidson's Jewelry & Augur's Books

Books *and* jewelry are two of life's essentials conveniently available under one roof at Davidson's Jewelry and Augur's Books. Could it get any better? As a matter of fact, *it does*. This enjoyable dual shop can please everyone on your gift list with their diverse and original inventories.

Davidson's Jewelry is the primary source of baseball jewelry in Cooperstown, much of it made on premise. Beautiful gold and silver earrings, charms and pendants in a variety of baseball motifs make perfect gifts. For the ideal, original keepsake of Cooperstown, look for their striking new Kingfisher Tower charm, available in gold or silver. They also have watches, watchbands and batteries to help keep you on time.

Augur's Books has been an anchoring presence on Main Street for over a century. Bestsellers, special interests, children's, and a terrific selection of books by local authors fill their shelves. Fine gifts, including Schaeffer pens, Crane's stationery and Swiss Army Brand knives are more reasons to stop and browse.

These two businesses combine to form one marvelous shop. Located by the Village flag pole, at the corner of Main and Pioneer streets, this always-interesting emporium should not be missed.

Brian Nielsen and Becky Davidson-Nielsen
73 Main Street
Cooperstown, NY 13326
607-547-5099
cooperstownjewelry.com

# Braised Short Ribs
## Davidson's Jewelry & Augur's Books

This meat-and-potatoes favorite takes very little hands-on effort, but it does demand enough time to make the meat tender and succulent. The slow cooking takes a good part of the afternoon, but it makes the house smell wonderful and the result is well worth it, especially on a wintry day.

| | |
|---|---|
| 2½ to 3 pounds beef short ribs | ½ cup diced carrots |
| ½ cup diced celery | 2 bay leaves |
| 2 cloves garlic, chopped | 6 cups beef broth (3 cans) |
| ¾ cup good red wine | 3 tablespoons vegetable oil |
| 4 tablespoons butter | 4 tablespoons flour |

In a Dutch oven, brown short ribs in vegetable oil. Work in batches, so not to crowd the pan. When all short ribs are browned, return to Dutch oven and add carrots, celery, bay leaves, and garlic. Cover with beef broth and bring to a boil. Reduce heat, cover pot and let simmer slowly for about two hours.

Remove meat and set aside. Strain stock and let fat rise to the top. Skim fat from broth, or, if you are making the ribs the day before and have time, refrigerate broth and remove the fat that solidifies on top.

Melt butter in Dutch oven and whisk with flour. Slowly whisk in 3 cups strained stock, adding water if necessary to make 3 cups. Let cook over medium heat until thickened. Salt and pepper the gravy to taste.

Place warm ribs on a serving platter and pour gravy over all. Garnish with chopped parsley, if desired.

Serve over noodles, mashed or boiled potatoes, or rice.

> *Let the stoics say what they please, we do not eat for the good of living, but because the meat is savory and the appetite is keen.*
>
> —Ralph Waldo Emerson

# Dog Wild Canine Supply

Dogs are a wonderful component of farm life, or any life for that matter. Specific breeds, and many of the ever-favorite mutts, are effective hunters, herders and protectors. As any dog lover or child knows, there is no better companion than a beloved pup.

Dogs have been humankind's best friend for thousands of years, for the same intangible and invaluable reasons: loyalty, partnership, unconditional love, and pure joy. Who else is supportive when we're down on our luck, in a foul mood, frumpy and miserable, or otherwise unfit for human company? Who else do we trust utterly, confide in completely, and rely on absolutely? What other creature can uplift flagging spirits with a mere flick of his tail, a happy pant, or a warm lick of palm or cheek?

Dog Wild Canine Supply offers a terrific array of dog needs. Dana and Ray have treats and leashes, travel supplies, tug and fetch toys, and lots of advice for meeting your dog's desires. They stock Wellness brand dog and cat food, a superior blend free of wheat products. They also carry goods to support your dog's well being; including grooming and dental supplies, and Safe Paw ice melt and dog booties to protect paws from rough winter conditions. Meet Blu, the Dog Wild shop dog and emissary of the enterprise. Inquire here how you can also rescue such a fine companion as Blu.

Dog Wild is located in Doubleday Court, just three doors down from Cooper Country Crafts. Dogs are welcomed and customers appreciated.

Dana Rice
8 Doubleday Court
Cooperstown, NY 13326
607-547-5261
dogwildsupply.com

> *If there are no dogs in Heaven, when I die I want to go where they went.*
> —Will Rogers

# Cheddar Canine Cookies
## Dog Wild Canine Supply

"*If you think dogs can't count, try putting three dog biscuits in your pocket and then give Fido only two of them*" – Phil Pastoret

Preheat oven to 400 degrees

**3 cups flour**
**2 cups shredded New York State cheddar cheese**
**2 cloves garlic, finely chopped**
**½ cup oil**
**¼ cup milk**
**Broth (any flavor) or water, as needed**

Combine all ingredients in a large bowl, adding broth if mixture is too dry to mix easily. Roll dough onto a floured surface ¼ inch thick, and cut into desired shapes (Tin Bin Alley on Main Street, Cooperstown, has great cookie cutters). The biscuits may also be shaped by hand.

Place one inch apart on a prepared (greased or lined with parchment paper) cookie sheet and bake 10-15 minutes.

*If you don't own a dog – at least one – there is not necessarily anything wrong with you, but there may be something wrong with your life.*
   —Roger Caras

# Ellsworth and Sill

Every Main Street in America was once home to at least one "ladies shop"; boutique havens of current style, enhanced with personal attention and good manners. Hats matched gloves, jewelry was tasteful, and there was a department, mysterious to most men, discreetly known as "foundation garments."

While the corsets may have gone by the by, the best of that wonderful tradition, with its superior service, still flourishes at Ellsworth and Sill. Their revolving inventory of seasonal fashions is attractively displayed on tastefully turned-out mannequins. The experienced staff is available to help with fittings and creating ensembles. There's even a Bargain Basement, with great buys and enticing browsing.

Long a fixture on Main Street, near the Village Flagpole, Ellsworth and Sill also stocks some men's and children's selections, making it a must stop when shopping in Cooperstown. Check with Marti and her staff if you need a cocktail dress, a bathing suit, a Fair Isle sweater or a gentleman's tie.

You'll find a satisfying tradition of style and service and a dependable inventory of casual and dressy clothing and accessories for the classic woman. Ellsworth and Sill is a "ladies shop" in the best retro-Main Street definition.

Marti Jex
79 Main Street
Cooperstown, NY 13326
607-547-9277

*A tremendous middle-of-the-night fire, origin unknown, gutted the Ellsworth and Sill shop and building in the late 1930s.*

# New York Cheese Spread
## Ellsworth and Sill

*T*his spread is easy to make and great to have on hand. Experiment with the flavor by substituting various shredded cheeses, such as Mexican, pizza, or chipotle blends.

1½ cups Miracle Whip salad dressing
One 4-ounce jar diced pimientos
1 tablespoon Worcestershire sauce
2 tablespoons chopped onion
¼ teaspoon ground black pepper
One 8-ounce package New York Sharp shredded cheddar cheese
One 8-ounce package New York Extra Sharp shredded cheddar cheese

Mix all ingredients and refrigerate at least an hour, allowing flavors to blend. Serve on crackers, or stuff into celery sticks.

*Miracle Whip was introduced at the 1933 World's Fair in Chicago. The term originally referred to the "Miracle Whip" emulsifying machine that made a less expensive substitute for mayonnaise, during those Depression days. As it happens, Miracle Whip has half the fat of mayonnaise, for these calorie-conscious days.*

# Fly Creek General Store

The country store is a priceless component of daily life in rural New York. In towns and villages mercifully still not invaded by fast-food franchises and convenience shops, these marketplaces fill the needs of locals and visitors, personally and proficiently. The Fly Creek General Store is an exemplary model of that bucolic commodity, providing food, fuel, supplies, and a crucial crossroads for country communications.

The Fly Creek General Store is also a great stop for locally-made products. On hand are Dancing Veggie Farm's garlic and handmade brooms, BlueStone Farm granola, jams, local apples, pumpkins and vegetables in season, and a bevy of books by local authors.

Tom Bouton's General Store is located just three miles from Cooperstown, at the off-center four corners in Fly Creek. It is the place to stop, heading north from Cooperstown on Route 28. Their deli features ample sandwiches and wraps, homemade sides, New York cheddar, and baked goods. Green Mountain coffee is hot and fresh all day long. Pull in for gas, hormone-free milk, Roger Vaughn's farm fresh eggs, bait, beer, snacks, and greeting cards. Don't go home without an article of one-of-a-kind Fly Creek apparel.

Tom Bouton
State Route 28
Fly Creek, NY 13337
607-547-7274

# Potato Tomato Salad
## Fly Creek General Store

S alt potatoes are an Upstate favorite, created near Syracuse during the heyday of salt mining. Look for them in area grocery stores in 5-pound bags - 4¼ pounds of potatoes and ¾ pound of salt. Boiled in the briny bath the potatoes make great potato salads, home fries, side dishes, and soups. They are served, with butter, at many New York fairs.

This Mediterranean potato salad is a bright change from the familiar mayonnaise-based varieties. While it shares some elements with a classic French salad Niçoise, this recipe is inspired by the Italian *insalata pantasca,* named for caper-producing Pantelleria, a tiny dot of an island off the coast of Sicily.

**Half a bag of boiled salt potatoes, cubed (refrigerate the remainder for later)**
**1 pint cherry tomatoes, halved**
**1 small red onion, thinly sliced**
**¹/₃ cup good olives, pitted and halved**
**2 tablespoons capers, well rinsed and drained**
**¹/₃ cup chopped flat-leaf parsley**
**Pinch of crushed red pepper flakes**
**1 tablespoon chopped fresh oregano, 1 teaspoon dried**
**¼ cup olive oil**
**One can (3 to 4 ounces) can sardines in olive oil**

Cut potatoes in a large dice when they are cool enough to handle. When the potatoes are cool, add the tomatoes, onion, olives, capers, parsley, and red pepper. Toss gently. Sprinkle the oregano over the top, pour in the oil, and toss gently.

Transfer the salad to a large serving dish. Drain the sardines; blot the excess oil with paper towels. Arrange them over the salad. Cover and let salad rest a half-hour so flavors may develop. Serve at room temperature.

# Glimmerglass Opera

Gracefully reposing on the shores of Otsego Lake, Glimmerglass Opera presents outstanding summer repertory in an intimate and idyllic setting. The 900-seat Alice Busch Opera House provides the perfect venue, set on 43 splendid acres at the north end of the lake.

Born of the collective desire and nurturing of its Cooperstown founders, Glimmerglass Opera has enjoyed over thirty glorious seasons offering more than 50 new productions of traditional favorites, along with rarely-heard compositions and innovative new works. Four operas are carefully chosen for each summer season.

A tantalizing menu of related activities enhances the world-class productions. The Young Artists Program recitals feature the most promising new talents from across the country. First Nights invite you to get to know the cast and crew after each opening. Gala Weekends present all four productions over three days and Seminar Weekends offer in-depth panel discussions and lectures. Be sure to take advantage of a tranquil Glimmerglass picnic complete with champagne and dessert, creating a scene befitting a Tissot painting.

Wrap yourself in a mesmerizing Glimmerglass performance under the luminous summer sky of this beautiful rural setting. Attending Glimmerglass, for the opera novice or veteran, is a singular experience.

*The Glimmerglass Opera season runs during July and August.*

Ticket Office:
607-547-2255
18 Chestnut Street
Cooperstown, NY 13326

PO Box 191
Cooperstown, NY 13326
glimmerglass.org

*Holiday (The Picnic) by James Tissot 1876*

# Classic Utica Chicken Riggies
## Glimmerglass Opera

*I*n Central New York, nearby Utica is as well-known in for this delicious chicken-rigatoni dish, as Buffalo, New York is known for their wings. There are as many variations of the dish as there are chefs, but it always calls for chicken and rigatoni. A number of Utica restaurants claim to have the best recipe and the town has recently introduced a "Riggiefest."

4 tablespoons butter (Some recipes
   call for margarine, but *Home Plate*
   prefers butter from New York cows)

5 cloves garlic, minced

3 hot cherry peppers, sliced
   (from a jar in oil, seeds removed)

4 tablespoons olive oil

½ onion, minced

1 small shallot, minced

1 bell pepper, seeded and sliced

2 pounds boneless chicken
   breast, cubed

One 15-ounce can chicken broth

1 teaspoon cornstarch

2 cups tomato sauce
   (homemade, or one 15-ounce jar)

Salt and pepper to taste

1 pint heavy cream, or half and half

1 small can sliced black olives

1 cup Parmesan cheese,
   divided in half

1 to 1½ pounds rigatoni

Heat butter and olive oil in a large skillet. Sauté onion, shallot, garlic, and peppers until onion softens. Add chicken and continue cooking until onion is translucent and chicken is partially cooked.

Stir cornstarch thoroughly into cream. Add to chicken, along with broth, tomato sauce, olives, and ½ cup Parmesan cheese. Simmer over low heat about an hour, stirring occasionally. Season to taste with salt and pepper.

Cook rigatoni in a large pot of salted water until *al dente*.
Serve chicken over rigatoni and enjoy.

# Goldpetals

**E**llen White Weir's story is a classic account of how a passionate avocation became a bustling cottage industry. When she gave friends gifts of the soothing balms and lotions she made from the organic flowers that grow on her farm, she was barraged with requests and offers to pay for her products. She transformed her hobby into a business she named Goldpetals. Ellen coined the term based on her extensive knowledge of *calendula officinalis L. Compositae*. The sunny orange flower is more commonly known as pot marigold.

Looking more like a daisy than the familiar marigold bedding plant, Calendula has been valued for centuries for its healing and soothing properties. Calendula balms may be applied to almost any skin irritation from minor burns to babies' bottoms. Mediterranean in origin, it thrives in Upstate New York, scattering sunny hues over the hillsides.

**Marigold**

Ellen uses only quality natural components in her superior formulations, including olive oil, beeswax, witch hazel, and aloe. Divinely scented lavender grows on the Goldpetals farm and is used in many blends, as are essential oils, and shea and mango butters.

Check the Goldpetals website for their calendar of programs related to herbs, flowers and biodiversity. Goldpetals products are available online, at the Cooperstown Farmers' Market, Cooperstown Natural Foods, at special events, and Wednesdays at the Goldpetals Farmstand, June through October.

Ellen White Weir
539 Christian Hill Road
Cooperstown, NY 13326
 607-547-8425 or 607-293-6106
goldpetals.com

*Kaley Manikas (left) and friends
enjoying Goldpetals products.*

# Maple Ginger Chicken
## Goldpetals

"What's for dinner?" is a question frequently asked, and this easy, flavorful chicken is a dependable reply. The simple ingredients are easy to keep on hand and it takes no special equipment, or much attention, either. It's great when life demands that you multi-task.

1 chicken, cut up
5 tablespoons fresh ginger, peeled and chopped
5 tablespoons soy sauce or Bragg Liquid Aminos
¼ cup real maple syrup
Salt and pepper
Olive oil

Preheat oven to 375 degrees.

Generously coat a 9" x 13" baking dish with olive oil. Coat the chicken pieces with olive oil, rolling as you place them in the pan.

Stir soy sauce and maple syrup together. Pour evenly over chicken. Place fresh ginger on chicken pieces and salt and pepper to taste. Bake uncovered for about 45 minutes.

*"Ginger" is from a Sanskrit word meaning "horn-shaped". It is not a root at all, but a rhizome. Ginger has numerous culinary uses, especially in baking and in Asian cuisines. Most ginger is grown in China and India, where the entire plant, with its pink and white buds that bloom into yellow flowers, is used in landscaping. Ginger has long been believed to be effective on motion sickness, but the scientific results are mixed.*

# Haggerty Ace Hardware

**H**aggerty Ace Hardware is the great retail equalizer. Whether seeking springtime bedding plants, trudging through the slush for more ice melt, or picking primer and paint for your latest project, practically everyone's path eventually crosses at Haggerty Ace Hardware.

Real service is one reason people flock to this friendly store. The red-vested staff knows their stuff! They are well-versed about their merchandise and they are happy to offer advice about your project, painting, gardening, plumbing, or chainsaws. When spring finally breaks through our Upstate winter, paying a visit to the Haggerty gardening center is a local ritual. Fine quality nursery stock, vegetable seedlings, hanging plants, and all manner of garden tools help make the most of the growing season.

If your chores demand more than hand tools, The Haggerty Rental Center on Route 28 is the area source for roto-tillers, log-splitters, steam cleaners, backhoes, even a popcorn machine. Their ample inventory of power tools and machinery makes any task lighter.

Haggerty Hardware is also a boon to the cook. They stock small appliances, OXO tools and gadgets, canning supplies and the also offer a knife sharpening service. Don't miss their selection of men's and women's work clothes to look your best while happily laboring.

Jeff Haggerty
5390 State Highway 28
Cooperstown, NY 13326
607-547-2166
haggertyhardware@stny.rr.com

# North and South Salad
## *Pumpkin and Black-Eyed Peas*
## Haggerty Ace Hardware

*A* colorful salad, full of nutrients, that shows the versatility of two underused foods – that wonderful Southern legume, black eyed peas, and vitamin-rich pumpkin, a major New York crop. Save time with this recipe by using canned or frozen black-eyed peas and finding pumpkin or butternut squash cubes in the produce section.

*Peas and Pumpkin*

2 cups cooked black-eyed peas
   (if using canned peas,
   drained and rinsed)
Olive oil

1½ cups pumpkin or
   butternut squash cubes
1 garlic clove, minced

*Salad Base*

1 cup thinly sliced red or
   Empire sweet onion
¼ cup diced cucumber,
   peeled and seeded)
3 tablespoons extra-virgin olive oil
Salt and pepper

¼ cup chopped bell
   pepper (any color)
1 terrific tomato, seeded and diced
A few fresh basil leaves, chopped
1½ tablespoons lime juice

Preheat oven to 400 degrees. Place pumpkin or squash cubes in an 8" square baking pan and drizzle with a few tablespoons of water and about a tablespoon of olive oil. Bake about 15 minutes, stirring occasionally, until the cubes are tender. Remove from oven, stir together with garlic and let cool.

Whisk together olive oil and lime juice in a small bowl; season to taste with salt and pepper. In a serving bowl, combine salad ingredients with black-eyed peas. Toss with dressing, adding salt and pepper to taste. Toss in pumpkin cubes.

*Most cultures celebrate New Year's Day with traditional foods thought to bring luck for the coming year. In parts of Pennsylvania its pork and sauerkraut; potatoes and cabbage are common in Eastern Europe, and the Dutch like doughnuts. In the American South, black-eyed peas (often in the form of Hoppin' John) served with collards and cornbread brings good fortune.*

# Harmony House
# Café and Antiques

Richard and Mary Lou's spacious renovated building, situated at Fly Creek's off-kilter four corners, is the flagship of this hamlet. Richard's pleasant café is country comfortable and warmly inviting, with fresh coffee and the best iced tea available all day. It's almost like entering a friendly home; sit, rest awhile, have something to eat. Study the local art and historic photos gracing the walls. The food is reliably delicious and the atmosphere relaxing. Richard, a native of Long Island, has a way with clams and seafood, and they are frequently featured specials. Breakfast, lunch and dinner, too, are available in season. Harmony House Café is the perfect stop when antiquing and shopping.

Next door is Mary Lou's Harmony House Antiques, the ideal balance to the Café. Annie, the happy shop Springer spaniel adds to the charm and welcome of this intriguing and sweetly-scented shop. The neatly displayed and well-chosen inventory draws you to explore every shelf and nook. Find great antiques and country ware in this pleasant store.

Located just three miles from Cooperstown and easy to find, just follow Route 28 north (Glen Avenue off of Chestnut Street in Cooperstown, by the Methodist church) to the flashing yellow light in Fly Creek.

Richard and Mary Lou Votypka
6208 State Highway 28
Fly Creek, NY 13337
Café: 607-547-5077
Shop: 607-547-4071

# Baby, It's Cold Outside Chicken Soup

## Harmony House Café and Antiques

*A*ctually, this is a year-round soup, easily accessorized depending on the season. During the frosty New York winters, adjust the cayenne pepper accordingly. Remember that soup is a flexible art and a wonderful field of creativity; add and subtract as you like. This soup is another good reason to maintain a kitchen herb garden.

### Soup

2 tablespoons vegetable oil
1 medium onion, diced
2 cloves garlic
6 cups chicken broth
One 15-ounce can of tomato sauce
One 15-ounce can black beans, rinsed and drained
1-2 cups fresh or frozen corn kernels
1 teaspoon cayenne pepper, or to taste
Freshly ground black pepper to taste
1-2 tablespoons fresh basil and fresh cilantro, chopped
2 cups cooked chicken (or pork)

### Garnish

Tortilla chips
Shredded cheese (New York cheddar, Monterey Jack, manchego, etc.)
Sour Cream
Diced avocado
Salsa

In a soup pot over medium heat, heat oil and sauté onion and garlic until softened. Add broth, cayenne pepper, beans, corn, and tomato sauce. Let simmer; add chicken and chopped fresh basil and cilantro. If using dried herbs, use only a third of what you would use of the fresh. If more liquid is needed, add water, broth, or even beer. To serve, crumble a few tortilla chips in the bottom of a soup bowl and top with shredded cheese. Ladle soup into bowl and top with more chips, sour cream, avocado, and/or salsa.

# Hoffman Lane Bistro

In the first volume of *Home Plate*, Hoffman Lane Bistro is noted, of course, for its excellent food, but also for the beautiful *espaliered* tree growing on the side of their building. A number of our appreciated readers politely asked, "A what?" According to Brookwood Garden expert Pat Thorpe, an *espaliered* tree is one that is trained to grow flat against a wall or fence. It is usually done with fruit trees and it makes a dramatic appearance, especially when the tree is in bloom.

That striking tree echoes the attractive presentation and impressive flavors of the Bistro's fine fare. Open since 1999, Hoffman Lane offers dinner only and reservations are recommended. Their menu changes seasonally, reflecting the best fresh ingredients. Favorite signature dishes such as the Maple Lamb Brochette and Jumbo Crab and Crawfish Cake appetizers, Chopped Iceberg Salad, and the Classic Bistro Meat Loaf are usually available, along with their tantalizing specials. Their welcoming full bar is ready to complement your choice with beer, wine, or cocktails. Catering and private parties are available, and their back room can accommodate 60-100 comfortably.

Live music and other performances are frequently featured at the Bistro, including jazz, blues, Celtic, folk, and rock, and also occasional theatrical stagings. Check their website for entertainment schedules.

Be sure to look for the large praying mantis sculpture, created by local metal artist Don Gailanella.

Mark Loewenguth
2 Hoffman Lane
Cooperstown, NY, 13326
607-547-7055
Hoffmanlanebistro.com

*"A restaurant is a fantasy — a kind of living fantasy in which diners are the most important members of the cast."*
—Warner LeRoy, creator of Tavern on the Green and The Russian Tea Room

# Seared Duck Breast with Cheddar Grits and Cherry Port Wine Sauce
## Hoffman Lane Bistro

**D**uck is increasingly available at farm markets and grocery stores, with many duck farms on Long Island. The dark, moist meat is prized for entrees, appetizers, and dinner salads.

### Duck

4 boneless duck breasts                    Cooking oil

### Sauce

1 cup dried cherries                       1¼ cups ruby port wine
1 tablespoon balsamic vinegar              ¾ cup sugar
Salt and pepper to taste

### Grits

1 cup grits                                2 cups water
1 cup cream                                1 tablespoon butter
½ cup shredded white cheddar cheese        Salt and pepper to taste

Preheat oven to 400 degrees.

Sear duck breast quickly in hot pan coated with oil, until just rare. Set aside.

Place sauce ingredients in saucepan and simmer for 20 minutes. Puree sauce and keep warm.

In a separate saucepan, bring water, cream, and butter to a boil. Stir in grits and cook until smooth and creamy. Add cheddar cheese and season with salt and pepper. Remove from heat.

Finish roasting the duck breasts in the oven until medium rare. Check every few minutes so they do not overcook. Slice.

Present on four warmed plates. Make a base of grits, top with sliced duck breast and finish with cherry sauce. Very pretty and very good.

*In 1873, nine ducks were imported to Long Island, NY, and these prolific fowl went on to become the predecessors of all the Peking duck in the country. They are also known as Long Island duckling.*

# Ladybug

*I*n North America, the term "ladybug" refers to a colorful, friendly beetle that gardener's encourage to take up residence in their roses. In England, they are called ladybirds; a scientist will know these symbols of good luck as *Coccinellidae*. But in Cooperstown, Ladybug is a terrific little boutique downstairs from Main Street.

Doris Mark's shop is such a pleasure. Genial sounds and scents greet you as you descend the stairs to the neatly displayed goods. Variety, so the saying goes, is the spice of life, and certainly the attraction of Ladybug. Doris's eclectic tastes have filled this cheery store with unique kitchen goods and gifts for the home. Her jewelry selections include creations from local artist Karen Burgess, and the local products theme continues with handcrafted soaps and candles, and New York honey and maple syrup. Find fancies for babies, beautiful Christmas ornaments, garden décor, and free-flowing ladies' fashions designed to flatter.

You won't forget which shop you're visiting; the ladybug motif is subtly and cleverly repeated throughout the store. They are nicely stenciled on the walls, as jewelry in pins and necklaces, among the special greeting cards, in the shape of coin purses, and more. As always, gift wrapping is complimentary with your purchase.

Doris Mark
108 Main Street
Cooperstown, NY 13326
607-547-1940

# New York Cheddar Puffs
## Ladybug

These light and cheesy snacks are marvelous to keep on hand for spur of the moment gatherings. They freeze well and bake to a beautiful golden brown from a frozen state. Serve them with pre-dinner drinks or with soup or salad. They are terrific with Heirloom Tomato Salad.

1 cup water
¼ cup (half a stick) butter
½ teaspoon coarse salt, plus more for sprinkling
1 cup, plus 2 tablespoons all-purpose flour
4 large eggs
1½ cups (packed) NY extra-sharp white cheddar cheese, grated
½ cup minced green onion

Preheat oven to 375 degrees. Line baking sheets with parchment paper.

Place water, butter and ½ teaspoon salt in a medium saucepan and bring to a boil. Remove from heat and mix in flour. Return to heat for a few minutes and stir until the dough becomes shiny and pulls away from the pan.

Transfer to a mixer and add eggs, one at a time. Mix in cheese and minced onions. The dough is sticky, so use two small spoons to make the puff ovals. Drop onto to a lined baking sheet, one inch apart. Either cover with plastic wrap and foil and freeze at this point, or bake for about 30 minutes.

> *A cheese may disappoint. It may be dull, it may be naïve, in may be oversophisticated. Yet it remains cheese, milk's leap toward immortality.*
> —Cliff Fadiman

# Lake Road Motels
## *Route 80 Cooperstown to Springfield*

Human beings are unquestionably drawn to water. Almost all of us live near an ocean or major waterway. Lakes, rivers and oceans provide recreation, transportation, food, and, ultimately, life itself.

For many generations, Cooperstown visitors have drawn from all that the treasured Otsego Lake offers. Summer swimming, sun-dappled sailing, even winter ice fishing beckon. Thousands of memories are embroidered with the quiet lapping of gentle waves on the banks; the shimmering reflection of the moon on a cloudless night; a new day promised with each sunrise over the Sleeping Lion; a child's delighted squeal at catching a trout or a sudden, perhaps unexpected, immersion.

Gather your own Otsego Lake experiences with a stay at any of these locally-owned motels on the Lake. They are all between Cooperstown and Glimmerglass Opera and all are accredited by the Cooperstown Chamber of Commerce.

Aalsmeer Motel & Cottages
7078 St Hwy 80 – 607-547-8819
aalsmeermotelandcottages.com

Bayside Inn & Marina
7090 St Hwy 80 – 607-547-2371
cooperstown.net/bayside

Hickory Grove Motor Inn
6854 St Hwy 80 – 607-547-9874
hickorygrovemotorinn.com

Lake 'N Pines Motel & Cottages
7102 St Hwy 80 – 607-547-2790
cooperstown.net/lake-n-pines

Lake View Motel & Cottages
6805 St Hwy 80 – 607-547-9740
lakeviewmotelny.com

Terrace Motor Inn
6439 St Hwy 80 – 607-547-9979
terrace-motor-inn.com

# Zucchini Spoon Bread
## Lake Road Motels

Not a bread at all, but a savory casserole that uses some cornbread ingredients and lots of vegetables. A perfect side dish for lake trout or barbéqued entrees.

Preheat oven to 350 degrees.

1 cup corn kernels, fresh or frozen
½ cup chopped onions
½ cup diced bell pepper, any color
½ cup water

1 cup diced zucchini
1 cup NY cheddar cheese, shredded
½ cup cornmeal
1 cup chopped fresh tomatoes
2 eggs, beaten
½ cup milk
Salt and pepper to taste
A few dashes of Tabasco or other hot sauce

Combine corn, onions, bell pepper and water in a large saucepan and bring to a boil. Reduce heat, cover and simmer about five minutes. DO NOT DRAIN. Add zucchini, cheese, cornmeal, and tomatoes, stirring to combine. Set aside.

In a small bowl, beat eggs, milk, Tabasco and salt and pepper. Stir into vegetable mixture. Put into a greased casserole dish (1½ quart) and bake uncovered about 40 minutes. Let stand at least five minutes before serving.

# Lilac Cottage

*I*n the years immediately following the creation of the Dreams Park baseball tournament camp, Cooperstown area weekly rental homes have sprung up like woodland mushrooms on the hot morning that follows a spring rain.

Among all the daunting choices, you can rest assured leasing Lilac Cottage. This neatly-kept house is located on Route 28, within eyesight and walking distance of the Dreams Park. Cooperstown Commons is located directly across Route 28, giving easy access to banking, groceries and restaurants. Lilac cottage is about an eight minute drive from the Village of Cooperstown and about 20 minutes from Oneonta, with many restaurants and attractions along Route 28 in both directions.

This refurbished two-story home has a charming front porch and back deck. Mature trees and their signature lilacs' heady perfume envelop it every Cooperstown spring. Lilac Cottage sleeps six comfortably and boasts an upgraded kitchen, bath and laundry room. It is the perfect place to rest and rejuvenate between and after games.

Conscientious owners Bob and Connie Lanz attend to the details, large and small, that ensure a pleasant stay. Their hospitality, thoughtful touches, and little extras — what they call "lagniappe" in New Orleans — are all ways the Lanz's say, "We're glad you're here!"

Bob and Connie Lanz
4697 Route 28
Cooperstown, NY 13326
914-584-0094
203-938-9977

# Farm Fresh Salad Buffet
## Lilac Cottage

**S**alads are a sure and delicious way to get a lot of nutritious food in a single meal. Vitamin rich greens provide a colorful base that invites endless additions and variations of fruit, nuts, grain, and meats. Salads are welcome dining relief in the summer heat, and a blissful reminder of more clement days during winter's drudgeries.

### Farmhouse Dressing

1 cup mayonnaise (low fat is fine)
¼ cup sugar, NY honey or maple syrup*
½ cup milk (lower fat is OK here, too)
¼ cup white vinegar

This is an easy dressing, made with ingredients usually kept on hand. It will thicken upon refrigeration. Thin with a little milk or vinegar, to taste.

*If using honey or syrup, reduce the milk 2-4 tablespoons

### Salad Base

Spinach leaves, washed, dried, and torn. Or,
   use a mix of your favorite greens.
Fresh Bean Sprouts, washed and dried
One small sweet red onion, thinly sliced
Several strips of bacon, diced, cooked and drained

Toss ingredients together and keep refrigerated. Dress immediately before serving.

*Salad by the Calendar (add to the salad base):*
*Spring — sliced strawberries, green onions, and toasted pecans*
*Summer — farm fresh tomatoes, cucumbers, sliced onion, and crumbled goat cheese*
*Autumn — Cubes of New York cheddar and New York apples*
*Winter — Citrus segments (oranges or grapefruit segments, or drained mandarin oranges,) thinly-sliced pears, toasted walnuts.*
*Avocadoes are a great addition anytime, as is your imagination.*

# Little Bo'Tique

*A*ny destination that attracts as many families as Cooperstown has to have a shop filled with the whimsy, charm and joy that is childhood. Just a half a block west from Cooperstown's only stoplight is such a place. Toys, games, clothing, and all the warmth of a Mary Cassatt painting greet you at Little Bo'tique.

Find quality children's products that last, such as Playmobil, Manhattan Toy and the delightful interactive wooden toy and puzzle fun of Melissa and Doug. They also carry organic cotton clothing, accessories by the likes of Baby Bjorn and Petunia Pickle Bottom, Robeez shoes, and the most adorable bunny slippers. In fact, there is an abundance of items in this enjoyable shop that will make you emit "cute attack" sounds.

Travel toys and distractions are available to make trips more pleasant, and they carry baseball-themed gifts, of course. The experienced staff is on hand to help choose just the right gift for birthdays or any other occasion, and the gift wrapping is free. Personal shopping is also available.

Celebrate the special child in your life with a browse of this well-tended, carefully stocked little shop. Take home a new favorite toy or a special memory.

Renee LaFond
175 Main Street
Cooperstown, NY 13326
607-547-8687

# Otsie Cups
## Little Bo'tique

Practically every body of water has a legendary "sea monster." Scotland's Loch Ness famously has "Nessie," beautiful Lake Champlain has "Champie," and local lore tells of "Otsie" in Otsego Lake. Variously thought to be a large fish or a beaver, believers in Otsie know better. Take a cruise of beautiful Otsego Lake, described as "Glimmerglass" by James Fenimore Cooper, and keep a sharp lookout. You never know what might emerge from the 165-foot depths!

These colorful frozen cups are great for children's parties. Full of healthy fruit, they have far less refined sugar than so many children's treats. Hide the gummy worm "sea creature" in one cup and make a game of "Who Finds Otsie?"

**2 cups chunky or regular apple sauce**
**2 cups diced strawberries (thawed, if frozen)**
**Two 11-ounce cans mandarin orange segments, drained**
**1 cup blueberries**
**1 cup grapes**
**¼ cup of juice concentrate (apple, orange, white grape, etc.)**
**or sweeten to taste with honey or real maple syrup**
**1 gummy worm**

Combine all ingredients in a medium bowl. Divide into individual dishes, hiding the gummy worm in one dish. Or, line a muffin tin with paper liners and spoon fruit mixture into each. Freeze until firm. <u>Remove from freezer about 30 minutes before serving</u>, to soften and allow flavors to heighten. Or, they can be microwaved briefly (about a minute on low or medium, depending on wattage) to soften sufficiently.

*Look for photographer Richard Duncan's stunning coffee table book, <u>Otsego Lake</u>, available at bookstores and shops throughout the area.*

# Main Street Bed and Breakfest

You'll feel instantly at ease just standing on the front porch of the Main Street Bed and Breakfast. An inviting entryway, seasonal flowers, and attractive wicker furniture all say "Welcome."

Professional innkeepers Susan and Ron Streek have owned and operated their handsome Victorian inn (complete with ornate gingerbread) for twenty memorable years. Their experience means that your stay is reliably comfortable and pleasant. They can impart information about Cooperstown history and area nuances, and their unique recollections of seasons past make the difference between a mere visit and an unforgettable experience.

Main Street's full country breakfast, an attentively prepared meal from Sue's creative kitchen, begins the day in fine style. Then, perfectly fortified for the day's excursion into Leatherstocking Country,* venture forth to visit the National Baseball Hall of Fame and Museum, the Railroad Avenue shops or Main Street, or Otsego Lake. Their in-village location is perfect for visiting attractions, restaurants and shopping.

Look forward to comfortable rooms, amiable hosts, a tranquil and pleasant atmosphere, and tempting food at Main Street Bed and Breakfast.

Ron and Susan Streek
202 Main Street
Cooperstown, NY 13326
800-867-9755
cooperstownchamber.org/mainstreetbb

*Why "Leatherstocking?" It's an illustrious reference to the works of Cooperstown native James Fenimore Cooper and his celebrated Leatherstocking Tales.

# Baked Eggs
## Main Street Bed and Breakfast

Eggs may well be the world's most nutritious, economical and versatile food. They can be used for any meal and are quickly transformed into a vast number of dishes. One of the many benefits of country living is the availability of fresh, country eggs. Look for local eggs from Vaughn's Poultry Farm at Danny's Market and the Fly Creek General Store.

This is an easy and flavorful recipe. It is a particularly good choice when the stovetop burners are occupied cooking other breakfast favorites.

Preheat oven to 400 degrees

**2 eggs**
**Chives or scallions, finely chopped**
**¼ cup sharp cheddar cheese, shredded**
**Fresh thyme and sage, finely chopped**

Butter individual ramekins or custard cups, or coat with cooking spray. Put a sprinkling of thyme and sage in the bottom of baking cup. Add a layer of chopped chives. Break two eggs on top of greens, and then top with shredded cheese. Bake for 10 minutes.

Serves one. Multiply as needed; experiment with different herbs and cheeses according to your flavor preferences.

*Eggshell colors are determined by the breed of chicken. Basically, white chickens lay white eggs, and brown chickens lay brown eggs. The egg inside is the same regardless of shell color. Brown shells are usually a bit thicker than white shells, making them preferable for boiling.*

# Mickey's Place

Baseball memorabilia is a special genre of retailing. Far more than caps and t-shirts, to meet the criteria the shop must specialize in "objects associated with a famous person or event, especially considered as collectors' items."

Mickey's Place fits that description with style, offering not only "the cards your Mother threw away," but items especially for the baseball connoisseur. There are baseball caps, to be sure; in fact Mickey's Place boasts the largest selection anywhere, including current, old-time and minor league teams. You'll also find great team jerseys (regulation and reproduction), street signs, the Cooperstown Collection, and Yankee specialties. Mickey's Place has terrific items representing your favorite baseball team and era.

Mickey's Place is Cooperstown's only source of genuine Louisville Sluggers, those legendary bats that have born the names of baseball greats since Honus Wagner. Bats can be engraved with a name or special inscription while you wait.

You can shop with enthusiasm and confidence at Mickey's Place. The autographs are authentic, the Major League Baseball apparel is licensed, and the inventory is diverse and fascinating. This shop is a bonanza for the baseball lover.

Vin Russo
74 Main Street
Cooperstown, NY 13326
607-547-5775
1-800-528-5775
mickeysplace.com

> *In the great department store of life, baseball is the toy department.*
> —Unknown

# Cheesy Veggie Bread
## Mickey's Place

Need an easy appetizer? This is perfect and the showy presentation belies how easy it is to make. Keep the ingredients on hand, and you can throw it together for impromptu parties. This hearty bread can also be served with a light dinner.

**One 10-ounce tube refrigerated pizza dough***
**1 carton (at least 6 ounces) garlic and herb cheese spread**
**¾ cup grated Parmesan cheese**
**3 tablespoons chopped fresh Italian parsley**
**1 small red onion, sliced into rings**
**1 or 2 small green or yellow zucchini, sliced into rounds**
**Cooking spray**
**Olive oil**

Preheat oven to 400 degrees.

Line a baking sheet with parchment paper and coat paper with cooking spray. Unroll pizza dough onto parchment. Spread garlic and herb cheese on half of dough, leaving about a half-inch border. Sprinkle half of Parmesan and 2 tablespoons of chopped parsley over cheese. Pick up edge of parchment paper and fold plain half of dough over filled half. No need to seal edges.

Spread top half of dough with more cheese and remaining Parmesan. Arrange onion rings and zucchini rounds in rows or other pattern, or scatter randomly. Drizzle with a thin stream of olive oil and sprinkle with salt and freshly ground pepper. Bake about 20 minutes, until bread is puffed and edges are browned. Scatter chopped parsley over top. Let cool until sliceable and try not to eat it all in one sitting (good luck)!

*The pizza dough recipe for New York Blue Pizzettes works well for this recipe. Adirondack cheese spreads are also available at Cooperstown Cheese Company.*

# National Baseball Hall of Fame and Museum

More American films have been made about baseball than any other sport. You've likely seen *The Natural* or *Bull Durham*, *A League of Their Own*, or *Field of Dreams*, even if you don't consider yourself a baseball fan. You probably know the phrases "If you build it, he will come," or "There's no crying in baseball!" even if you haven't set foot in a stadium since Wrigley Field still went dark at sundown.

You're aware of the phrases, the films, and Babe Ruth, because baseball and Americans are inseparable. This unparalleled game has been played and held fast by every generation since we were still paying our taxes to England. As James Earl Jones says in his memorable speech in *Field of Dreams*, "the one constant through all the years has been baseball… this game is a part of our past."

As with any long-term relationship, Americans and baseball have had their ups and downs. We love the game when it is heroic and generous, get angry when it disappoints, and we tend to take it for granted due to its comforting and reliable presence. But, like any couple who experiences soaring heights, chilly distances and warm embraces – the vicissitudes of love – baseball and America are still together. We are a part of each other and as indivisible as the country itself.

Since 1939, The National Baseball Hall of Fame and Museum has astutely safeguarded our memories of baseball and its inextricable bond with American history. Carefully tended artifacts, displays, interactive exhibits, and the Hall of Famer's venerable plaques are presented with joy and deserved reverence. The Museum's diligent archivists meticulously maintain clippings, films and photos of anyone who ever crossed a big league infield.

Historically, baseball has been a barometer of the American temperament. The National Baseball Hall of Fame is the judicious custodian of the people and events that paint our past, color our language, and define America.

25 Main Street
Cooperstown, NY 13326
1-888-HALL-OF-FAME
607-547-7200
baseballhalloffame.org

# Company Chicken Rolls
## National Baseball Hall of Fame and Museum

**S**avory and satisfying, these chicken rolls make a wonderful company dish. They are delicious for your guests and easy on the cook! Most of the steps can be done the day before, giving you time to enjoy your own party. *Home Plate* thanks Ann Petroskey, wife of National Baseball Hall of Fame and Museum President Dale Petroskey, for sharing this home run recipe.

| | |
|---|---|
| 3 whole, boneless and skinless chicken breasts | 1 teaspoon garlic salt |
| ½ teaspoon crushed oregano | 1 teaspoon onion salt |
| 2 teaspoons vinegar | ½ teaspoon pepper |
| ¼ cup New York State white wine | 2 teaspoons vegetable oil |
| 6 slices of bacon | 3 ounces Monterey Jack cheese, sliced into six pieces |

Preheat oven to 375 degrees.

Cut chicken breasts in half and flatten, using a rolling pin on a non-wood cutting board.

Mix together onion and garlic salt, oregano and pepper. Sprinkle half of mixture evenly on chicken.

Starting at the narrow end of the flattened breast, place a piece of cheese and roll tightly. Sprinkle rolled breasts with remaining salt mixture. Wrap each chicken roll with a slice of bacon. Place in a shallow baking dish. If not baking immediately, cover with foil or plastic wrap and refrigerate.

Immediately before baking, mix the oil, vinegar and wine together, and pour evenly over chicken. Bake uncovered for 30-45 minutes, until chicken is completely cooked.

> *This is a game to be savored, not gulped. There's time to discuss everything between pitches or between innings.*
> —Bill Veeck

# National Pastime

You can almost feel the pulse of baseball history when you walk through the door of National Pastime. The old gloves that caught legal spitballs, advertising articles that recall the heyday of a player's popularity, balls smudged with the dirt of infields long since developed into condos. National Pastime offers respected vestiges of baseball heritage.

The National Pastime inventory includes the upper echelon of baseball nostalgia. Their stunning art gallery of Arthur Miller baseball works includes portraits of celebrated players such as Lou Gehrig, Josh Gibson, Rogers Hornsby, and Joe DiMaggio among many others. Check here also for Induction Day Cards, Major League Baseball souvenirs, and Ebbets Field flannels.

Leisurely study the display cases of rare items and learn as you shop. Their entire section devoted to the All-American Girls Professional Baseball League picks up where "A League of Their Own" left off. You'll find great shirts, pins, patches, bobbleheads, and autographed photos of the Rockford Peaches.

A multifaceted store, National Pastime also offers custom embroidery on shirts and more, on the mezzanine. Custom framing is available, too; just ask for Barb.

National Pastime is located on Main Street, a block from the Hall of Fame, and just a foul ball from the Village Flagpole.

81 Main Street
Cooperstown, NY 13326
607-547-2524
national-pastime.stores.yahoo.net

# Heirloom Tomato Salad
## National Pastime

S alads come in a variety of categories. There are the popular *tossed* greens, *layered* salads so familiar in Mexican cuisine, *congealed* salads made with a gelatin base and beautiful *arranged* salads, such as this glorious summer celebration of heirloom tomatoes. If heirloom tomatoes are unavailable, get the best quality tomatoes you can find, from your own garden or at the farmers' market.

This is so easy and absolutely gorgeous. Put it on a pretty platter and let the tomatoes take the spotlight.

**3 pounds assorted heirloom tomatoes**
**1 small sweet onion**
**1 farm fresh seedless cucumber**
**Chopped Italian parsley, if desired**

**3 tablespoon extra virgin olive oil**
**2 tablespoon white wine vinegar**

Whisk oil and vinegar together, seasoning with salt and freshly ground pepper. Set aside.

Core tomatoes and slice into thin rounds. Slice onion thinly and separate into rings. Slice cucumber into thin rounds. Arrange cucumber rounds on platter and drizzle with dressing. Place tomatoes on top of cucumbers and drizzle with more dressing. Top with onion rings and finish with remaining dressing. Sprinkle with chopped parsley, if using.

*Heirloom vegetables (and a debt of gratitude) are owed the farmers and gardeners who, in the wake of the post-World War II mega-agriculture trends, preserved the seeds of flavorful native plants that taste fabulous, but tend to travel poorly. Hundreds of varied and delicious types of vegetables and fruits might have been lost to the few mass-marketed strains, had it not been for their effort.*

# Nicoletta's Italian Café

*I*talian fare, like any cuisine, can run the gamut of disappointing (heavy, salty and nondescript) to magnificent (fresh, appealing and near perfection). Nicoletta's Italian Café is the epitome of the latter. Their handcrafted food is beautifully presented, and their carefully selected ingredients ensure a splendid dinner.

Wonderful Italian wines, kitchen-made sausage, fragrant, warm bread, and signature dishes such as Lobster Pomodoro or Bisteca Bianco Gorgonzola make Nicoletta's a flawless choice.

This welcoming Main Street restaurant is within shouting distance to the National Baseball Hall of Fame, and has fed a number of players and celebrities. Take a moment and enjoy perusing their framed photos featuring Nicoletta's employees with Ferguson Jenkins, Bob Gibson and Gary Carter, to name a few.

Their neatly-attired waitstaff serve you smartly in this lovely building, with its hardwood floors and decorative tin ceiling. Brilliantly merging Italian and American cultures, Nicoletta's ambience features art and Frank Sinatra's crooning to enhance your calamari. The music and décor befits this sophisticated, family-friendly place. A charming rear dining room is available for private parties.

Phillip Andrews
96 Main Street
Cooperstown, NY 13326
607-547-7499
nicolettasitaliancafe.com

> *Cooking is at once one of the simplest and most gratifying of the arts, but to cook well one must love and respect food.*
> —Craig Claiborne

# Seared Bay Scallops Florentine
## Nicoletta's Italian Café

This recipe is quick, easy, and devastatingly delicious. In New York, scallops are available from Long Island or from the vast Chesapeake Bay. The Bay is fed by the Susquehanna, the longest river in the eastern United States. Otsego Lake at Cooperstown forms the headwaters of the Susquehanna River.

**1 pound bay scallops**
**2 tablespoons butter**
**3 cloves garlic, minced**
**⅛ cup minced red onion**
**¼ cup minced bacon**
**1 cup heavy cream**
**¼ cup diced tomato**
**1 cup chopped, fresh spinach**
**3 cups cooked penne pasta**
**Salt and pepper**

Melt butter in a large sauté pan; add scallops and bacon. Sear scallops until golden brown. Add garlic and onion, sautéing until onion is translucent. Stir in heavy cream; when it begins to thicken, add tomato, spinach and penne. Adjust seasonings with salt and pepper and serve.

*Some culinary titles indicate the ingredients to come. Anything "Florentine" means the dish contains spinach. "Genovese" indicates pesto. If a recipe is "Dubarry," expect cauliflower, usually with cheese sauce. If the recipe is "Milanese," the main ingredient has been dipped in egg, breadcrumbs and Parmesan, and browned in butter. A "Bolognese" sauce is the rich ground meat and tomato ragu usually associated with spaghetti. If asparagus is topped with browned breadcrumbs and chopped hardboiled egg it is served "Polanaise."*

# NYSHA

## *Fenimore Art Museum and The Farmers' Museum*

The New York State Historical Association (NYSHA) undertakes the joyous, daunting task of looking after New York's fascinating past. Set on picturesque Otsego Lake, they document the contributions of Native Americans, early settlers, and New York's key role in the development of the country. NYSHA honors agriculture at the working village of The Farmers' Museum, and they magnificently illustrate American History with works at Fenimore Art Museum.

Enjoy a memorable day wandering the 11 galleries of Fenimore Art Museum, including collections of American fine and folk art, and the Eugene and Clare Thaw Collection of North American Indian Art. Their collection of more than 125,000 photographs gives a priceless look at New York's history. Many images, including the remarkable Smith and Telfer visions of a changing Cooperstown, are available online.

The Farmers' Museum is a working, living history of our agrarian heritage. Stroll the village and enjoy the livestock, gardens and barns; Todd's General Store and the delightful Empire State Carousel. Guides in period dress enthusiastically convey life in the pre-electric, pre-automobile nineteenth century. The meticulously detailed shops and buildings are authentic down to the butter molds and hand planes.

The Farmers' Museum and Fenimore Art Museum offer wonderful gift shops and casual dining. Lunch on the terrace overlooking Otsego Lake at Fenimore Art Museum makes a pleasant outing on a fine day.

Visit www.nysha.org for information regarding the many special events and exhibits of both museums, the Research Library and the Cooperstown Graduate Program.

5775 State Highway 80 (Lake Street)
Cooperstown, NY 13326
607-547-1450
nysha.org

*Every spring greets new lambs at The Farmers' Museum*

# Cup Cake
## The Farmers' Museum

*T*he *American Frugal Housewife: Dedicated to Those Who Are Not Ashamed of Economy* is a fascinating read, addressing all manners of domestic issues from the position of stalwart thrift and indispensable good sense, applicable even today. Its author, Mrs. Child, was a journalist and women's rights advocate. She espoused wisdom far beyond cleaning kid gloves and how to keep butter through the winter. Her book is once again available in special editions; check your local bookstore.

*Home Plate* thanks the Farmers' Museum for the following:

The Cup Cake is a favorite recipe that the open-hearth cooks in the Lippitt Farmhouse at The Farmers' Museum enjoy making. Cup Cake is sometimes called "One, Two, Three, Four Cake" for the amounts and order of ingredients. This cake is tasty and easy to make.

This version of the recipe was printed in *The American Frugal Housewife* written by Lydia Maria Child. First published in 1829 and going out of print in 1850 after thirty-five editions, *The American Frugal Housewife* was one of the more popular recipe books published in the 19th century.

Cup cake is about as good as pound cake, and is cheaper. One cup of butter, two cups of sugar, three cups of flour, and four eggs, well beat together, and baked in pans or cups. Bake twenty minutes, and no more.

In all cakes where butter or eggs are used, the butter should be very faithfully rubbed into the flour, and the eggs beat to a foam, before the ingredients are mixed.

Lydia Maria Child, *The American Frugal Housewife*, Boston 1833

*A child of six years old can be made useful; and should be taught to consider every day lost in which some little thing has not been done to assist others.*
    —From the Introduction of *The American Frugal Housewife*

# Otesaga Hotel

The Otesaga Hotel is the flagship of accommodation and hospitality on Otsego Lake.

Elegant and refined, the Otesaga offers an incomparable stay when visiting Cooperstown. "Otesaga" (Oh-te-sah-gah) derives from the Iroquois language and means "a place of meeting." Appropriate to its name, the Otesaga Hotel provides the perfect venue for gatherings of all kinds, from weddings and parties to business meetings and receptions.

Partake of sophisticated repasts in the upstairs Dining Room (jackets for gentlemen required for dinner, please), enhanced by stellar service and piano music in the background. For great food in a more casual setting, try the Hawkeye Grill downstairs, and enjoy al fresco dining lakeside on fine days. After dinner, relax in the Templeton Lounge with cocktails and live music six nights a week.

The Leatherstocking Golf Course is one of the best links in the Northeastern United States. The par 72 championship course, with its lake vistas, is as beautiful as it is challenging (70.8 rating,) hosting special tournaments throughout the golf season, including the Hall of Fame match on Induction Weekend. Leatherstocking Golf Course is open to the public and PGA pros Dan Spooner and Ron Philo are on hand for game turning instruction.

Operating since 1909, the Otesaga Hotel is part and parcel of Cooperstown's rich history. A perfect Sunday summer afternoon on the Otesaga's sweeping veranda, with tea or a cocktail, overlooking the ever-tranquil Otsego Lake and Star Field, is the definition of graceful living.

60 Lake Street
Cooperstown, NY 13326
1-800-348-6222 or 607-547-9931
otesaga.com

*For several decades the Otesaga was the site of the elite Knox School for Girls.*

# Steamed Clams
## with Chorizo, Fennel, and Corn
### Otesaga Hotel

Courtesy of the Otesaga's talented chef, David Lockwood, this traditional summer celebration of steamed clams and farm fresh corn takes an adventurous turn with the addition of spicy Spanish sausage and aromatic fennel.

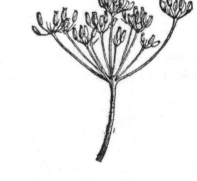

1 tablespoon extra virgin olive oil
½ pound chorizo sausage, cut in ¼" slices
½ cup finely chopped onions
1 tablespoon finely chopped garlic
½ cup julienned* fennel bulb
1 cup dry white wine
1 cup fresh corn kernels
40 fresh clams
¼ cup chopped flat leaf (Italian) parsley
Juice of one lemon
2 tablespoons cold butter
Salt and pepper to taste
1 loaf best quality French bread (i.e. Danny's, Heidelberg,
    Black Cat,) sliced ½" thick and toasted

*"Julienne" means to cut in matchstick pieces

In a medium-sized stock pot, heat olive oil over medium heat. Add the chorizo slices and sauté until golden brown on both sides. Remove chorizo and drain on paper towels. Drain all but about 2 tablespoons of fat from pot. Return to heat and add onion, fennel and garlic, and sauté until soft. Add the white wine and reduce by half. Add the corn and clams; Season with lemon juice, salt and pepper.

Cook until the clams open, then whisk in cold butter. Remove from heat and add the parsley. Serve in bowls with bread.

# Springfield Tractor and Implement

Upstate rural living takes a different attitude, considerable fortitude, and the right equipment. Vast gardens need tilling, feet-high snow needs removing, and lawns are mowed by the acre.

In a region where the family farm is a hallowed institution and the land is held in reverence, Springfield Tractor and Implement is housed, fittingly, in the former Light of the World Church. Cub Cadets are respectfully displayed on the apse where the preacher once gave sermons. Here at the two-lane Springfield Center crossroads of Routes 20 and 80, Iver Lindberg ranks as the second largest retailer of Club Cadets in the entire country.

Beyond offering a terrific selection of lawn tractors, tillers, snow removers, and the service for them, Springfield Tractor also serves as a community gathering place. Locals come in throughout the day, picking up sparkplugs, exchanging pleasantries and news of neighbors. It is also the site of a number of popular community events. Carhartt clad residents from far and wide gather under huge tents for the annual Open House, used equipment auction or annual tractor show. Complete with food (the sales benefit local churches) and camaraderie, these events paint a profile of the character that makes Upstate work. Don't miss Iver's Big Pot o' Chili. It's a community event, too, with all suggestions for additions considered as it cooks throughout the day.

If you're relocating or already a resident, when it's time to "cultivate your dreams," Springfield Tractor and Implement is a must stop.

Iver Lindberg
State Route 80
Springfield Center, NY 13468
315-858-2578

*Antique Steam Plow*

# Vegetable Venison Soup
## Springfield Tractor and Implement

*T*his meat-and-potatoes recipe is absurdly easy to make and a hunter's favorite. Like most soups, it lends itself to substitution and experimentation. Try adding wine, root vegetables, winter squash cubes, herbs, or most anything you find appealing. The soup is also delicious made with beef, though it will be higher in fat than when made with the leaner venison.

1 tablespoon vegetable oil
1 pound venison, cut into cubes
1 yellow onion, diced
2 cloves garlic, chopped
One 16-ounce package frozen mixed stew vegetables
2 (14 ½ ounce) cans diced tomatoes, with juice
3 cups potatoes, washed and cubed (peeling is optional)
4 cups water
1 tablespoon honey or maple syrup
2 teaspoons beef bouillon granules
1 teaspoon salt
½ teaspoon ground black pepper
Hot pepper sauce, to taste

Heat oil in a stock pot, over medium high heat. Brown venison in hot oil; add onion and garlic. Reduce heat and cover pot; cook about 10 minutes, stirring occasionally, until onions are translucent.

Add the mixed vegetables, tomatoes and potatoes. Stir the water, honey and bouillon into the soup. Season with salt, pepper, and hot pepper sauce. Cover and simmer for at least one hour, or until the meat is tender. Adjust seasonings and serve.

*"Numble" is an old term for the entrails of a deer. In 17th century England, the heart, kidneys, etc., were combined with apples, spices, currants, and sugar and baked into "numble pie." After the curious treatment British speakers of English sometimes give the letter "H," it became "'umble pie," and then "Humble Pie." Humble was eaten almost exclusively by the servant class, while the landowners enjoyed the venison, much the same as slaves had chitterlings, while slave owners ate "high off the hog" in the pre-Civil War American South.*

# Straws and Sweets

Every Main Street needs a sweet shop to complete its charm, and Cooperstown's Straws and Sweets fills the bill beautifully. From their focal point chocolates and confectionaries case to the eclectic giftware and sweet fragrances, they have been a favorite Cooperstown stop for nearly a decade.

Straws and Sweets is one of those intriguing shops that offer something different on every shelf and in each corner. It's a fine place to while away a pleasant hour just exploring the kitchenware and home decorations, or sampling the array of scented lotions and soaps, or choosing a unique piece of jewelry.

Perfectly located on Main Street, near the Village Flagpole, Straws and Sweets is within doors of the National Baseball Hall of Fame, bookstores, Wilber Bank, and baseball memorabilia shops. Relax in this oasis of appealing merchandise that runs the gamut from local artist's creations, to mementoes sure to warmly recall your trip to Cooperstown. Look here for just the right gift for just the right person.

Be sure to visit the newly-opened second Straws and Sweets location in Cooperstown Commons, south from Cooperstown on Route 28, near the Dreams Park.

Gail McManus
70 Main Street
Cooperstown, NY 13326
607-547-5365

*All you need is love. But a little chocolate now and then doesn't hurt.*

—Charles M. Schulz,
***Peanuts*** creator

# Chocolate Raspberry Cake
## Straws and Sweets

**R**ich, indulgent and decadent are words aptly used to describe desserts such as this Chocolate Raspberry Cake. It is a fitting recipe from Straws and Sweets, with its candy case brimming with fine chocolates.

### Cake

| | |
|---|---|
| 1 cup all-purpose flour | 1 cup sugar |
| ½ cup (1 stick) butter, softened | 4 eggs |
| ¼ teaspoon baking powder | 1½ cups Hershey's dark syrup |

### Raspberry Cream Center

| | |
|---|---|
| 2 cups powdered sugar | ½ cup (one stick) butter, softened |
| 2 tablespoons raspberry flavored liqueur (Chambord) or ¼ cup raspberry preserves | 1 teaspoon water |
| | Red food coloring, if desired |

### Chocolate Sauce Topping

| | |
|---|---|
| 6 tablespoons butter | 1 cup semi-sweet chocolate chips |

Fresh raspberries

Preheat oven to 350 degrees.

*To Make Chocolate Cake:* In a large bowl, cream butter and sugar together, and then add eggs one at a time, until thoroughly combined. Fold in flour and baking powder until completely mixed. Stir in syrup. Pour batter into a prepared 9"x13" pan. Bake 25 to 30 minutes or until tester comes out clean. Cool completely in pan on wire rack. Cover and refrigerate several hours.

*To Prepare Raspberry Cream Center:* Beat butter and powdered sugar together. Beat in liqueur and water to desired consistency. Add a few drops of coloring, if desired. Spread on cool cake and refrigerate.

*To Make Chocolate Sauce Topping:* Melt six tablespoons butter and 1 cup Hershey's semi-sweet chips in a small sauce pan over very low heat. Remove from heat, stir until smooth. Pour over chilled cake.

*Finishing Cake:* Place as many fresh raspberries as you like on top of cake. Cover and chill at least one hour before serving. Cover and refrigerate leftover (if any!) cake.

# Sunny Slope Bed and Breakfast and Dairy Farm

In Upstate New York, it serves us well to be fond of cows; there are so many of them. Dairying accounts for more than half of the agricultural production of our fine state, and for generations it was provided by the family farm. Cliff and Patti Brunner's Sunny Slope still works in that fine tradition and represents it grandly.

The Brunner's place, in its picture-postcard setting, has everything a model dairy farm should have: a neat farmhouse, a huge barn (look for the 1883 date), a pond, Chester, their Golden Retriever, truly contented cows, and an absolute devotion to what they do. If that weren't idyllic enough, their organic certification is soon to come.

Stay with them during your visit to Cooperstown and enjoy life at Sunny Slope. Rolling hills, starlight, wildflowers, and the Brunner's hospitality are available at their farmhouse accommodations or at Tansy Cottage. Revel in all that country goodness in the morning when Patti serves the farm's own bounty of milk, eggs, sausage, and maple syrup in her hearty homemade breakfasts.

Sunny Slope is a beautiful place, in spirit and being. It is all a New York family farm ought to be.

Cliff and Patti Brunner
211 Brunner Road
Cooperstown, NY 13326
607-547-8686
sunnyslope@mymailstation.com

"The friendly cow, all red and white,*
I love with all my heart;
She gives me cream with all her might,
To eat with apple-tart."
–Robert Louis Stevenson

*If you see a "red and white" cow, as Mr. Stevenson describes, you're looking at a Guernsey; the black and white cows, more common in our area, are Holsteins.

# Peaches and Cream Muffins
## Sunny Slope Bed and Breakfast and Dairy Farm

These muffins are an easy and sunny start to the morning. In August, look for fresh peaches at local farmers' markets and at Sunnycrest Orchard.

Preheat oven to 425 degrees

2 eggs
½ cup vegetable oil
3 cups flour
2 cups chopped peaches,
fresh or frozen

1 cup sour cream
1 cup sugar
4 teaspoons baking powder
1 teaspoon salt

In a large mixing bowl, combine eggs, sour cream, oil, and sugar. Mix well. In a separate bowl, stir together flour, baking powder and salt. Stir together wet and dry ingredients until combined. Fold in peaches.

Spoon batter into prepared muffin tins. Grease tins well, or line them with muffin papers. Use an ice cream scoop to transfer batter into muffin tins, evenly and cleanly. Bake muffins 20-25 minutes, or until a toothpick inserted comes out clean. Makes 18-20.

*Do I dare to eat a peach?*
*I shall wear white flannel trousers,*
*and walk upon the beach.*
*I have heard the mermaids singing,*
*each to each.*
– T.S. Eliot, The Love Song of J.
Alfred Prufrock

# Reiss Enterprises

- **Ledges Pin Shop**     • **A Cooperstown Christmas**     • **Moving and Storage**
- **Car Wash**            • **South Meadow Accommodations**

Howard and Doris Reiss are in contention for being the two busiest people in the Cooperstown area. Their conglomerate of activities, next door to the Dreams Park, fills the needs of visitors and residents alike with services, accommodations and pleasant shopping.

*Ledges Pin Shop* – Terrific Cooperstown baseball pins, buttons, shirts, and remembrances. Their baseball clocks are a great way to say, "Thanks, Coach!" with lots of space on the clock face for player's signatures. Moms and sisters – look for the line of attractive jewelry Doris has added.

*A Cooperstown Christmas* – Ornaments are a great way to remember your special time in Cooperstown, year after year. Look for the festive tree and house adornments, especially made to commemorate your time here. Their themed trees are sure to suit whatever the hobby, including baseball, fishing, pets, and much more.

*South Meadow Accommodations* – When looking for a place to stay, it's important that the owners offer a top-notch place, with attention paid to the details. Not only are the Reiss's accommodations clean and comfortable, *Doris even irons the sheets*. Enough said.

*Reiss Moving and Storage* – The Reiss professional service can handle large and small moves, locally and farther. New to the area? Store your goods with Reiss while looking for the right place to live.

*Reiss Car Wash* – This is the only car wash on this section of Route 28, and a valuable antidote for travel road grime or winter salt.

Howard and Doris Reiss
Route 28 (next door to Dreams Park)
Milford, NY 13807
607-547-6187

# Blueberry Stuffed French Toast
## Reiss Enterprises

This recipe is a sure favorite for breakfast or brunch. It can be prepared the night before to help make a busy morning less manic, and it uses two New York favorites – blueberries and maple syrup. Wonderful blueberries are available in late July or early August across Route 28, just a tenth of a mile from the Reiss shops, at Ingall's Pick Your Own Blueberries.

### French Toast
12 slices good quality white bread (your own homemade, Danny's, Heidelberg, or Black Cat Café)

1 cup blueberries, rinsed and drained (or more, if you like)

2 cups milk

Two 8-ounce packages cream cheese, cut into cubes while cold

12 large eggs

⅓ cup New York State maple syrup

### Blueberry Sauce
½ cup sugar

½ cup water

1 tablespoon butter

1 tablespoon cornstarch

½ cup blueberries

½ cup maple syrup

Butter a 9" x 13" baking dish. Layer half the bread cubes on the bottom and evenly scatter the cream cheese cubes and blueberries over all. Place the remaining bread cubes on top.

In a large bowl, whisk together eggs, milk, and maple syrup. Carefully pour over bread layers. Cover and refrigerate overnight.

To bake, preheat oven to 350 degrees. Cover pan with foil and bake for 30 minutes. Remove foil and bake up to an additional 30 minutes, until puffed and golden.

While the casserole bakes, make the sauce: Whisk sugar, cornstarch and water together in a small saucepan. Cook over medium heat until mixture begins to thicken. Add blueberries and simmer until they begin to pop. Stir in butter and maple syrup and serve over Baked French Toast.

*The blueberry is one of three fruits native to the United States. The cranberry and the Concord grape are the other two.*

# Riverwood

Eclectic… inspired…quirky… distinctive… FUN. If Santa and his elves were to establish a Cooperstown branch it would be at this delightful shop on the corner of Main and Pioneer. Just try not to smile as you explore the merchandise that ranges from upscale gifts to curious trinkets.

There aren't enough adjectives to sufficiently describe Rick Gibbons' treasure house of a shop. The endearing river otter statuary greets you at the door and sets the tone for your stay. The Brighton leather selections are ideal gifts, as are American Fine Crafts. Or, stop by just to play with the toys. As Rick is fond of saying, "At Riverwood, the fun is in the discovery."

Riverwood invites you to spend some stress-reducing time. Gadgets, games and puzzles command your happily undivided attention. You'll also find quality jewelry, hats, kitchenware, local pottery, and other intriguing inventory reflecting Rick's idiosyncratic tastes. Locally created SoapRocks are beautiful aromatherapy. The Bats baseball game and custom Cooperstown home plate slates are perfect keepsakes.

Toys for all ages are found throughout Riverwood, but Rick sets the back room aside for the young ones. Books, stuffed animals and enchanting playthings are waiting to fascinate a favored child.

Treat yourself to this wonderful shop; take a magical stroll through Riverwood.

Rick Gibbons
88 Main Street
Cooperstown, NY 13326
607-547-4403
riverwoodgifts.com

# Mushroom Leek Croquettes
## Riverwood

**M**ake these delectable croquettes several hours prior to serving. They benefit from the resting time and you benefit from one less thing to do just before dinner. They are perfect served on a bed of greens (escarole, spinach or Swiss chard) sautéed in olive oil, garlic and a little onion, with a whiff of red pepper flakes.

**1 stick of butter, halved**
**10 ounces of your choice of mushrooms, coarsely chopped**
**1½ cups (packed) shredded cheddar cheese**

**4 cloves of garlic, chopped**
**1½ cups finely chopped leeks (white and pale green parts only)**
**1½ cups bread crumbs**

**4 eggs, beaten**
**1 tablespoon steak sauce**

**2 tablespoons fresh thyme, chopped**
**1 tablespoon chili sauce**

**Flour for coating croquettes**

**About a cup of oil, for frying**

In a large skillet over medium heat, melt half of butter. Add chopped mushrooms and garlic; sauté until mushrooms are quite soft. Transfer to a medium bowl and set aside. Melt remaining butter in the same pan and add leeks, sautéing until soft. Add to mushrooms and let cool. Stir in breadcrumbs and cheese.

Whisk eggs, thyme, steak sauce, and chili sauce together. Stir into mushroom mixture and season with salt and pepper. Scoop mixture and shape into patties. Place on baking sheet, cover and refrigerate for at least one hour, and up to four hours.

Just before dinner, preheat oven to 350 degrees. Coat mushroom patties with flour. Heat oil in a large frying pan over medium heat, and then cook patties until brown, about 2 minutes per side. Transfer patties to a baking sheet and finish cooking in the oven, about five minutes.

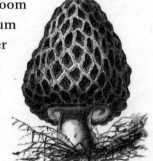

Serve one or two patties on sautéed greens as a first course, or luncheon entrée.

# Rose and Thistle Bed and Breakfest

The Rose and Thistle Bed and Breakfast provides an enchanting welcome to the Village of Cooperstown. This lovely, rose-colored Queen Anne Victorian home is the first B&B inside the Village, warmly greeting you as you enter from the south on Chestnut Street (State Highway 28).

The remarkably attentive innkeepers Steve and Patti D'Esposito see that their guests are satisfied, offering well-appointed rooms, generous breakfasts and the kind of personal service that make warm memories of a superior bed and breakfast stay.

Relaxation reigns at the Rose and Thistle. Oftentimes you can see guests enjoying conversation on the front porch, surrounded by Steve and Patti's award-winning flowers and landscaping, contentedly letting time go by after breakfast, between games or before the opera.

Their convenient location to Main Street Cooperstown and many Village attractions, the cozy warmth, the home-like ambience, and wonderful breakfasts – there are so many reasons to choose The Rose and Thistle. Relax in Steve and Patti's inn-keeping know-how.

Steve and Patti D'Esposito
132 Chestnut Street
Cooperstown, NY 13326
607-547-5345
roseandthistlebb.com

# String Bean Salad
## Rose and Thistle Bed and Breakfest

"Green beans," "string beans" and "snap beans" are all synonymous terms for the same valuable vegetable. Before the current hybrids were available, green beans had a fibrous string that ran along the seam. The beans were broken in half, to remove the inedible string. The "snap" sound fresh beans make when broken is the source of the third name.

This easy salad is great to make ahead of serving time.

1 pound string beans
1 medium red onion, thinly sliced
6 hard-boiled eggs
6 red new potatoes

Olive Oil
Balsamic vinegar
Fine chopped oregano, a tablespoon
    if fresh, or a teaspoon if dried
Salt and pepper

Boil potatoes until tender and set aside to cool.

Trim tops and tails from beans and quickly boil or steam until tender.

Cube potatoes and chop boiled eggs.

In a large bowl, combine green beans, sliced onion, eggs, and potatoes.

Drizzle olive oil and balsamic vinegar over all, according to taste, and sprinkle with minced oregano and salt and pepper. Toss gently until combined. Refrigerate two hours. Toss again and adjust seasonings just before serving.

*"Buon appetito!" from the D'Espositos.*

# The Barnwell Inn

Just a short walk from Cooperstown's Main Street, the Barnwell Inn is as graceful as a summer debutante at a garden party. This tidily kept bed and breakfast offers four elegant rooms, comfortably furnished and adorned with antiques.

Built in 1850, the dignified Victorian house is painted the same soft shades of yellow as a pound of New York State's best butter (a color you can confirm should you visit the butter sculpting at the New York State Fair in Syracuse). There is a neatly trimmed front lawn and an apple tree in the back, perfect for sitting under with a cup of coffee and your quiet thoughts, or with a glass of sherry, wooing your best girl.

Breakfast is a lovely morning ritual at the Barnwell Inn. Tara and Mark "Barney" Barnwell place beautifully prepared food before their guests, the result of Mark's uncanny knack with quality ingredients. Returning guests tell splendid tales of savory quiches; warm breads and fresh, ripe fruit; eggs in all guises, and Mark's indulgent baked goods.

You'll appreciate the Barnwell Inn's private baths, off-street parking, cable TV, and air-conditioning. You'll remember Mark and Tara's warm reception and hospitality.

Tara and Mark Barnwell
48 Susquehanna Avenue
Cooperstown, NY 13326
607-547-1850
Barnwellinn.com

> *"What is there more kindly than the feeling between host and guest?"*
> —Aeschylus

# Black and Blue Chicken
## The Barnwell Inn

*T*he zingy pepper makes it black, the Gorgonzola makes it blue, and the ingredients joyously clamor to make this chicken mouth-watering and succulent.

**3 or 4 boneless chicken breasts, halves, cut up into strips lengthwise**
**3 or 4 garlic cloves, pressed or chopped**
**8 ounces sliced mushrooms**
**1½ teaspoons black pepper**
**8 ounces (one-half pound) blue or Gorgonzola cheese, crumbled**
**1½ sticks butter, plus more for sautéing**
**Good French or Italian Bread (Heidelberg, Black Cat or**
  **Danny's Market,) sliced and lightly toasted**

Preheat oven to 350 degrees.

In a large skillet, lightly brown chicken breasts in a bit of oil, but do not cook completely. Remove chicken and set aside. Add a knob of butter to the skillet and sauté mushrooms until liquid is reduced.

Melt 1½ sticks of butter in a 2-quart casserole dish. Add garlic and black pepper (Mark and Tara swear the more, the better!) and stir together. Add browned chicken breast strips and cover with sautéed mushrooms. Salt to taste. Crumble blue or Gorgonzola cheese over the top.

Bake for 45 – 50 minutes, until bubbly.

To serve, spoon chicken and cheese mixture from the bottom of the casserole over the toasted bread. This simple entrée is great with a simple salad and fresh tomatoes. Bon Appetit!

*Gorgonzola cheese is named for an area near Milan, Italy, and is one of the finest of the cheeses incorporating blue-green veins. Due to the greenish marble of the interior, the London Stock Exchange is sometimes called "Gorgonzola Hall."*

# SSPCA Better Exchange Thrift Shop

The Susquehanna Society for the Prevention of Cruelty to Animals is a tremendous community asset. They take great care of Otsego County's dogs and cats, of course, and they are also the mother lode of the area's best bargains.

The Better Exchange Thrift Shop is the ongoing fundraising branch of the SSPCA. It is an Aladdin's Cave of great buys with a continually changing inventory. Household goods, clothing, books, and giftware are just some of what you may find during a pleasant meander of the shop. Proceeds from The Better Exchange Thrift Shop benefit the SSPCA's animal care programs, including long-term stays, adoptions and education, and feral cat spay and neuter projects.

The Better Exchange is operated by a dedicated group of volunteers who keep it organized and tidy, and the merchandise rotated. They accept and display only quality donations, providing their customers great selections. Your purchases help keep the area's dogs and cats healthy and sheltered until they are placed in responsible, caring homes.

The Better Exchange Thrift Shop is located on Route 28, within a mile of the Cooperstown Dreams Park. It is open Tuesday through Saturday, from 10AM-5PM.

4841 State Highway 28
Cooperstown, NY 13326
607-547-8111
sspca.petfinder.org

*Adopt!*

# Homemade Pet Fare
## SSPCA Better Exchange Thrift Shop

How did we feed pets before all those cans and bags took up an entire row in the grocery store? In the light of tainted pet food incidents, it's good to remember that there are alternatives to heavily advertised products that contain unfamiliar ingredients. Be sure to check with your vet regarding your pet's special needs.

### Feline Fish Fancies
½ cup canned sardines or mackerel, drained
1 cup whole grain bread crumbs
1 tablespoon oil
1 egg, beaten
½ teaspoon brewer's yeast, optional (check the natural foods store)

Preheat oven to 350 degrees.

Place all ingredients in a food processor and combine briefly. Alternately, mash fish well and stir in remaining ingredients thoroughly. Drop by dots (¼ teaspoon) onto a greased cookie sheet and bake about 8 minutes. Cool. Store in an airtight container in the refrigerator.

### Fido's Favorite
1½ pounds chicken meat, minced
1¼ cups frozen mixed vegetables, finely chopped
2 cups rice
3¼ cups water or salt-free broth (3¾ cups, if using brown rice)

Place chicken, vegetables and rice in a soup pot. Stir in water, combining well. Place pot over medium-high heat and bring to a boil, stirring frequently.

Reduce heat and cover pot. Simmer until the rice is tender and the liquid is absorbed, about 25 minutes for white rice; 35-40 minutes for brown rice. Cool before serving; dogs prefer food at room temperature. Store refrigerated.

# TJ's Place: The Home Plate

**T**J's Place is a grand mix of baseball, burgers, cocktails, country décor, and good friends. Ted and Diane's welcoming shop and restaurant is American at every turn, from their many Coca-Cola items, to the framed and autographed photos of baseball icons, to country ware gifts for your home. You'll find terrific sports memorabilia for sale and the baseball greats themselves signing autographs and greeting fans during Induction Weekend and special events.

Spacious and friendly, TJ's offers ample casual fare in a comfortable, casual atmosphere. Open year round, TJ's easily accommodates groups (up to 50) for breakfast, lunch and dinner. Their extensive menu features classic favorites such as eggs and home fries for breakfast, sandwiches and salads for lunch, and steak, spaghetti and specials in the evening. Special menus are available for seniors and kids, as are vegetarian selections. Their full bar invites you and your friends to relax with a favorite round, and their big screen TV gives you a place to catch a game.

TJ's Place has been a favorite fixture on Main Street for nearly 20 years, marking memorable Inductions and Cooperstown celebrations. Its history is on the walls, on the menu, and captured in the stories of the many locals who make TJ's: The Home Plate their home base.

Ted Hargrove and Diane Howard
124 Main Street
Cooperstown, NY 13326
607-547-4040
tjs-place.com

*Need a place to stay? TJ's offers accommodations next door at The Stables. E-mail thestablesinn@yahoo.com.*

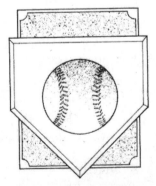

# TJ's Pot Roast
## TJ's Place: The Home Plate

**M**any beef cuts make a great pot roast, particularly from the chuck. Arm roasts, seven-blade roasts, chuck eye roasts, bottom rounds, and others work well. Check with the local meat cutter for more suggestions.

TJ's owner, Ted Hargrove, makes this American classic every Saturday night.

**One good-sized beef roast (3-30 pounds)**

*Seasoning mixture*
**(The amount needed will depend on the size of the roast)**
**Garlic Salt**
**Onion Salt**
**Paprika**
**Black Pepper**
**Worcestershire Sauce**
**Soy Sauce**

Rub the entire roast well with the salts, paprika and pepper. Place in a deep roasting pan with a cover. Douse well with the Worcestershire and soy sauces. Add water halfway up the roast. Add more Worcestershire and soy sauce to water. Cover the pan and place in a 175 degree oven for at least 3 hours (up to overnight, if it's a big roast).

When the roast looks like it will fall apart, remove it from the stock and place meat on a platter. Cover with foil to keep warm.

*To Make Gravy:*
Put beef stock into a pot, skimming fat if you prefer. Allow a scant tablespoon of flour per cup of stock. In a cup, blend flour with a small amount of cold water to form a liquid paste, free of lumps. Bring stock to a boil and slowly whisk flour mixture into stock. Gently boil until nicely thickened. Add more stock if gravy is too thick; cook down if too thin. Serve with tender beef, traditionally over mashed potatoes.

# The White House Inn

*I*n an increasingly demanding world it is easy to overlook the value of the home and hearth elements that contribute to a peaceful soul. Paying attention to those details define a premium bed and breakfast. The well-made beds; a hand-painted table; carefully filled bookshelves, or a lace-edged tablecloth all represent a haven of tranquility. The White House Inn welcomes and envelops their guests with the comforts of "home."

Ed and Margie Landers' Greek revival home (reputedly built by a former pirate) and adjacent Carriage House accommodate guests warmly, comfortably and memorably. Located in the heart of Cooperstown, they are a few minutes walk from Main Street shopping, dining and attractions. The White House Inn's full-sized pool and gardens are a wonderful respite on a summer's day. Or, get cozy next to the gathering room fire on a cool evening.

The day begins in hearty fashion with the White House Inn's gourmet breakfast. Daily specials, seasonal fresh fruit, and home baking remind you, in delicious style, why breakfast truly is the most important meal of the day.

Surrounded by antiques and tasteful furnishings, the White House Inn promises a gracious stay. Their personal advice and guidance, cable television and wireless internet service, promises a convenient one.

Open year round, the White House Inn is a grand ambassador of Cooperstown.

Marjorie and Edward Landers
46 Chestnut Street
Cooperstown, NY 13326
607-547-5054
thewhitehouseinn.com

> *Pray you bid*
> *These unknown friends to's welcome, for it is*
> *A way to make us better friends, more known.*
> —William Shakespeare,
> *A Winter's Tale*

# Country Soufflé
## The White House Inn

*I*f you need a great brunch recipe, check with a bed and breakfast. It's their business to feed a dozen or so people at a time, every morning. Good ones, like The White House Inn, make it look as if it's no effort at all.

**6 large eggs, beaten**
**1 cup Bisquick baking mix**
**1 cup milk**
**½ stick butter, melted**
**24 ounces cottage cheese**
**8 ounces Monterey Jack cheese, shredded**
**8 ounces Monterey Jack cheese with jalapeno peppers, shredded**
**Chopped fresh tomatoes**
**Chopped fresh scallions**

Preheat oven to 325 degrees.

Add baking mix to beaten eggs, along with milk and melted butter. Mix well. Reserving about a ½ cup of the shredded cheese, add cottage cheese and both Monterey Jacks to egg mixture, mixing well. Coat a 9" x 13" baking pan with cooking spray and pour in egg and cheese mixture.

Bake for 30-35 minutes.

Top with chopped tomatoes, scallions and reserved cheese. Bake an additional 5-10 minutes.

The recipe is especially good made with New York State's McCadam Cheese.

> *Cheese has always been a food that both sophisticated and simple humans love.*
> —M.F.K. Fisher from *How to Cook a Wolf*

# Tin Bin Alley

Nostalgia is defined as a mix of warm reminiscing, combined with a bit of wistful longing. Just treading the old wooden floors of Tin Bin Alley, surrounded by their inventory of beautiful giftware, metal signs depicting advertising of yore, and old-fashioned candies evokes that pleasant feeling.

Open year-round and an easy stroll from the National Baseball Hall of Fame, Tin Bin Alley offers the type of special merchandise you'll want to take home. Their well-chosen goods from small manufacturers include Buck Hill pancake mixes and Arbor Hill grape products from New York (grab the Grape Twists, if they have any of this bestseller,) Ann Clark cookie cutters from Vermont, Erda bags from Maine, gorgeous holiday gourds from Pennsylvania, and stunning stoneware from Poland. They also offer the Lang Companies appealing note cards, calendars, and giftware, and Boyd's Bears. Tin Bin Alley is the only source for the attractive Cooperstown Commemorative afghan, and their baseball artwork is perfect for the collector of quality goods. Many of their products are also available online.

Every tourist destination needs a fudge shop! Tin Bin Alley meets that requisite with a variety of enticing flavors. The candy counter is also laden with Jelly Bellys and the "penny candy" memories of root beer barrels and licorice pipes, among the traditional favorites.

The fudge and candy counter greets you at the entry, and the clever merchandise entreats you to keep exploring to the far wall of this deep and spacious shop. Tin Bin is a must stop on Main Street, located between TJ's and Ladybug.

Ian and Jennifer Porto
114 Main Street
Cooperstown, NY 13326
607-547-5565
TinBinAlley.com

# Bourbon Meatballs
## Tin Bin Alley

With a bold current of bourbon running through the sauce, these sweet and sassy meatballs are especially easy when made with already prepared frozen meatballs. Just a few pantry staples and a browse of the liquor cabinet make this terrific appetizer perfect for parties and impromptu get-togethers. The flavors improve the longer the meatballs swim in the whiskey-infused sauce.

**2 pounds of Italian seasoned meatballs, appetizer size**
**2 cups barbecue sauce (Brooks, Arbor Hill or other New York-made sauce)**
**1½ cups bourbon**
**1 cup local honey**
**1 cup Dijon-style mustard (check for local varieties)**
**Splash of Worcestershire sauce**

In a large skillet, brown meatballs in a small amount of oil. Set aside. In a mixing bowl, whisk remaining ingredients together. Combine sauce and meatballs and simmer in a saucepan over low heat, or in a crockpot set on low. On top of the stove, let meatballs simmer at least a half-hour so flavors can meld. The meatballs can stay in a crock pot for several hours, making them perfect for parties.

*Bourbon is a distinctly American spirit, as proclaimed by a 1964 Congressional act. It must be made in the United States, contain at least 51% corn, and age in new, charred oak barrels. Bourbon whiskey plays a fascinating role in the history and culture of the state of Kentucky. Hall of Fame pitcher Jim Bunning is the junior Senator representing the Bluegrass State.*

# Tom and Kelly's

Named for the owners, Tom and Kelly's is one of those great area landmarks that functions as a rural positioning device. Located at the crossroads of Routes 20 and 80 in Springfield Center, they are on the way to and from Albany, Glimmerglass Opera, and Richfield Springs. This convenient stop offers food, fill-ups, the *New York Times*, local eggs and maple syrup, and pleasant chatter all the while. Tom and Kelly's is the kind of place where the service includes giving directions to wayfaring travelers and pumping gas at no extra charge. If you are a fan of *The Andy Griffith Show* and Barney Fife, this is "the fillin' station" where you'd go to get "a bottle of pop."

Like many rural general markets, Tom and Kelly have a "Round Table" where locals and visitors alike can gather and discuss current events and sip gourmet coffee. They also feature a corner dedicated to "summer fun beers"– diverse ales and lagers from regional breweries, and a deli case, available in the summer season, for convenient and tasty take-out. If you are a fan of fishing or gardening, stop by the bait refrigerator for fish fancies, or worms for lures or the compost pile.

For Red Sox fans, don't fret; they also carry the *Boston Globe*.

Tom and Kelly Mabie
4964 US Highway 20 (at Route 80)
Springfield Center, NY 13468
315-858-1108

# Maple Sugar Nuts
## Tom and Kelly's

This is the simplest of recipes, calling for only two ingredients. Don't even consider making these festive nuts with anything other than pure maple syrup. That sticky brown stuff sold as "pancake topping " is primarily corn syrup and will never sugar correctly– making a mess and wasting good nuts. Properly made, Maple Sugar Nuts are a wonderful holiday or hostess gift.

A candy thermometer is useful when making these nuts.

**3 cups pure New York maple syrup**
**6 cups nuts (walnuts, almonds, cashews, hazelnuts,**
    **peanuts, or your preference)**

Butter a large roasting pan, or coat it with cooking spray. Spread nuts in a single, even layer.

In a large pot, heat the maple syrup to 240 degrees on the candy thermometer, or until it reaches the soft to firm ball stage. Once it reaches this stage, boil a minute longer, stirring constantly.

Pour boiling syrup over nuts, and start stirring. The mixture will be sticky at first. Continue to mix until syrup granulates and hardens. Store nuts in an airtight tin.

*Walnuts are one of the exceptionally good-for-you foods. Just a few nuts, with their high fat content and Omega 3 acids, quell appetite and promote cardiovascular health. Other foods bursting with health-promoting and health-protecting nutrients include blueberries, broccoli, oats, pumpkin, salmon, tomatoes, and yogurt – all New York State products.*

# Triple Play Café

Newly and beautifully renovated, this snug, comfortable eatery features natural brick and warm wood, creating a relaxing, comfortable atmosphere. It's friendly, fresh design is reminiscent of metropolitan café. Triple Play offers three meals and, a rarity in Cooperstown, delivery within the Village.

Just a line drive across Main Street from the National Baseball Hall of Fame, and next door to Wilber National Bank, Pat Governale's place is renowned for his homemade soups. Steaming pots of Italian Wedding, Manhattan Clam Chowder, Chicken Vegetable or chili simmer on the back burners, ready to satisfy the most ravenous appetite.

Exceptional soups are just the starting point. Eye-opening breakfasts greet the day with omelets for the breakfast lover, or muffins for lighter appetites. Hearty sandwiches and specials are lunchtime favorites and casual dinners feature fine steak cuts and salads. Check the daily specials on the blackboard displayed in their picture window. A word of advice: if meat loaf or chicken and biscuits are listed, stop by before they run out!

Wine and beer are available to enhance your meal and Pat is usually on hand to make sure you're well-served. Catering is available.

Pat Governale
64 Main Street
Cooperstown, NY 13326
607-547-1395
607-547-1355 for fax orders

*The unassisted triple play is one of rarest feats in baseball, occurring just 13 times in the major league baseball history, 12 times in regular season play and in the 1920 World Series by Cleveland Indian Bill Wambsganss.*

# Manhattan Clam Chowder
## Triple Play Café

Manhattan clam chowder is the estranged cousin of its creamy New England relative. The rivalry between fanciers of either type of this hearty soup has existed since tomatoes were added, possibly by Portuguese immigrants. The enmity reached a peak in 1939 when a Maine assemblyman introduced legislation to make the addition of tomatoes to clam chowder illegal. (Maine's tax dollars at work).

**4 slices bacon, diced**
**1 onion, chopped**
**½ green pepper, diced**
**2 stalks celery, diced**
**2 boiling potatoes, peeled and diced**
**Two 8-ounce bottles of clam juice**
**One can (15 ounce) diced tomatoes, including juice**
**Three dozen chowder clams, scrubbed well**
**¼ cup chopped fresh flat-leaf parsley**

Cook and stir diced bacon in a heavy soup pot over medium heat, about 5 minutes. Reduce heat and add onion, bell pepper, and celery. Cook until softened, about 5 minutes. Stir in potato, bottled clam juice, and tomatoes and simmer, covered, until potatoes pierce easily. Add clams, cover pot and simmer, stirring occasionally until clams open, about 10 minutes. Discard any clams that do not open. Remove pan from heat.

Use tongs and remove most of clams. Detach clams from shells and return them to chowder. Leave a few in their shells to garnish chowder. Stir in parsley and salt and pepper to taste.

The chowder can be made a day ahead, without the clams and parsley. Bring the refrigerated soup to a simmer, add clams and follow remaining directions.

# Villa Isidoro

**V**illa Isidoro joins the roster of the area's premiere rural restaurants, those fabulous dining rewards awaiting you at the end of a short journey on scenic country roads.

Located on historic Route 20, near Springfield Center, Villa Isidoro is fewer than 10 minutes from the Glimmerglass Opera. This authentic Italian restaurant is all rustic stone and warm woods, set in a 1790's mansion. An elaborate lobby bar separates the tavern area with its open fire pizza oven, and the two-tiered fine dining side.

Isidoro "Izzy" Marra of Calabria is your affable host. His menu, in Italian, overflows with all those wonderful Romance language vowels, and reads as if it should be sung by one of the Glimmerglass stars. There are considerate English translations, if your Italian is less than fluent.

The food itself overflows with fresh flavors and sumptuous, even extravagant ingredients. *Flan di fegato doca e porri croccanti con il ragu di mele cotogne, foglia d'oro* contains goose liver custard, crispy leeks, quince ragu, Port reduction and edible gold leaf. If you're feeling a shade less adventurous, they make a great pizza in the Tavern. All breads and pastas are made in-house. Reservations are appreciated.

As the character Red says to Roy Hobbs, as they dine in an upscale restaurant in the baseball classic, *The Natural*, "You can't spell it, but it eats pretty good, don't it?"

Isidoro "Izzy" Marra
3941 Highway 20
Richfield Springs, NY 13439
315-858-3500

# Potato Lake Soup
## Villa Isidoro

"Izzy" Marra of Calabria (at the "toe" of Italy's "boot" on a map) makes his potato soup Florentine with the colorful addition of spinach. This classic potage is uniquely presented, with the potato and onion soup forming a "lake" around the spinach center. The flavor is nicely enhanced with a finish of infused oils.

Spinach is a remarkable green, noted as a "super food" for its hefty cargo of vitamins. Whether or not spinach really makes you "strong to da finach" is best left to Popeye.

**4 large white potatoes, peeled and diced**
**3 large white onions, diced**
**Chicken stock**
**2 bay leaves**
**Chunk of prosciutto or smoked pork hock**
**Salt and pepper**
**2 cups (or more) torn fresh spinach**
**Olive oil for sautéing**
**Basil oil**
**Chipotle oil**

Place potatoes and onions in soup pot and add stock, covering completely. Add prosciutto and bay leaves. Bring to a boil and then gently cook until potatoes and onion are soft. Salt and pepper to taste.

When potatoes are done, remove meat and bay leaves. Puree soup until smooth.

Saute spinach in a little olive oil; salt and pepper to taste. To serve soup: place a mound of spinach in the center of the serving bowl, and drizzle basil and chipotle oils around it. Ladle a "lake" of potato soup around the spinach.

*Creative cooking oils are available infused with herbs, spices, pepper, garlic, citrus essence, and more. Look for them in larger markets and specialty shops.*

# Village Cobbler

This captivating little red shop, tucked behind Schneider's Bakery off Chestnut Street, is a Cooperstown gem. Best quality merchandise, superior service and delightful surprises are the hallmarks of the Village Cobbler.

Splendidly meeting the need for a local shoe store, Wayne and LauraJane Alexander's carefully selected inventory includes premium brands such as Clark, Merrill, Rockport, UGG, Stonefly, Timberland, and Dansko. To entice you further, Laura Jane also stocks the shelves with whimsical kitchenware, fabulous jewelry and stylish clothing.

The Village Cobbler offers the professional experience that makes for satisfying purchases. Unlike warehouse shoe stores, where you are left to muddle on your own, rummaging to find the style, size and color you really want, and hoping the shoes do more than just "sort of fit," Wayne meticulously sees that your shoes are comfortable and suit your style. Devoting time and attention to the customer's needs, the Village Cobbler's success is evident by their impressive number of loyal patrons.

No shopping excursion in Cooperstown is complete without a stop at this pleasant shop. Wayne's experience makes certain that your shoes fit properly and Laura Jane's unerring sense of style ensures that your purchases are completely flattering.

Wayne and LauraJane Alexander
25 Chestnut Street
Cooperstown, NY 13326
607-547-6141

# Giambotta (Vegetable Stew)
## Village Cobbler

This vegetable medley is very easily made and full of attractive vegetables. As a side dish, giambotta complements practically any entrée, or it can be extended to serve as a vegetarian main dish. Stop by The Village Cobbler for beautiful bowls and plates to serve LauraJane's Giambotta, or other great dishes.

2 red bell peppers, seeded, cored and cut into bite-sized pieces
2 large tomatoes, cored and cubed
2 medium potatoes, peeled and cubed
1 medium eggplant, cubed
1 medium zucchini, cubed
1 large onion, diced
Salt and freshly ground pepper, to taste
¼ cup water
2 tablespoons olive oil
4 or 5 fresh basil leaves, torn in pieces

In a large pot, combine all ingredients, except basil leaves. Cover and cook over medium heat, stirring occasionally, about 30 minutes, until the vegetables are very tender.

Remove from heat and stir in basil. Serve hot, or at room temperature, with chicken, pork, lamb, or pasta.

> "Eating is not merely a material pleasure. Eating well gives a spectacular joy to life and contributes immensely to goodwill and happy companionship. It is of great importance to the morale."
> —Elsa Schiaparelli, fashion designer

# Willis Monie Books

*J*ust as you would expect from an excellent antiquarian bookstore, every available square foot of Willis Monie Books is filled with fascinating volumes. Appropriately tucked in an alleyway off of Main Street, Willis Monie Books' location and character befits any shop on London's Charing Cross Road.

A bibliophile's paradise, you'll find hundreds of categories ranging from Africa to Zen. Appropriate to Cooperstown, there are extensive selections in Baseball, Opera, Americana, and New York History, plus wonderful, collectible ephemera. There are literally thousands of titles in Mystery and Science Fiction alone. The Willis Monie Web site, www.wilmonie.com, lists over 70,000 books available online, with an astounding variety offered in the store.

A treasure in the Cooperstown area for over a quarter-century, Willis Monie Books' reputation is well-known and respected in book lovers' spheres everywhere. They are an organizer of the annual Cooperstown Antiquarian Book Fair, held every June at the Clark Sports Center.

Beguiling to a booklover anytime, there is something magical about taking refuge among stacks of utterly absorbing books during a sudden cloudburst. If you are on Main Street and the skies happen to open, there is no better place to wait it out than Willis Monie Books.

*A member of the Antiquarian Booksellers Association of America.*

139 Main Street
Cooperstown, NY 13326
607-547-8363
wilmonie.com

# Will's Favorite Zucchini Bread
## Willis Monie Books

A traditional summer favorite when zucchini are abundant, this moist and flavorful bread is always appreciated. As Barbara Monie attests (and *Home Plate* agrees), it is perfect with tea and a good book.

Preheat oven to 350 degrees. Prepare two loaf pans. Grease and flour, or coat non-stick pans with cooking spray.

**3 eggs**
**2 cups sugar**
**1 cup cooking oil**
**2 cups peeled and grated zucchini**
**1 tablespoon vanilla**

**3 cups flour**
**1 teaspoon baking powder**
**1 teaspoon baking soda**
**1 tablespoon cinnamon**
**1 cup walnuts**

In a large mixing bowl, thoroughly combine eggs, sugar and oil. Stir in zucchini and vanilla. In a separate bowl, stir dry ingredients together. Add to egg mixture and combine. Fold in walnuts. Divide evenly into the loaf pans and bake for about an hour, until a toothpick inserted into the loaf comes out clean. The bread also freezes quite well.

> *Where is human nature so weak as in the bookstore?*
> —Henry Ward Beecher

# *On the Side*

## Neighboring Communities
Cherry Valley, Oneonta, Sharon Springs, Worcester

# Cherry Valley
## An Introduction

Cherry Valley is as picturesque as its name implies. It was the first English-speaking settlement in the area, founded in 1738. It boasts an impressive link to telegraph inventor Samuel B. Morse, and is reported to have naturally elevated levels of the feel-good element lithium in its water supply. Because of its topography, Cherry Valley played a critical role in the development of New York's early transportation systems. It is home to the oldest bank in New York west of Albany, and it provided writers Allen Ginsberg and Jack Kerouac a rural escape.

Still, with all of Cherry Valley's pleasant attributes the first thing anyone learns, and everyone remembers, about this village of approximately 600 residents is the massacre of 47 of them in 1778. The horrifying incident occurred during the Revolutionary War, when a Tory regiment combined forces with Native Americans and assailed Cherry Valley inhabitants. Forty-seven people were bludgeoned and hacked, 32 of them women, children, and non-combatants. The vicious episode influenced the course of General Washington's troop deployment, focusing more on the New York frontier, and eventually leading to General Clinton's campaign through Cooperstown.

Cherry Valley often commemorates its dramatic role in the Revolution with reenactments of the Cherry Valley Massacre. Frequent Civil War encampments remember Company H of the 76th Infantry Regiment. Other village events include Memorial Day Weekend festivities and Dancin' in the Streets in July. To learn more about the big impact of this little place, tour the *Cherry Valley Museum,* stop by the *Plaide Palette* and chat with owner and local historian, Sue Miller, or visit the *Cherry Valley Chamber of Commerce* Web site at www.cherryvalleyny.com.

### *Getting There*

Cherry Valley is well marked and easy to find from Route 20. Just look for the big green highway signs. To get to Cherry Valley from Cooperstown, follow Main Street east over the bridge (that's the headwaters of the Susquehanna River you're crossing) and turn onto Estli Avenue (Route 31). Stay on 31 for about a mile, and then turn left onto Route 33. Travel 33 for about eleven miles, and turn left onto Route 166. Follow 166 for two miles to Cherry Valley.

# 42 Montgomery Bed and Breakfast

Some elements are just expected of a preferred bed and breakfast. Personal service, special touches, and a warm welcome are essential. If you offer superior coffee too, guests return again and again. If your sun doesn't shine quite as brightly without a French roast espresso or cappuccino, 42 Montgomery Bed and Breakfast is tailor-made for you.

Innkeeper Melanie Crawford puts her guests at ease with comfortable rooms, a contented atmosphere, and the pleasant hiss of the cappuccino machine. Sunlight streams through the dining room windowpanes, setting the table's warm wood aglow and heralding the start of a good day. Plush robes, indulgent breakfasts, and friendly conversation add to your stay in her Victorian Cherry Valley home.

Whether you've come for the Glimmerglass Opera, a country stop on the way to Albany, or a quiet summer accommodation, 42 Montgomery suits your purpose. Sit on the porch and hear the birds, the lyric opera voices in practice, or the church bells nearby.

The warm elegance of gracious living is difficult to achieve in a fast-paced world. Grace and style take time – the time, care, and attention to details that are the hallmarks of 42 Montgomery Street.

Melanie Crawford
42 Montgomery Street
Cherry Valley, NY 13320
607-264-9974
42montgomery.com

> *Good friends, good books and a sleepy conscience: this is the ideal life.*
> –Mark Twain

# Apple-Cinnamon Bread Pudding
## 42 Montgomery Bed and Breakfast

**M**any of the recipes in Savor New York books come from cooks who "neveruse recipes", preferring to cook by intuition. Once you're comfortable with ingredients and basic processes, "throwing a dish together" is creative, enjoyable time spent in the kitchen.

This classic bread pudding is a perfect example of cooking creativity. Maple sugar may be substituted for brown sugar, dried cranberries for raisins, pears or blueberries for apples, and honey for maple syrup. The possible combinations are numerous. The only constant ingredients in this favorite comfort food are good bread for the base, and milk and egg for the custard. Everything else is up to you. Play!

Preheat oven to 350 degrees.

**Leftover good quality bread (Danny's or Black Cat,) cubed or torn**
**Cinnamon**
**Dark brown sugar**
**Raisins**
**New York cooking apples**
**New York maple syrup**
**3 eggs per every cup of whole milk**
**Butter**

Butter a baking dish of desired size. Generously cover the bottom with torn bread. Top with sliced apples, dot with raisins, and sprinkle sugar and cinnamon over all. Drizzle with maple syrup. Repeat the layer again, and then one more time, if you'd like.

Whisk three eggs into each cup of milk, making enough to saturate entire bread mixture. Dot with butter and bake until middle is set and top is browned.

To gild this lily further, serve with sauce of sour cream thinned with a little orange juice, and sweetened to taste with maple syrup, honey, or brown sugar.

*Good choices among baking apples are Crispin, Cortland, Empire, Ginger Gold, Idared, Jonagold, Northern Spy and Rome. These are just a sampling; visit Sharon Orchards for an impressive listing of the many apples grown in New York State.*

# A Rose is a Rose Flowers and Gifts

The *"earth laughs in flowers"* wrote Ralph Waldo Emerson. His concept of nature's mirth is expressed in every beautiful bouquet and arrangement at A Rose is a Rose.

Owner Jackie Hull and her talented floral artists fill every blooming need for any occasion, offering traditional and innovative displays. Whether it's a single romantic rosebud or extravagant arrays for weddings or banquets, A Rose is a Rose is the area's professional choice for flowers, plants and eclectic gifts.

A sure choice for Valentine's Day, Christmas and the usual occasions, A Rose is a Rose shines with their custom designs of fresh and dried wreaths, bouquets and table arrangements. Take a leisurely look through the shop's nooks for unique articles and garden statuary.

Located in an historic 1852 stone building, A Rose is a Rose is a keystone of Cherry Valley's Main Street. They make daily deliveries to Cooperstown destinations, including the Otesaga Hotel, Bassett Hospital and Glimmerglass Opera. They also deliver to Richfield Springs, Fly Creek, Milford, and most other area destinations.

Sometimes, the best floral gifts are the ones given for no reason other than their own loveliness. In the words of Hans Christian Andersen, "Just living is not enough... One must have sunshine, freedom, and a little flower."

Jackie Hull
17 Main Street
Cherry Valley, NY 13320
607-264-3100
800-243-9501
aroseisarose17@hotmail.com

# Frosted Pumpkin Squares
## A Rose is a Rose Flowers and Gifts

Pumpkins and autumn frost are celebrated companions, symbolizing both Halloween and Thanksgiving. There's no reason to wait until the leaves change to enjoy these luscious bars. The availability of canned pumpkin makes it possible to serve them year-round.

*Squares*

One 16-ounce can pumpkin

1²⁄₃ cup sugar

2 cups flour

1 teaspoon baking soda

1 teaspoon salt

4 eggs

1 cup vegetable oil

1 teaspoon baking powder

2 teaspoons cinnamon

*Frosting*

One 3-ounce package cream cheese, softened

3 cups confectioner's sugar

Chopped nuts, optional

½ cup soft butter

1 teaspoon vanilla

Dribbles of milk for consistency

Preheat oven to 350 degrees.

Beat pumpkin, eggs, oil, and sugar together. Sift together dry ingredients and stir into the pumpkin mixture. Pour into a prepared 15" x 10" jelly roll pan and bake 25-30 minutes, or until squares spring back with touched in the center. Lining the sheet with parchment paper makes clean-up easier. Let cool completely.

Beat together frosting ingredients and spread on cooled pan. Sprinkle frosting with chopped nuts, if desired. Cut into squares and indulge.

*Championship pumpkins that weigh in at the 800+ pound mark grow 10-15 pounds per day. Look for them at Cooperstown's yearly Pumpkin Fest.*

# Bates Hop House

*I*f you love lilacs, you owe yourself a sweet-scented trip to the Bates Hop House.

Well-supplied and well organized, visiting George and Alicemae Alverson's lilac labyrinth is a fragranced-filled springtime ritual for those familiar with this Cherry Valley tradition. The also carry a good supply of blueberry plants.

During the deep-freeze days of February, thoughts of the Bates Hop House's field, filled with multiple shades of redolent lilacs, buoy flagging Upstate spirits. The Bridal Veil whites, Lincoln blues, variegated pinks, magentas, yellows, and deepest purples, graced with tantalizingly light to intoxicatingly heavy perfume, trigger pleasurable anticipation of spring.

Spend a lovely day in Cherry Valley; Browse the TePee and the Celtic wonder of the Plaide Palette, have a spectacular dinner at The Rose and Kettle and wander the Alverson's lovely lilacs in between.
To find them, look for the round, Civil War-era stone Bates Hop House, about a half-mile on the right, up the Lancaster Street hill beyond The Rose and Kettle restaurant. Just beyond the Hop House is the lilac field.

George and Alicemae are on hand to guide you through the many varieties and help you make the best selections among the different colors, fragrances and blooming times for your garden. Lilacs are available for ten weeks only; May, June and the first two weeks of July.

George and Alicemae Alverson
54 Lancaster Street
Cherry Valley, NY 13320
607-264-3450

# Alicemae's Recipe for a Beautiful Spring Garden
## Bates Hop House

**W**atching spring unfold Upstate is like reveling in a long-anticipated meal after fasting over the winter. The spirit-lifting snowdrops, crocus and lily-of-the-valley are served first, perhaps as early as March. April brings beds overflowing with daffodils, hyacinths and tulips. The magnificent, fragrant lilacs scent the valleys with every May breeze, and by June the irises and peonies bloom.

Follow Alicemae Alverson's suggestions and, with a little planning during the fall bulb-planting months, and some time well-spent in the flower beds when the snow melts, your yard can color profusely in spring and tumble into a vivid summer.

*Ingredients*
   **Lilacs**
   **Daffodils**
   **Lilacs**
   **Tulips**
   **Lilacs**
   **A mixture of spring perennials — lily of the valley,**
      **crocus, irises, bleeding hearts, edelweiss, etc.**

Make lilacs the focal points and choose from the wide selection of these hardy, perennial favorites at the Bates Hop House. Contrast dark purple Ludwig Spaeth, blue President Lincoln, magenta Charles Joly and blue and purple Nadezhda; include delicate pink and white Beauty of Moscow and yellow Primrose. Add a selection of the many sparkling white lilacs and add special interest with some of the Alverson's unusual varieties.

Scatter many shades bright daffodils and lots of colorful tulips around the heady lilacs.

*Tulips are a deer favorite, so plant them in protected areas. Deer do not eat daffodils, so plant them **everywhere**. Gather suggestions from the Alversons or from Ruby Mitchell at **Home Plate** favorite Perennial Field, or check with local gardeners.*

# Plaide Palette

There are a number of famous Gaelic phrases. *"Cead Mile Failte,"* popular on front door plaques everywhere, means "a hundred thousand welcomes;" *"Slainte,"* heard in Irish pubs worldwide, means "Cheers!" Of course, *"Erin Go Bragh"* is "Ireland Forever." Less familiar, but so appropriate to the Plaide Palette, is *"Ta agam le rudai cheannach,"* which means, "I have to do some shopping."

The Plaide Palette is Celtic browsing at its finest. This one-of-a-kind regional shop is filled with terrific woolens, Irish music and instruments (including bagpipes), beautiful jewelry, flags of Celtic lands, and a complete selection of tartans. Their front porch pantry is filled with choices, including fine British biscuits, Irish oats, sweets, and a plethora of teas and tea accessories.

The Plaide Palette's resident artists create many of the wonderful Celtic gifts. Discover hand-painted tartans, ceramics, sculpture, birdhouses, handcrafted jewelry, and the most incredible cake toppers. They offer locally-made knitted goods, candles, porcelain, and the especially fine McGilliduddy's soaps. The Plaide Palette's collections also include carefully selected goods imported from Ireland, Scotland and Wales. Don't miss their Celtic figurines of angels, Santas, chess pieces, and more.

From claddagh doorknockers to Scottish jigsaw puzzles to Welsh flag afghans, everyday is a Celtic festival at the Plaide Palette. Treat yourself to a visit to the store, or shop online.

45 Main Street
Cherry Valley, NY 13320
607-264-3769
plaidepalette.com

*One should either be a work of art, or wear a work of art.*
—Irishman Oscar Wilde

# Scottish Shortbread
## Plaide Palette

Sue Miller is the area's resident expert on all things Celtic, including the rich, buttery goodness that is Scottish Shortbread. The name reveals much about its origin: This classic butter cookie did originate in Scotland (something had to make up for haggis) and it does call for a large percentage of fat to flour, making it, in culinary terms, "short." The oven time is also "shortened," so the cookies are not baked into "hockey pucks" (Sue's term).

Though obviously not bread, the shorter baking time classified the cookies as such historically, and Scottish bakers held fast to the term because it exempted them from the tax levied on "biscuits" (Britspeak for "cookies"). Scottish Shortbread is a large, round cookie with notched edges (symbolizing the sun's rays,) served in pie-shaped wedges. Though once associated mainly with Christmas and with the Scottish New Year's Eve, Hogmanay, it is available year-round and, thanks to Sue's recipe below, from your own oven anytime.

Preheat oven to 300 degrees

1 cup real butter, at room temperature (use only pure butter)
½ cup fine sugar (Pulse granulated sugar in a blender or food
   processor to make it finer, or use confectioner's sugar)
2 cups all-purpose flour
¼ teaspoon salt
A few drops of vanilla, almond, or orange extract (optional)

Cream together butter, sugar, salt, and optional extract until silky smooth. Lightly fold in the flour until just coated, being careful not to over mix.

Roll out about a ½-inch thick, into the shape and size of a pie, evening the edges with the flat of your hand. Place on an ungreased cookie sheet and bake for about 45 to 60 minutes, until just beginning to brown.

Remove from oven and cut into wedges. Cool completely. Shortbread will keep quite a long time if kept in a tin and away from humidity.

*In Shetland and Orkney, shortbread becomes "Bride's Bonn" with the addition of caraway seeds. During holidays, shortbread is commonly adorned with almonds and citrus peel.*

# Pleasant View Breakfast House

Pleasant View Breakfast House owners Andy and Judy Carson have served fabulous breakfasts for nearly two decades, investing the time that truly good food requires.

If you are on the run, have to dash, gotta go, or are generally in a hurry, The Pleasant View Breakfast House is not the place for you. As the framed statement in their foyer declares, they are not fast. They are courteous, but not fast. If you want fast, go to New York City. Pleasant View is "north of the tension line".

While you wait for your breakfast, browse the many local products in their gift shop. Play with the hematite magnets on each table. Peruse the antiques, stencils and lace curtains in both dining rooms. Talk to your family, or strike up a conversation with the county folk or travelers at the next table. Relax and enjoy.

Pleasant View also offers comfortable accommodations in the Inn's Suite or Cottage. Visitors of the Farmers' Museum in Cooperstown will recognize Pleasant View's building – it is a replica of the Bump Tavern in the Museum village. Gift certificates are available, as are home-baked goods.

Located on Route 54 in Cherry Valley, Pleasant View is just 20 minutes from Cooperstown. The "pleasant view" is 75 miles of the Mohawk Valley, the Adirondacks, and even the Green Mountains of Vermont. Route 54 runs between Route 20 and Cherry Valley. Take Route 54 from Cherry Valley's Main Street or, from Route 20, turn onto Route 54 at the Sharon Orchards and Mohawk Campground signs. Turn right toward Cherry Valley.

The Carsons
1524 County Hwy 54
Cherry Valley, NY 13320
607-264-3980
breakfasthouse.com

# Apple Pancakes
## Pleasant View Breakfast House

Take the time to make these dressed-up pancakes on a leisurely morning. The apple filling can be made ahead of time and kept refrigerated for up to a week.

### Basic Pancakes

| | |
|---|---|
| 1¼ cups sifted flour | 1 tablespoon baking powder |
| 1 tablespoon sugar | ½ teaspoon salt |
| 1 beaten egg | 1 cup milk |
| 1 tablespoon vegetable oil | |

Stir dry ingredients together in a large bowl. In a separate bowl, combine egg, milk, and oil. Add to dry ingredients and stir until just combined. Batter will be lumpy.

### Apple Filling

| | |
|---|---|
| 3 pounds of cooking apples, such as Macintosh | ¼ cup sugar |
| 5 tablespoons butter | 1 teaspoon cinnamon |

Core, peel, and slice apples. Melt butter over low flame; add apple slices and gently sauté. Add cinnamon and sugar. Cook, stirring occasionally until apples are soft, but not mushy.

### Cider Sauce

| | |
|---|---|
| ½ cup sugar | 2 tablespoons cornstarch |
| ½ teaspoon pumpkin pie spice | 2 cups apple cider |
| 2 tablespoons lemon juice | ¼ cup butter |

Mix dry ingredients together in a saucepan. Whisk in cider and juice. Cook over medium heat, stirring constantly, until mixture thickens and boils. Remove from heat and stir in butter.

Heat oil on a pancake griddle. Mix a ladleful of pancake batter with a tablespoon of prepared apples and pour onto hot griddle. Flip pancakes when bubbles appear and edges turn brown. Serve with Cider Sauce.

# Rose and Kettle Restaurant

The Rose and Kettle would be equally at home in rural Europe as it is in rural New York. When traveling the countryside in France, amid what appears to be only rolling farmland populated by cows, incredible restaurants offering beautifully prepared local fare and carefully selected wines pop up as if in a child's storybook.

The Rose and Kettle illustrates that cherished culinary experience. In tiny, charmingly historic Cherry Valley, the Rose and Kettle is a magical find. Chef-owner Clem Coleman applies his masterful touch to distinctive entrees, soups, and luscious desserts. Local and regional farm bounty distinguishes every dish, including fresh greens and herbs, organic beef and free range chicken, and just-picked berries. Enjoy local brews, New York State wines and signature cocktails from R&K's intimate bar.

The Rose and Kettle's building has witnessed two centuries of Cherry Valley history. It stands directly across Lancaster Street from one of the oldest bank buildings in New York. Just a beautiful 10 miles from Glimmerglass Opera or a scenic 12 miles from Cooperstown, you'll enjoy the journey to this epicurean destination.

Maitre d' and co-owner Dana Spiotta oversees your courteous table service. Reservations are recommended for this dining gem.

Clem Coleman and Dana Spiotta
4 Lancaster Street
Cherry Valley, NY 13320
607-264-3078
roseandkettle.com

> *Ponder well on this point: the pleasant hours of our life are all connected by a more or less tangible link, with some memory of the table.*
> —Charles Pierre Monselet

# Braised Lamb Shanks
## Rose and Kettle Restaurant

This recipe requires little hands-on time but a long, fragrant afternoon to prepare. Lamb shanks are a cut similar to a pork hock and essentially stewing meat, which accounts for the long cooking time. The shanks are the perfect fusion of everything wonderful about lamb – the deep earthy flavors and tender, delicate texture are rich, but subtle. This preparation is especially good in early spring or in deepest winter.

One lamb shank (8-10 ounce) per person
One bottle dry white wine (<u>not</u> one with oaky or vanilla overtones; avoid California vintages)
A handful of chopped garlic, rosemary and chives

Pepper and kosher salt
4 cups chicken stock
1 onion and 1 carrot per guest, chopped
Rosemary sprigs for garnish
One pint heavy cream

Preheat oven to 400 degrees.

Rinse and dry the lamb shanks. Salt and pepper generously. Place shanks, vegetable and herbs in an ovenproof pot or casserole dish. Pour in wine to top off shanks, adding some stock as necessary. Put lid on pot (or cover with a double layer of foil, tightly sealed) and place in oven for 2½ hours. Check the shanks once or twice, turning to ensure even cooking. Add more wine or stock if cooking liquid is low. The lamb should be very tender. Remove cover and cook another 30-45 minutes.

Remove the well-braised lamb to a platter to cool about 20 minutes. Meanwhile, pour cooking liquid into a container, refrigerate and let fat rise to the top. Remove fat and put broth in a pan over high heat. Reduce stock by about half and add cream; lower heat and continue reducing until sauce is thick and rich to touch and taste. Add salt and pepper to taste.

To finish shanks, heat about two tablespoons of butter in a cast iron skillet and heat to browning, but not burning. Add shanks and toast surfaces nicely; or briefly turn out onto a heated grill. Shanks may be returned to oven for a quick reheat. Serve shanks over mashed potatoes, risotto, or other starch. Pour reduction over all and garnish with rosemary and chives. Accompany with a green salad and crisp vegetables.

# Serenity Day Spa

*I*t's a hectic world out there. When there's too much tension, too much noise, too much stress, and just *too much*, Serenity Day Spa provides a nurturing and sublime escape. Amy Russo's personal attention provides the basic ingredients of rejuvenation: a peaceful retreat, a relaxing atmosphere, and sublime treatments.

Serenity Day Spa's therapeutic services include a personal line of skin treatments and an array of hand and foot care, waxing, a variety of facials, and professional make-up application. All of Amy's ministrations are designed to make you feel *good* — quiet the noise, ease the mind and body, and uplift the spirits. Spend an hour or three at Serenity Day Spa and leave feeling renewed and attractive.

Your peaceful retreat begins with the leisurely and beautiful drive to Cherry Valley. You'll find Serenity Day Spa at 39 Main Street, next door to Limestone Mansion. Wonderful music and aromatherapy greet you as you cross the threshold, and a feeling of ease envelops you as you ascend the stairs of this welcoming century-plus home. Beautiful music, pleasing fragrances, and Amy's personal and professional consideration await you in lovely, calm surroundings. To further sweeten this idyllic experience, she even has chocolate. Gift certificates are available for spa treatments and Amy's products, including Bare Escentuals Mineral Makeup.

Take refuge in the Serenity Day Spa experience. Rest and relax; restore your spirit and outlook on life. Call for reservations.

Amy Russo
39 Main Street
Cherry Valley, NY 13320
607-264-8226

# Honeyed Baked Apples
## Serenity Day Spa

*A*utumn in New York brings snappy temperatures, stunning colors and orchards full of apples. Fortunately, pick-your-own orchards and cider mills are strewn throughout the state, providing marvelous fruits and enjoyable experiences. Spend a sunny afternoon wandering the trees and bring home a bushel or two of New York fruit (the orchard can make appropriate suggestions) for this terrific take on traditional baked apples. Remember the cider!

### Apples
4 large baking apples (Cortland,
    Macintosh, Macouns, etc.)

¼ cup apple cider
Greek yogurt

### Filling
¾ cup chopped and toasted almonds
2 tablespoons New York honey
1 teaspoon ground ginger

¼ cup (packed) brown sugar
1½ teaspoons grated lemon peel
½ cup whipping cream

To toast almonds, place in a dry skillet over medium heat and stir constantly for a few minutes. Be careful not to burn. They will turn slightly brown and aromatic.

In a small bowl, combine almonds with brown sugar, honey, lemon peel and ginger. Stir in cream and let stand until thickened and sugar is dissolved.

Preheat oven to 350 degrees. Using a small melon baller or a sharp paring knife, core apples and remove seeds. Leave about a half inch at the base of the apple. Place apples upright in an 8" square baking dish. Stuff apples with filling, mounding remaining filling on top. It's okay if it overflows. Pour cider around apples. Butter one side of foil and loosely tent over apples, buttered side down.

Bake about an hour, until apples are getting tender. Remove foil and continue to bake another 10-20 minutes, until sauce bubbles and apples are quite tender. Place apples and sauce in individual serving dishes and add a dollop of Greek yogurt.

# SweetTooth SchoolHouse

A deserving recipient of an Historic Preservation Award, Harriet and Dick Sessler's SweetTooth SchoolHouse is a tidy testament to their vision and hard work, and a niche of fine dining in the country. Their renovated one-room schoolhouse and church are the showpieces of the tiny hamlet of Pleasant Brook, near Cherry Valley and about 13 miles from Cooperstown.

When you need a break from the ballgames, feel like a little exploring, or appreciate afternoon tea that is British down to the Devonshire cream and cucumber sandwiches, the SweetTooth is the ideal destination. The Sessler's red schoolhouse welcomes you with an appetizing array of well-prepared lunches, high teas, special themed dinners, and luscious desserts.

The poetic white church in the dale is a wonderful venue for weddings and the SweetTooth's unique dress-up parties. Beautifully restored with stained glass, polished pews and Harriet's hand-stenciled walls, the church is also filled with fancy outfits, feather boas and costume jewelry for an afternoon of play for girls of all ages.

The SweetTooth SchoolHouse is in the same vicinity of Breezie's Maple Products. It is just six miles from Cherry Valley, following Route 166. To find SweetTooth, follow the directions to Cherry Valley, turning right onto Route 166, and then left onto Route 165 for two miles.

Harriet and Dick Sessler
540 State Highway 165
Pleasant Brook, NY
607-264-3233
sweettoothschoolhouse.com

*There's a church in the valley by the wildwood,*
*No lovelier spot in the dale;*
*No place is so dear to my childhood,*
*As the little brown church in the vale.*

                    –William S. Pitts

# Frank Mendl's Hamburger Soup
## SweetTooth SchoolHouse

*T*his is one of Harriet and Dick Sessler's most popular soups, a gift from the old country from their octogenarian Czech friend, Frank Mendl. This recipe makes a lot, and can easily be halved, but it is perfect as written for a large group. It also freezes well for easy dinners on busy days.

**4 slices bacon, chopped**
**1 cup chopped onion**
**3 pounds ground beef**
**Four 28-ounce cans crushed tomatoes**
**2 cups potato buds**
**2 cups beef broth**
**3 cups sliced carrots**
**2 cups fresh celery leaves**
**1 tablespoon salt**
**1 teaspoon salt**
**One 14 ½ ounce can chopped tomatoes with green chilies**
**½ cup sherry**
**1½ tablespoons sugar (optional)**
**Grated Parmesan cheese**

In a large stockpot, sauté onion in bacon until onion is translucent. Add ground beef and brown. Drain fat. Add remaining ingredients, except sherry and Parmesan, and simmer for 45 minutes, stirring occasionally. Add sherry and simmer another 15 minutes. Adjust seasonings and serve with freshly grated Parmesan cheese.

*Soup puts the heart at ease, calms down the violence of hunger, eliminates the tension of the day, and awakens and refines the appetite.*

–Auguste Escoffier

# The TePee and TePee Pete's Chow Wagon

This fun family-run gift shop and eatery is a marvelous throwback to the days before the Interstate Highway System commandeered travel and cluttered roadways with all-too-familiar restaurants and shops.

The TePee is a Route 20 original, and a splendid vestige of the novel and curious attractions that once made your journey as interesting as your destination. It is actually a four-story tepee, stocked with Native American and New York State goods. Jewelry, footwear, books, and gifts fill the TePee shelves.

"TePee Pete" Latella is "just a guy with a pot of chili and a dream." And dream big he does, with a variety of "nearly famous" chilis, including 7-Pepper and Vegetarian, and an assortment of fruit and bean salsas. Pete runs a terrific chow wagon, providing homemade and hearty food.

The TePee and TePee Pete's is a must-stop when visiting Cherry Valley, traveling from Albany, or on the way to Sharon Springs. Across Route 20 is a panoramic view of the Mohawk Valley. On a clear day, this photogenic vista extends to the Adirondacks.

Dale, Donna, and Pete Latella
7632 US Highway 20
Cherry Valley, NY 13320
607-264-3987
thetepee.biz

*Thanks to the Interstate Highway System, it is now possible to travel from coast to coast without seeing anything.*
*—Charles Kuralt*

# TePee Pete's Apple Harvest Chili
## The TePee and TePee Pete's Chow Wagon

Wow. Pete's recipe contains a startling amount of great stuff, resulting in a creative amalgam of this cold weather favorite. It's quite different with the addition of the Upstate fruits, and is entirely delicious.

### The meat
1¼ pound ground beef

¼ pound bacon

¾ pound diced chuck roast

### The tomatoes
2 cans (14 ounces) diced tomatoes

1 tablespoon tomato paste

1 can (20 ounces) crushed tomatoes

### The vegetables and fruits
1½ green peppers, diced

Diced jalapeno pepper to taste (entirely optional)

2 cooking apples (i.e. Cortland, Rome, MacIntosh) diced

1 yellow bell pepper

1½ Granny Smith apples, diced

½ large yellow onion, diced

1 cup dried cranberries

¼ cup minced garlic

### The spices and such (adjust to taste)
¼ cup brown sugar

¼ cup Jiffy Corn Muffin Mix

2 teaspoons red pepper

Pinch of cumin

¼ cup oregano

2 teaspoons cayenne pepper

1 tablespoon chili powder

½ teaspoon cinnamon

In a large pot, brown meats over medium heat. Drain fat. Add all those chopped fruits and vegetable and sauté until they begin to soften. Add a bit of cooking oil, if necessary. Add tomatoes and simmer. Mix together the spices and such and add to pot. Continue to simmer, stirring occasionally, for about an hour. Thin with water, if it begins to thicken too much. As with most chili, this gets better with age.

> *Next to jazz music, there is nothing that lifts the spirit and strengthens the soul more than a good bowl of chili.*
> —Harry James

# Oneonta
## An Introduction

The commonly mispronounced (Oh-knee-on-ta) "City of the Hills" is the only city in Otsego County. The name may derive from an Iroquois word meaning "place of open rocks." Just a half hour from Cooperstown, on the Susquehanna River, Oneonta is the usual destination when residents of smaller surrounding communities want to take in a movie or watch a minor league baseball game.

The newly renovated **Damaschke Field**, located in the city's attractive Neahwa Park, is home to the Oneonta Tigers, the Single A division team of the Detroit Tigers. Oneonta is the smallest city to host a minor league team and Damaschke Field is the only park not to sell alcohol. Since 1939, spectators have witnessed the youthful play of such future major leaguers as Don Mattingly, Bernie Williams, Jorge Posada, and football great, John Elway.

The National Soccer Hall of Fame pays homage to the world's most popular sport, through displays, videos and interactive exhibits. This handsome museum with its extensive grounds is a great place to take your budding Marcelo Balboa or Mia Hamm.

Oneonta once thrived as a bustling hub of the Delaware and Hudson Railroad, and was the site of the world's largest roundhouse. The availability of rail transportation supported a huge milk industry and cigar manfacturing. The railroad base has since been replaced with higher education offered at Hartwick College and the State University of New York (SUNY) –Oneonta. Fox Hospital is a major service provider and employer. The Foothills Performing Arts Center, www.foothillspac.org, is emerging as one of Central New York's finest state-of-the-art performance and educational venues.

Oneonta counts among its favorite sons former Washington Redskins lineman Mark May and "Mr. Bojangles" composer Jerry Jeff Walker. Local historian Mark Simonson's series of books recounting various facets of Oneonta history are available in local shops, or visit oneontahistorian.com.

*A busy Oneonta in 1899*

# Annuttos Farm Stand and Cider Mill

Whatever the calendar may say, it's truly spring when the Annuttos open their doors. This father-daughter enterprise packs a lot of farm and garden activity at their location on Route 7 in Oneonta. From garden seeds to prepared garden salads, the Annuttos cover every step of growing plants, from sowing to serving.

Bedding plants and hanging baskets spill out of several greenhouses, and their lush vegetable and herb plants give your garden a great head start. Their nursery stock includes fruit trees, ornamentals, shrubs, and about anything your backyard needs. They even have water hyacinths, if you're putting in one of their garden pool systems.

All of that, plus garden décor and equipment, is just on the outside. Walk in the door and find local fresh produce, a deli case and bakery goods. Annuttos has one of the largest bulk food departments in the area, including beans, rice, grains and the like, and a terrific selection of baking sugars and confections. They carry regional specialties such as McCutcheon's jams from Maryland and Mrs. Miller's Amish noodles from Ohio. Look for local honey and maple syrup, and cider pressed from their in-house cider mill during apple season.

Annuttos is a great stop for filling the pantry, the birdfeeder, or the garden beds.

Tony Annutto and Debbie Annutto Dauenheimer
5396 Main Street (Route 7)
Oneonta, NY 13820
607-432-7905

# Arugula Pear Salad
## Annutto's Farm Stand

The peppery, pungent green arugula (aka "rocket") dances in perfect step with the sweet and mellow pear. Red onion, toasted *pignoli* (pine nuts) and piquant blue cheese join the chorus line, making agile additions to the flavor choreography. Adding grilled chicken or shrimp extends the salad to make an entrée.

Like most salads, use your intuition to make it. The amounts given are suggestions only, and will vary depending on taste and servings needed.

**Fresh arugula**
**1 Red onion, sliced thinly**
**1 or 2 Bosc (or other) pears**
**¼ cup pine nuts, toasted**
**½ cup blue cheese, or Gorgonzola, crumbled**

**Olive oil**
**Seasoned rice vinegar (available in the Asian food section)**
**Salt and pepper to taste**

To toast pine nuts, place in a dry skillet over a medium-low heat and stir constantly for a few minutes. The heat heightens their flavor and gives them an attractive color.

Combine all ingredients in a large salad bowl. Drizzle with olive oil, sprinkle with vinegar, add salt and pepper to taste and toss. Taste and adjust seasonings.

*Pine nuts are the seed of Pinyon pine trees in the United States, and of other pine varieties in Europe and Asia. In Italian they are called pignoli or pinocchi – Pinocchio means "pine nut" – and are used in, among other specialties, pignoli cookies. They contain more protein than any other nut or seed.*

# Artisans' Guild

In our relentlessly automated world, the term "handcrafted" rarely applies, and goods created by the human hand (and guided by the human heart) are especially prized. Visit the Artisans' Guild and explore their cache of completely original gifts, articles, and warm reminders of Upstate New York.

The Artisans' Guild is a brilliant shop, located on Oneonta's Main Street. Well-stocked and diverse, it specializes in one-of-a-kind items, made by hand, by home-grown talent. This consortium of more than 50 of the best local artists and craftspeople create fine pottery, jewelry, photography, candles, wood products, children's toys, knitwear, chocolates, and more.

Many New York State agricultural products, edible and inedible, such as flowers, wool, alpaca fiber, beeswax, honey, wood, etc., are used in the Artisans' Guild creations. One or more of the artists is on hand to answer questions about products, the processes that made them, and how to place custom orders. It is the perfect place to find a practical work of art.

Art is the outcome of a compilation of intangibles. Creative energy, inspiration, insight, talent unleashed – components difficult to define, but unmistakable when you see their results. At the Artisans' Guild, they are evident at every turn.

Deborah Blake
148 Main Street
Oneonta, NY 13820
607-432-1080

> *It is art that makes life, makes interest, makes importance . . . and I know of no substitute whatever for the force and beauty of its process.*
>
> —Henry James

# Deb's Squash Delight
## The Artisans' Guild

This is a wonderful main dish for vegetarians, and anyone else, for that matter. Simultaneously savory and sweet, it sings with flavor and textures, and is bolstered by vitamins and nutrients.

1 butternut squash, cubed
1 large apple, cubed
1 large red onion, diced
¾ cup walnuts
¾ cup dried cranberries
1 tablespoon olive oil
1 tablespoon butter (optional)
½ cup apple cider
Salt, pepper, and cinnamon to taste

In a large skillet, sauté the squash and onion in olive oil until they begin to soften. Add apple, walnuts, cranberries and optional butter. Cook about 5 minutes, until fruit softens.

Stir in apple cider and spices and cook an additional two minutes or so.

Serve over rice or pasta, or as a side dish.

*Butternut is a superior winter squash. The size is right, it keeps well, it's easy to peel, and the orange flesh is sweet and flavorful, enhancing soups, entrees, side dishes, and desserts. Butternut squash can generally be used in place of pumpkin or sweet potatoes. The term "squash" comes from the Narranganset word "asquatasquash."*

# Autumn Café

Fresh cooking and live entertainment are the constants that have made the Autumn Café a favorite Oneonta tradition for over a quarter century.

This popular gathering place is a preferred stop while strolling Main Street Oneonta. The "Specials" blackboard outside is your first stop. Once inside, a more elaborate version is available to the right of the handsome cherry bar, which serves good value wines, hard cider and domestic and imported beer on tap.

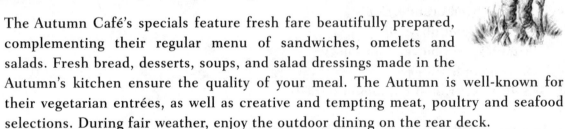

The Autumn Café's specials feature fresh fare beautifully prepared, complementing their regular menu of sandwiches, omelets and salads. Fresh bread, desserts, soups, and salad dressings made in the Autumn's kitchen ensure the quality of your meal. The Autumn is well-known for their vegetarian entrées, as well as creative and tempting meat, poultry and seafood selections. During fair weather, enjoy the outdoor dining on the rear deck.

Located in an early 20th century building with high, embossed tin ceilings, the Autumn's warm, informal setting is the perfect backdrop for monthly featured artwork. The Café regularly features quality live music, hosting blues, jazz, rock, swing, and reggae bands from New York City, Boston and other venues.

Go to autumncafe.com to check the calendar of events for upcoming entertainment.

The Autumn Café is closed on Mondays.

Tim Johnson
244 Main Street
Oneonta, NY 13820
607-432-6845
autumncafe.com

# Greek Chicken Salad
## Autumn Café

Feta cheese and Kalamata olives make this dinner salad unmistakably Greek. Simple and satisfying, it has been an Autumn Café favorite for over twenty years. *Home Plate* congratulates owner Tim Johnson for sharing it.

*Chicken*

2½ pounds boneless, skinless chicken breasts
1 cucumber, peeled, seeded and diced
¼ cup chopped Kalamata olives
Oregano and basil, dried or fresh
Salt and pepper

*Dressing*

1 cup mayonnaise
1 cup plain yogurt, regular or Greek
1 cup crumbled feta cheese

Fresh greens
Toasted pita triangles or French bread slices

*Gently* poach chicken breasts in salted (1-2 teaspoons) water for 15-20 minutes. It's easy to overcook white meat, so just let the water simmer, not boil. Let cool and dice. Combine with cucumber and olives. Add herbs to taste. Remember to use three times as much fresh herb as you would dried. One teaspoon dried oregano = one tablespoon fresh oregano. Add salt and pepper and toss; let ingredients stand for about a half-hour. After resting, toss again and adjust seasonings. Add dressing and mix thoroughly.

Serve on a bed of fresh greens with the pita or French bread. Serve with wedges of farm fresh tomatoes, and pasta or potato salad, if desired.

# Brooks' House of Bar-B-Q

Barbecue may be humankind's first attempt at culinary skill. Some clever cave dweller threw a bit of mastodon brisket on the newly-introduced fire, and thenceforth deemed it much preferable to the *tartare* version.

Brooks' Bar-B-Q and their variety of sauces has a well-deserved reputation for miles around. When you're hankering for the unmistakable smoky succulence of tender grilled meat, Brooks' is the place. A local restaurant icon, thousands of hungry patrons, including campaigning politicians and visiting celebrities, have devoured Brooks' St. Louis style ribs, chicken halves, pulled pork, and satisfying sides. If you can't get to Brooks,' Brooks' might well come to you with their extensive catering, serving about 450 events every summer.

The word "barbeque" translates from a Caribbean word for "sacred fire pit," according to one purported word origin. Brooks' 38-foot charcoal "fire pit" is the largest in the Eastern United States. Their substantial cooking facilities, ample seating and efficient service make Brooks' perfect for large groups.

Barbeque techniques are, indeed, an art form, and respected as such by regional masters, purveyors and consumers everywhere. The Brooks family has practiced their craft and perfected their sauces for three generations, perfecting the rib-sucking satisfaction of man's original cookery.

Ryan and Beth Brooks
5560 State Highway 7
Oneonta, NY 13820
607-432-1782
800-498-2445
brooksbbq.com

> "Grilling, broiling, barbecuing — whatever you want to call it — is an art, not just a matter of building a pyre and throwing on a piece of meat as a sacrifice to the gods of the stomach."
>
> —James Beard

# Barbecue Pork Chop Casserole
## Brooks' House of Bar-B-Q

Easy and succulently delicious, this recipe is meat-and-potatoes satisfying, and smoky barbeque irresistible. It multiplies easily, depending on size of crowd or appetite.

**1 pound boneless country spareribs or pork chops**
**2 to 3 large potatoes, sliced**
**2 apples, peeled, cored and cut in chunky slices**
**2 large onions, halved and cut in thick slices**
**1 bottle Brooks' pork Bar-B-Q sauce**

If desired, marinate the pork the night before, using about a half bottle of Brooks' Sauce.

Preheat oven to 350 degrees.

Place potato slices in bottom of a large casserole dish. Drizzle with sauce and follow with layers of onions, and then apples, drizzling more sauce between layers. Top everything with the pork and more Brooks' Sauce, if desired.

Bake the casserole, uncovered, for 45 minutes to an hour, or until done. Check occasionally and add more sauce, if desired. Expect the house to smell enticing and appetites to be ravenous.

> *"Vegetables are interesting but lack a sense of purpose when unaccompanied by a good cut of meat"*
> —Fran Lebowitz

# Cooperstown/Otsego County Tourism

Cooperstown/Otsego County Tourism welcomes you to this beautiful part of the Empire State. Their office acts as the marketing organization for Otsego County, and the catalyst that puts the wonderful attractions and events together under one helpful umbrella. Go to VisitCooperstown.com for lots of useful information.

Everyone knows Otsego County as the Birthplace of Baseball, but Otsego Tourism lists other fascinating facts about this area:

- Otsego County is located within a 750-mile radius of 50 percent of the North American population.

- Our region boasts an internationally acclaimed opera, an emerging performing arts center, several summer theater production companies and festivals, and one of the country's top folk art collections.

- James Fenimore Cooper, son of Cooperstown founder William Cooper, immortalized our area in his great American novels, *The Leatherstocking Tales.*

- Cooperstown is located at the southern end of Otsego Lake, known in Cooper's novels as "Glimmerglass." Otsego Lake is the headwaters of the Susquehanna River.

- Boy Scout Troop #1 in Unadilla is the longest chartered troop in the US.

- The National Baseball Hall of Fame opened its doors June 12, 1939; the first sports Hall of Fame in America. The Museum has drawn more than 13 million visitors since opening.

- Oneonta is also home to the National Soccer Hall of Fame.

Contact them for more information and get the most from your visit!

Deb Taylor
242 Main Street
Oneonta, NY 13820
Phone: 800-843-3394
Fax: 607-432-5117
VisitCooperstown.com

# Comfort Food Stuffed Peppers
## Cooperstown/Otsego County Tourism

Comfort foods are distinctly personal choices, usually recalling a favorite cuisine, family tradition or childhood memory. Chicken noodle soup, macaroni and cheese, kugel, gingerbread, meatloaf and mashed potatoes – the list is long and highly subjective. For Cooperstown/Otsego County Tourism Director Deb Taylor, it's these stuffed green peppers.

**6 fresh, firm green peppers**
**2 ½ pounds ground sirloin**
**1 large sweet onion, diced**
**6 garlic cloves, minced**
**1 cup of uncooked rice (more or less, depending on preference)**
**Four cans tomato soup**
**Salt**
**Black pepper**
**Crushed red pepper flakes**

Sauté beef, onion and garlic in a large pot (large enough to hold 6 peppers). Drain any fat. Add 1 to 1½ cans of undiluted tomato soup to the beef mixture. Stir in uncooked rice. Add salt, pepper, and crushed red peppers to taste.

Slice tops from green peppers, remove seeds and ribs, and salt the insides. Stuff the peppers with the prepared meat and tomato mixture. There will be stuffing mixture leftover.

Stir the remaining tomato soup and one can of water in the big pot. If desired, add more salt/pepper/crushed hot peppers to the soup mixture. Return the stuffed six peppers to the pot. Cook on top of the stove, partially covered, for an hour or so, until the peppers are soft.

*Bell peppers, or capsicum, come in a variety of beautiful jewel tones. Green peppers are actually the unripe produce. When ripe, peppers can be red, yellow, orange, and, more exotically, purple, white, blue, and brown. Regardless of color, the peppers are usually interchangeable.*

# Da'vida

*The Communities Center for Fair Trade*

D a' Vida surely carries the most internationally diverse selections in the area. Jewelry from nearby Mount Vision, silver from Vietnam, locally-made McGillicuddy's soap, fashions from Africa, the best of local farm products, local art and photography, and yarn from Uruguay (hand-painted in Upstate New York), this amazing non-profit venture offers great shopping that supports small producers, here and abroad.

Da' Vida means "gift of life." The name conveys this noble non-profit's philosophy of fair marketing practices. Da' Vida supports shepherds in Peru to yarnsmiths and farmers in New York, employing an inspiring symbiotic approach. Almost all of their fine quality merchandise is made by hand, the creations of single artists, family farms and small groups of craftsmen.

Located on Main Street in Oneonta, just across the street and a few doors down from the Artisans' Guild, Da' Vida is the place to find Fair Exchange coffee and chocolate, gorgeous alpaca throws, beautiful baby knits, and local maple, honey and dairy products among their diverse bill of fare. A visit here is consuming with a conscience and shopping for a better world.

179 Main Street
Oneonta, NY 13820
607-434-1962 Phone (00-1) 607-434-1962
davidafairtrade.org

# Thymed Pear Salad
## Da'vida

Roasting the pear slices accentuates their natural sweetness, complementing the complex flavors and textures of this brilliant start to dinner. Plus, much of this recipe is made ahead of time, making dinner that much easier. If the herb garden is abundant and thyme is a favorite, this salad is ideal. If available, add some arugula to the mixed greens to play off of the sweet pears.

### Dressing

3 tablespoons white grape juice

⅓ cup grapeseed oil

2 teaspoon fresh thyme leaves

2 tablespoons apple cider vinegar

1 large shallot, finely chopped

### Salad

3 bunches fresh thyme

¼ cup New York honey

½ cup chopped, toasted nuts (almond, hazelnuts, walnuts, etc.)

4 firm and ripe New York pears, unpeeled

Mixed salad greens

1 to 1½ cups blue cheese crumbles

Whisk dressing ingredients together in a small bowl, seasoning to taste with salt and pepper. Set aside.

Preheat oven to 400 degrees. Stem pears and cut in half. Remove cores with a melon baller, place cut side down on a cutting board and slice pears, a quarter to a half-inch thick. Scatter thyme sprigs on a rimmed baking sheet and place pear slices on top of sprigs. Drizzle all with honey and sprinkle with salt and pepper. Bake about 10-15 minutes, until pears are tender. Let stand on baking sheet for at least a half-hour, or up to three.

Just prior to serving, toss mixed salad greens with dressing and divide onto serving plates. Place pear slices on and around greens, and garnish with cheese and nuts.

*Thyme is a perennial herb of the mint family. It is easily grown in sunny places, where it makes a fragrant ground cover. Thyme is a favorite of bees and thyme honey is highly prized.*

# Elena's Sweet Indulgence

There is good reason why some European cuisines – French, of course, Spanish, too, and certainly Italian – enjoy such enthusiastic praise. The simple explanation is that the food is fabulous. At its best, it is invariably based on fresh ingredients, skillfully prepared using classic techniques, and ingredients such as herbs and spices added with a practiced hand.

Elena Doyle brings the legacy of Italian country cuisine to her *pasticceria* and *rosticceria* on Oneonta's Main Street. If your Italian is a little rusty, read pastries and hot food. *Delicioso* and *succulento* pastries and hot food. If you need your meals fast, there is no need to resort to mass-produced substitutes. Elena's take out fare is exceptional; it's genuine food (including vegetables) that boasts a full palette of colors and flavors. The savory meats, sweet peppers, imported cheeses and olive oil all celebrate Italian cuisine. The cookies and pastries, made of pure ingredients and in reasonable serving sizes, put a sweet cap on your meal.

Open for breakfast, Elena's has a loyal AM following who enjoy morning starters, coffee, and conversation. Catering is an Elena's specialty. Consider her favorite Mediterranean entrees and sides for a delicious change at events and parties.

Elena Doyle
281 Main Street
Oneonta, NY 13820
607-431-9140

*Cooking is at once child's play and adult joy.*
*And cooking done with care is an act of love.*
– Craig Claiborne

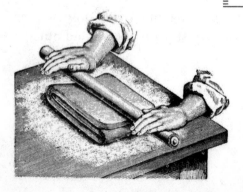

# Ommegang Summer Chicken
## Elena's Sweet Indulgence

Elena brings her expertise to the fore, using Belgian ales from Brewery Ommegang. The orange peel used in Ommegang ales infuses a subtle layer of citrus flavor into this fine poultry entrée.

Using a marinade and a separate glazing sauce makes this chicken intensely flavorful, with sunny orange overtones buoyed with the spicy heat of red pepper flakes.

1 large roasting chicken, cut up

_Marinade_

1 cup Ommegang

¼ cup olive oil

3 garlic cloves, chopped

3 tablespoons orange zest

1 teaspoon crushed red pepper flakes

¼ cup Dijon-style mustard

1 bunch of scallions both white and green parts, snipped

Salt and pepper to taste

_Orange Glaze_

Heat the following ingredients and combine:

1 cup orange marmalade

1 cup Hennepin

1 tablespoon brown sugar

⅛ teaspoon allspice

Place all marinade ingredients in a screw-top jar. Make sure the lid is on tightly and give it a good shake to combine them. Place chicken parts in roasting pan, in single layer. Pour marinade over all, turning pieces to cover completely. Marinate at least an hour. Sit back and enjoy a Hennepin while you wait. Preheat oven to 425 degrees. Oven-roast chicken 30-45 minutes, or cook chicken on the grill. Brush chicken frequently with the Orange Glaze.

# Fox Hollow Nursery

Fox Hollow Nursery keeps in tempo with all four seasons of nature's rhythms. The Monzeglio family fills their roadside farm stand with springtime strawberries, spinach and lettuces, a bounty of vegetables during the fruitful summer months, autumn squashes and acres of pumpkins, and in winter, that merriest of renewable resources – Christmas trees.

Located on Route 23 in West Laurens, Fox Hollow Nursery makes a perfect stop on the way to or from a visit to the classic cars in Norwich, the artists' enclaves in Gilbertsville or the Otsego County Fair in Morris. Garlic, tomatoes, fresh basil, potatoes, and cucumbers – you'll find those wonderful garden favorites and more, depending on the season. Neil adds new crops to the groaning board every year. If he or his family is busy working the farm, just leave the money in the box. Like many rural produce stands, paying is often on the honor system.

Plan a special holiday trip to Fox Hollow Nursery for the ideal jack-o-lantern pumpkin, and take a memorable Halloween snapshot of the children in the Fox Hollow Pumpkin Patch. Fox Hollow contributes to a traditional family Christmas with their selection of fresh, fragrant trees, wreaths and festive pine roping.

A professional landscaper, Neil is also available for consulting and contracting year-round.

Neil and Bonnie Monzeglio
2751 State Highway 23
West Oneonta, NY 13861
607-263-5764
bmonzeglio@stny.rr.com

> *"The garden suggests there might be a place where we can meet nature halfway"*
> –Michael Pollan, author of
> *The Omnivore's Dilemma*

# Cauliflower and Macaroni
## Fox Hollow Nursery

Neil and Bonnie Monzeglio contribute great recipes to Savor New York books, featuring their superb produce and reflecting their Italian heritage. Don't miss Spinach and Bowties in the first edition of *Home Plate*. Their dishes are wholesome, substantial and satisfying – much like Fox Hollow Nursery.

**½ pound of elbow or ditalini macaroni**
**½ to 1 whole head of cauliflower, chopped into medium florets**
**Several cloves (about a half bulb) fresh garlic, chopped**
**One or two 8-ounce cans of tomato sauce**
**Olive oil**
**Salt, pepper, Italian seasoning, and fresh parsley to taste**

Bring a good-sized pot of water to a boil and cook cauliflower until just tender. Drain and set aside.

Cook macaroni according to package directions. Drain and set aside.

Heat about 2 teaspoons of oil in a medium frying pan. Add chopped garlic and brown over low to medium heat for about 5 minutes.

Add sauce, Italian seasoning, parsley, and salt and pepper. Cook over medium heat until sauce thickens. Add cauliflower to sauce and cook about 3 minutes.

Pour sauce and cauliflower over cooked pasta, and stir until well mixed. Serve hot with freshly grated Parmesan or Romano cheese.

This quick and pretty dish is great for lunch or dinner.

You can substitute frozen green peas for cauliflower. Add peas to tomato sauce as it cooks. The green peas, red sauce, and white pasta recall the Italian flag.

*There are hundreds of pasta shapes, many with apt, and sometimes amusing, translations. Linguine, for example, literally means "little tongues." Cannelloni translates to "large reeds," orecchiette is "little ears," and fusilli means "little springs". Ditalini means "tiny thimbles."*

# Konstanty Law Office

With nearly 40 years experience, the Konstanty Law Office offers professional legal services in multiple specialties, together with counseling for a wide range of legal questions.

Consult the Konstanty Law Office for business litigation, real estate transactions, estate planning, matrimonial law, and general legal counsel and advice. A respected local firm throughout central New York, the Konstanty Law Office has handled litigation from coast to coast, as well as county, state and federal appeals courts.

Like a medical check-up is necessary to maintain your health, legal check-ups are necessary to maintain your legal affairs in good condition. Konstanty Law's experience and skill assures you that the decisions you make regarding your will, estate plan or health care proxy will be respected.

For routine legal issues to the most challenging life situations, consider the expertise and assurance of the Konstanty Law Office.

James Konstanty
Stephen Baker
252 Main Street
Oneonta, NY 13820
607-432-2245
866-432-2245
konstantylaw.com

*A lawyer's time and advice
are his stock in trade.*
—Abraham Lincoln

# Spicy Fish Fillets
## Konstanty Law Office

*S*picy and flavorful, these crunchy fish fillets are delicious and remarkably healthy. They are an ideal entrée for the gourmet weight watcher or diabetic.

½ **cup nonfat buttermilk**
**Dash of Tabasco sauce, or a pinch of cayenne pepper, to taste**
½ **teaspoon dried oregano**
½ **teaspoon chili powder**
¼ **teaspoon garlic salt**
2 **cups cornflakes**
½ **cup pecan pieces**
1 **pound fish fillets (tilapia, whitefish, catfish, etc.)**
   **about 1 inch thick, cut into 4 portions**

Preheat oven to 375 degrees.

In a shallow bowl, blend buttermilk, hot sauce (or cayenne), oregano, chili powder, and garlic salt.

Put cornflakes in a food processor and pulse to form coarse crumbs. Or, place cornflakes in a sealed plastic bag and crush with a rolling pin. Pour crumbs onto a large plate. Process pecans in short pulses, or chop finely with a knife. Mix pecans with cornflake crumbs.

Dip each catfish fillet in the buttermilk mixture, then coat both sides with the cornflake mixture. Line a baking sheet with foil and place fillets on sheet. Bake for 20-25 minutes, or until fish flakes easily with a fork.

# Lettis Auction Service

Thursday is auction day at Lettis Auction Service. Beginning at 1PM, a continuous parade of prospective buyers previews the week's cache of treasures, examining silver marks, furniture, art, household goods, and historic articles of practically every ilk. For over 50 years, the highly regarded Lettis Auction Service has been the source of distinctive finds and great buys.

By the 5:30PM sale time, the spacious (and heated — very important during Upstate winters!) Lettis Auction room is crowded with bidders, numbers in hand. This is more than a sale; it's a weekly social event, a gathering of regular buyers and wonderstruck visitors.

Auctions have been a part of human economies since Babylonia; they are the fair market in its purest form, and a big part of their allure is the prospect of getting just the right item at a terrific price. Lettis Auction Service offers a broad array of ever-changing, high quality inventory and, unlike many auction houses, they never charge a buyer's premium. What you bid is what you pay (plus New York tax, of course). Their auctioneering services are available offsite for any event.

Kevin Herrick
23 Reynolds Street
Oneonta, NY 13820
607-432-3935

*In the American South, auctioneers are sometimes called "Colonel," a title that emerged at the time of the Civil War, when auctioneers sold confiscated goods as the spoils of war.*

# Spinach Sauerkraut Dip
## Lettis Auction Service

*A* great take on a perennial party favorite, this spinach dip punches out flavor in all directions. The base of spinach and mayonnaise is enhanced with complex layers of sauerkraut and chutney. The chopped apple adds a mellow sweetness and the peanuts add texture and unmistakable flavor.

1 16-ounce package frozen chopped spinach
½ to 1 cup mayonnaise (low fat is okay)
1 apple, cored and finely chopped
½ cup chutney
½ cup peanuts, chopped
1 cup sauerkraut, with liquid

Place spinach in a strainer over the sink and squeeze until dry.

In a large mixing bowl, combine spinach and mayonnaise. Fold in apple, chutney, peanuts, and sauerkraut, adding more mayonnaise if preferred. Mix well and refrigerate. To be traditional, go ahead and serve in a hollowed-out round of rye bread. Or, serve this versatile spread on pita crisps, cocktail rounds, celery sticks, apple slices, etc.

*Tanna's Chutney Unlimited is especially good in this recipe.*

# McCoy's Pure Raw Honey

Honey is the only human food produced by an insect. Over the course of 40-odd years, John McCoy has perfected his relationship with these marvelous, industrious creatures, cajoling the most delicious honey from them. The McCoy honeyworks is set halfway up Franklin Mountain, just outside of Oneonta. Open on Thursday and Saturday afternoons, a visit to McCoy's observation hive is a child's delight and an adult's sweet reward.

The charming Bee House gift shop offers John's varieties of honeys in liquid, creamed, crystallized, and comb forms. There are also accessories, honey-themed gifts, candy and maple products, and beekeeping supplies.

The honey bee is priceless to agriculture and hardly respected enough. Bees are responsible for a third of the world's food production. Our gardens and orchards would be barren without them, so take care before swatting at everything that buzzes by. Think twice before spraying pesticides; tipping nature's balance upsets apple carts, beehives and our table's bounty.

To find McCoy's Honey (where bees are always treated respectfully), take Route 28 south from Cooperstown to Interstate 88. Travel west to Exit 15, and then get back on Route 28 toward Delhi. McCoy's is on the right, at the point where the passing lane begins. Enjoy the view!

John McCoy
307 State Highway 28
Oneonta, NY 13820
607-432-0605

> "...the only reason for making a buzzing-noise that I know of is because you're a bee..... And the only reason for being a bee that I know of is making honey.....
> And the only reason for making honey is so as I can eat it."
> —Winnie the Pooh (A.A. Milne)

# Honey Teriyaki Sauce
## McCoy's Pure Raw Honey

**K**eep this exceptionally versatile sauce/marinade in the fridge, ready to use for stir-frying, or for marinating and basting chicken, pork, beef, or fish. Its flavor is far better, fresher, and healthier than the bottled versions. It is also a better value.

1 cup **McCoy's Pure Raw Honey**
1 cup **soy sauce, regular or low sodium**
1 cup **sake or dry white wine (New York wine, of course!)**
1 clove **minced garlic, more or less to taste**
2 teaspoons **freshly grated ginger, more or less to taste**
1 teaspoon **sesame oil**

Stir the honey and soy sauce together. If you warm the honey a bit first, the two will blend more easily. Add the remaining ingredients and store in a jar or bottle with a tightly-fitting lid. The flavors will meld the longer it is stored. Keep refrigerated.

You can experiment with this sauce by substituting fruit juice for all or part of the wine. Pineapple or orange juice, apple cider, or apricot nectars are all possible, depending on your preferences.

*Never return leftover marinade to the jar once it has been used to marinate meat or fish, nor should you baste meats directly from the jar.*

# Regional Visitor Center
## *and Stuff*

This neat little tucked-away shop around the corner from Oneonta's bigger Main Street, pays off as promised. The Regional Visitor Center offers area visitors lots of information and selections of fine goods from this historic rural region. This is a perfect stop to choose from a variety of some of the best merchandise in the area.

The Oneonta Tigers sell their shirts and other products here, as does the National Soccer Hall of Fame. If you have hankering for Walker's Shortbread or fine teas and can't make it to Cherry Valley, don't fret; Sue Miller offers some of her favorite Plaide Palette merchandise. Local foodstuffs are available as well, including Laura' Chocolates, Bubba's BBQ Rub and Sauce, Johnson's Honey, and maple products from the Otsego Maple Producers.

Local craftspeople are represented, too, with Pat Crowe's jewelry and Roy Bartoo's hand-tied fishing flies. Find works by local authors and musicians, and something for your faithful friend with products by Faithful Friends of nearby Sherburne. Find a bit of The Farmers' Museum in their designated area.

This shop is well worth a stop, and just a half a block down and around the corner from the intersection of Main and South Main in the heart of Oneonta.

Cindy Reynolds
4 South Main
Oneonta, NY 13820
607-433-1451

# Rhubarb Custard Bars
## Regional Visitor Center

Certain ingredients invariably make a dish "rich." The components tend to be heavy in fat, often in sugar, and are customarily irresistible. This recipe makes the richness bell clang on several fronts: it contains butter, whipping cream, cream cheese and sugar. Keep the servings small, exercise a bit more, and enjoy.

*Crust*

2 cups all-purpose flour

1 cup cold butter

¼ cup sugar

*Filling*

2 cups sugar

1 cup whipping cream

5 cups finely chopped rhubarb,
   drained if frozen

7 tablespoons flour

3 eggs, beaten

*Topping*

Two 3-ounce cream cheese, softened

½ teaspoon pure vanilla extract

½ cup sugar

1 cup whipping cream, whipped

Preheat oven to 350 degrees.

To make the crust, combine the flour and sugar; cut in butter thoroughly. A food processor makes this step a snap. Press into a 9" x 13" baking pan. Bake for 10 minutes.

While the crust bakes, make the filling. Combine sugar and flour in a large mixing bowl. Whisk in eggs and whipping cream. Fold in rhubarb and pour over baked crust. Return to oven and bake for 40-45 minutes, until custard is set. Let cool completely.

*Vanilla pods and flowers*

Prepare topping. Beat whipping cream stiff and set aside. In a separate bowl beat cream cheese, sugar and vanilla together. Fold in whipped cream. Spread on top of cooled rhubarb custard. Cover and chill. Cut into bars to serve. Keep refrigerated.

# Private Drawers

As tempting as a French *patisserie*, the satin and lace confections at Private Drawers are a glorious indulgence. This lingerie shop on Main Street in Oneonta carries just the right garments and accessories to make you feel exceptional.

There is a story, probably apocryphal, about renowned showman Florenz Ziegfeld. Upon hiring a new dancer for his Follies, he would give her an astounding amount of cash for the sole purpose of buying pretty, sensuous underwear. His reasoning was that if she felt good about what she had on underneath, it would glow in her face. Whether or not the story is true, the sentiment surely is.

Silky kimonos, flattering sleepwear, adorable teddies, assorted bras and panties, and intimate *accoutrement*, plus personal service, make Private Drawers a delightful shopping excursion. Don't overlook the antiques, original art and perfumes too! As a brilliant service, Private Drawers keeps a file of their customer's sizes and preferences. Gentlemen, here is your opportunity to be a hero.

Each year Private Drawers puts out the calendars, *Beautiful Women* and *Marvelous Men*, featuring local citizens modeling their merchandise. In the beneficent spirit of community, proceeds from the calendar sales fund the Catskill Area Hospice.

Treat yourself to a leisurely stroll through Private Drawers, "where all women are beautiful."

M.D. Poole
269 Main Street
Oneonta, NY 13820
607-432-5335
privatedrawers.com

# Blueberry Cheesecake Pie
## Private Drawers

There was a warm exchange between the famous Southern authors William Faulkner and Katharine Anne Porter, referring to the warm nostalgia of food. Having dined on a sumptuous repast in Paris, Mr. Faulkner reminisces:

"Back home the butter beans are in, he said, peering into the distance, 'the speckled ones.' Miss Porter stared into space. 'Blackberries,' she said, wistfully."

Recollections of the simple fare of childhood are at the heart of comfort food. It can take all guises, from the favorite southern victuals remembered by Mr. Faulkner and Miss Porter, to Brooklyn pizza, to Midwestern corn casseroles. This sweet and delectable Blueberry Cheese Cake Pie, so perfect for summer, might well fit the category.

One 8-ounce package of cream cheese
1½ cups confectioner's sugar
1 teaspoon vanilla
1 cup whipping cream, whipped
One 9" baked pie shell, or graham cracker pie shell
2 cups fresh New York blueberries or blackberries
    (check the local farmers' markets)

Beat cream cheese, sugar and vanilla well. An electric mixer makes this task easier. Fold in whipped cream, and then gently fold in berries. Pile high and prettily in pie crust. Chill several hours. Enjoy with abandon.

*Blackberries are easily confused with black raspberries, and either could be used in this scrumptious pie. Black raspberries, like their red cousins, have hollow centers. Blackberries have a green or whitish core that extends almost through the fruit. Blackberries aren't even true berries. They are an amalgam of drupelets.*

# Sego Café

This is an ever-so-pleasant wine bar on Oneonta's Main Street. Big, cushy sofas in the front picture window beckon you to come in and try a fine vintage or good cup of coffee. Sit; read the paper; converse. Appropriately, "sego" is a Mohawk word meaning "welcome," and nothing conveys welcome as readily as warm, comfortable surroundings, good drink and good food.

*Good food.* It is that; it isn't particularly fast, but Sego isn't the place to rush. Swing in and out for a great cup of morning java and a crumb cake, but when it comes to dining, *relax.* They don't rush you, you don't rush them and lunch or dinner is a deliberate, delicious experience. The regular menu lists reliable favorites and the specials are reflections of the chef's imagination. Partake of the repasts at a civilized tempo.

*Tempo.* Let's talk music; there's live music most nights of the week. Sego offers real music, with real musicians playing it – jazz, Celtic, Cajun, blues, and more. Local and regional bands, open mike nights and acoustic jam nights encourage grown-ups to cut the cord to the television and get out on the town.

Food. Drink. Music. See you at Sego.

Al Cleinman
291 Main Street
Oneonta, NY 13820
607-432-0228
segocafe.com

# Salmon Dill Chowder
## Sego Café

*Chowder breathes reassurance. It steams consolation.* American food writer Clementine Paddleford beautifully and accurately pegged the allure of this hearty soup. A Kansas native transplanted to New York City, her 1960 book, *How America Eats,* illustrated the charm and history of American cuisine.

Lisa King's Salmon Dill Chowder certainly fits Ms. Paddleford's description. Easy and quick, this recipe makes a big pot, so halve it if you need fewer servings. The salmon responds best to gentle heat.

1 cup butter
2 large onions, chopped
4 cups chopped celery
2 pounds fresh salmon, cut in chunks
1 quart chicken stock
2 quarts half-and-half
1 cup chopped fresh dill
Salt and pepper to taste

In a large soup pot, melt butter over medium heat. Add onions and celery and sauté until softened. Add salmon chunks and cook briefly, just until it starts to lose some color.

Add chicken stock and bring to a simmer. Turn the heat off and add half-and-half and dill. Stir thoroughly and season with salt and pepper. Heat as needed, but do not overcook the salmon.

*Never grow a wishbone, daughter, where your backbone ought to be.*
also from Clementine Paddleford

# Stella Luna Ristorante

Try to describe Italian culture without reference to their marvelous cuisine. It can't be done. It would be like describing Yellowstone without Old Faithful, or Cooperstown without baseball. You could limp along and make an attempt, but the definition would be absent a key dimension.

Stella Luna embraces all those wonderful attributes frequently ascribed to Italian culture: fabulous fresh food based on the bounty of the Mediterranean; family ties reflected throughout the upscale surroundings, and the relaxed spirit of *la dolce vita* everywhere.

Brothers Antonio and Vincente Avanzato impressively renovated the former Market Street train station, creating the beauty and ambience that makes dining a memorable event. Their food is exceptional, of course. The bar is friendly with inviting spirits and, a rarity in New York State, they also offer a smoking room, with humidors filled with fine cigars. From Vinny's hand selected wines and premium spirits to Aunt Ruth's tiramisu to Giuseppa Avanzato's portrait gracing the bottles of olive oil at every table, Stella Luna brings old world style and relaxed elegance to dinner.

Located in the heart of Oneonta, next door to the Foothills Performing Arts Center on Market Street, Stella Luna is just a half hour from Cooperstown and just a step into the Old Country.

Antonio and Vincente Avanzato
58-60 Market Street
Oneonta, NY 13820
stellalunas.com
607-433-7646

# Chicken Cavatelli
## Stella Luna Ristorante

*C*hicken Cavatelli is one of Stella Luna's popular and satisfying dishes. The home version of the recipe is easy to make and serves up to 8, making it ideal for casual dinner parties. Serve with good wine, good bread and a green salad. The recipe is also excellent made with shrimp.

¾ **cup chopped prosciutto**
1¾ **cups white wine**
3 **tablespoons dried sage**
1½ **teaspoons salt**
1½ **teaspoons pepper**
2½ **cups heavy cream**
1½ **pounds boneless chicken breast, cubed**
3 **pounds cavatelli pasta**
**Freshly grated Parmesan cheese**

In a large saucepan, combine prosciutto, wine, sage, and salt and pepper. Cook until wine is reduced by half. Add cream and cook until reduced. Add chicken cubes and gently poach in cream sauce until cooked through. Set sauce aside. Cook pasta in rapidly boiling water until *al dente*. Drain and toss with cream sauce. Serve topped with grated Parmesan.

*Although it makes a good story, Marco Polo didn't really bring pasta to Italy upon returning from his famous trek to China. Romans were enjoying macaroni long before Marco Polo's eastern swing.*

# The Perennial Field

Spring is a season hard won in Upstate New York. When February snow falls by the foot, visions of hovering hummingbirds and scented blossoms can seem mighty far away.

But, after weeks of thawing, spring does come and Ruby Mitchell's Perennial Field emerges green and abundant. Her phenomenally well-used space is a wonderful destination for plant lovers. You'll find your favorite perennials and, more than likely, some you've never encountered. Ruby knows them all personally.

Wander her field, picking and choosing whatever you fancy. You'll find hostas, various lilies, bleeding hearts, poppies, ferns, and many sun and shade-loving plants. If you don't know the name, just point at something pretty. Ruby will tell you what it is, where to plant it, how often it blooms, and what to plant with it. She also digs it for you on the spot. These field-grown plants are acclimatized to Upstate New York, assuring you that the lush plants are hardy. Ruby's careful attentions assure you that they're healthy.

Bee balm, sedum, toad lilies, foxglove and more grow profusely. In fact, the only thing missing from Ruby's garden are the fairies. Then again... maybe they aren't.

To find The Perennial Field, travel I-88 west toward Binghamton. Take Exit 12 to Otego. Head toward Route 7 and turn left at the "T." The Perennial Field is seven-tenths of a mile on your right. Look for the sign and the blue mailbox.

Ruby Mitchell
25 Main Street
Otego, NY 13825
607-988-9009
perennialfield.com

# Lemon Balm Tea
## The Perennial Field

Lemon balm is one of the handsome perennials in the mint family. The herb is easily grown; it has a pleasant, lemony fragrance, and makes a refreshing tea. Its nectar-filled white flowers bloom in late summer and are a favorite of bees. Its Greek name *Melissa (officinalis,)* means "honey bee."

**20 sprigs of lemon balm**
**4 tablespoons New York State honey**
**10 whole cloves**
**1 quart boiling water**

Pour boiling water over lemon balm sprigs. Add remaining ingredients and steep 10 minutes. Strain and cool. The tea is best served over ice, garnished with mint.

### Lavender Lemonade

For a delicious twist to your favorite homemade lemonade or mix, add the following infusion:

Place 2 teaspoons lavender buds in a 2-cup glass measuring cup. Add 1 cup boiling water and steep for 5 minutes. Pour mixture through a fine mesh strainer and discard lavender buds into compost pile. Cool and add to lemonade; chill several hours to heighten flavors.

### Herbal Tea

Herbal infusions can be made from any herb, according to your preference. Those from the mint family are particularly good.

Per cup: pour 1 cup boiling water over 3 teaspoons of fresh herbs or 1 teaspoon of dried herbs.

Cover and steep 5-10 minutes. Strain; add honey and enjoy.

> *"Love and scandal are the best sweeteners of tea"*
>
> —Henry Fielding, author of *Tom Jones*

# Sharon Springs
## An Introduction

*I*n its nineteenth century heyday, Sharon Springs welcomed all manner of dignitaries to its soothing mineral baths and many large hotels. A pastoral escape from the grime and stifling air of summer in the city, Sharon Springs became the desired retreat of fashionable urbanites. The long-since demolished Pavilion Hotel accommodated ambassadors, wealthy merchants, playwright Oscar Wilde, and socialites from New York City's 400, including the Vanderbilts.

Time, changing trends and the New York State Thruway contributed to the decline of Sharon Springs. But the springs are still there, as is the spirit, and Sharon Springs is on the precipice of a renaissance. The *American Hotel* restoration marked the beginning of what promises to be more renovations of this richly historical area. Stroll Main Street and explore the gift-filled nooks at *Cobbler and Company*. Stop at the delicious *Black Cat Café and Bakery* for Vanessa's exquisite food before browsing the wonderful finds at *The Finishing Touch* (a local favorite) and *Moonlight Studio Graphics* at the American Emporium. Across Main Street is *Gino's* for authentic Italian fare, and the *American Hotel* for fine dining and accommodations. If a bottle of wine is on your list, stop at the *Liquor Cabinet* at the intersection of Routes 10 and 20. Visit sharonspringschamber.com for information about more shopping, events and attractions.

### *Getting There*

Sharon Springs is just 35 minutes from Cooperstown and an easy stop from Albany. It is situated at the intersection of Route 20 and Route 10. Turn north onto Route 10 to get to Main Street restaurants and shopping. From Interstate 90, take Exit 29 at Canajoharie and follow Route 10 to Sharon Springs' Main Street, stopping at *Sunnycrest Farm Market* just before reaching town. In Canajoharie, look for Church and Main Restaurant (518-673-CHEF) on the corner of Church and Main (of course) for excellently prepared local and organic fare.

*The Old White Sulphur Temple Sharon Springs*

# Black Cat Café and Bakery

The world has officially become a better place. The Black Cat Café and Bakery now supplies picnics for the Glimmerglass Opera. The partnership of these two talented enterprises creates a satisfying package of fabulous food for the body and inspiring food for the soul.

Tony and Vanessa Daou's dream child venture is a jewel of Sharon Springs. Their Black Cat Café and Bakery (named for a beloved ebony pet, Pinkie Purr) scales the upper register of culinary grace notes. The harmonious combination of skillfully prepared local ingredients plays delightfully on the tongue, and the unmistakable aromas emanating from their quality bakery makes the olfactory sing. From a simple loaf of bread to celebration cakes, Vanessa is a virtuoso comfortable in her medium.

Perusing the Black Cat's breakfast and lunch menu is as pleasant as reading the lyrics of a favorite song. Breakfast features James Beard's French Toast, an assortment of oatmeal enhancements, and great interpretations of eggs and herbs, lox, or applewood bacon. Lunch is a variety of international themes, with special solos of Mediterranean fare, including delicious Italian and Lebanese preparations. Their bravura coffee and dessert compositions are exceptional.

The Black Cat Café and Bakery is snug and welcoming and enjoys a well-deserved following. Their seating may be limited; the Daou's forte is anything but.

Tony and Vanessa Daou
195 Main Street
Sharon Springs, NY 13459
518-284-2575
blackcat-ny.com

# Vanessa's Huguenot Torte
## Black Cat Café and Bakery

This interesting recipe is neither Huguenot in origin, nor is it always made as a torte, although Vanessa's is with its many eggs, nuts, and very little flour. Similar to an Ozark pudding (which isn't a pudding, but a cake) Huguenot tortes are more common in the American South, especially in Charleston, South Carolina, where it was reportedly named in honor of the city's Huguenot settlers. It can be served with a glass of neat bourbon.

Preheat oven to 350 degrees.

4 eggs
8 tablespoons sifted flour
½ teaspoon salt
2 cups chopped walnuts
3 teaspoons vanilla
Whipped cream

3 cups sugar
5 teaspoons baking powder
2 cups peeled and
    coarsely chopped New York
    apples (Empires or Macintosh)

In a large mixing bowl, beat eggs and sugar well, until pale yellow in color.

Sift flour with baking powder and salt. Fold flour mixture into eggs, combining well. Stir in chopped apples, walnuts and vanilla.

Prepare two 9"x13" baking pans. Line each with aluminum foil, using enough foil so it extends past the edge of the pan. Butter the foil.

Pour half of the torte batter into each pan and spread evenly. Bake for 35-45 minutes, until set.

Let tortes cool completely. Using the aluminum foil, remove cakes from the baking pans, and turn them upside down. Carefully remove foil.

Place one cake right side up on a serving dish. Cover with freshly whipped cream, and then top with the second cake. Dust with confectioner's sugar and serve.

*The Huguenots, or French Calvinists, were the much-persecuted Protestants of 16th and 17th century France and Belgium. Huguenot immigrants founded New Paltz, NY in 1677. Huguenot Street in New Paltz is the oldest continually inhabited street in the current United States.*

# Gino's Italian Restaurante and Pizzeria

*When the stars make's you drool, just like pasta fazool, that's amore*
*When you dance down the street with a cloud at your feet, you're in love…*
*"That's Amore"*

So Dean Martin first rhapsodized in the 1953 film, *The Caddy. That's Amore* was made popular again in the 1987 film, *Moonstruck*, the Academy Award winning Best Film all about love, food, and an Italian family.

Gino's, the charming *cucina* of Sharon Springs, embraces that delicious Italian image. Gino's daughter, Marcia, owns and runs the place, nephew Nino is in charge of pizza and calzones, and Mama Cecilia makes fantastic entrees and, just as Dino croons, pasta fazool (pasta fagioli.) This classic Italian peasant dish of white beans, small pasta, carefully chosen tomatoes, and Parmesan is comfort food at its best, and a hallmark of any Italian restaurant.

Gino's is decked out with all things Italian and welcomes you with the heady aromas of garlic and tomatoes, oregano and Parmesan Reggiano. Jars of olives, panettone and biscotti, pottery and Italian music enhance the comfort of the casual dining room and the enjoyment of its fabulous food. Tin ceilings and old wood floors add to the ambience of the intimate setting. A cozy side dining area is open in the summer months. Relax, bring friends, and enjoy the food. Mangia!

Gino's is open Tuesday through Sunday. Take out and gift certificates are available.

Marcia Jaque
166 Main Street
Sharon Springs, NY 13459
518-284-2931

*Chi mangia bene, vive bene*
"He who eats well, lives well"

# Pasta Fagioli
## Gino's Italian Restaurante and Pizzeria

This is NOT Mama Cecilia's recipe, which is a justifiably well-kept secret, but it's still a good version. Quick and hearty, it's also economical and can be made vegetarian. Like most soups, it has a lot of latitude for creativity. Try adding a small amount of red pepper flakes for heat, or cooked and crumbled Italian sausage to make the soup even heartier.

**2 tablespoons olive oil**
**1 onion, chopped**
**A few cloves garlic, minced**
**Two 15-ounce cans *stewed* tomatoes, undrained**
**3 cups chicken or vegetable broth**
**One 15-ounce can white beans**
   **(cannellini or great northern)**
**¼ cup chopped flat leaf parsley, fresh**
**Fresh basil, or 1 teaspoon dried basil leaves**
**Fresh black pepper**
**4 ounces small pasta (shells, ditalini, etc.)**
**Freshly grated Parmesan cheese**

Heat olive oil in a large pot over medium heat; sauté onions and garlic for a few minutes. Stir in tomatoes, broth, beans, parsley, and basil leaves (if using dried). Add a few shakes or grinds of pepper, to taste. Bring to a boil, stirring occasionally, and then reduce heat. Cover and simmer about 10 minutes. Uncover and add pasta; simmer until pasta is tender, stirring occasionally. If using fresh basil, add it a few minutes before serving. Serve with freshly grated Parmesan.

# Sunnycrest Orchard Farm Market and Greenhouses

The Schilde family of Sharon Springs shines in apple production, glorious greenhouse goods, country market giftware, and marvelous monthly events. Their roots run deeply in Schoharie County, with the pick–your-own Sharon Orchards and Cider Mill, their sister company, begun in 1952. Milt and Carol Schilde started the Sunnycrest operation in 1975, after returning from the Peace Corps. Sharon Orchards and the Sunnycrest Farm Market are within easy proximity to each other, on either side of Route 20.

Sunnycrest opens in February and celebrates country bounty with shows, fairs, and plentiful plants and produce every month through Christmas. Attend their annual Open House in March, remember Mom in May, welcome the summer harvest of corn, tomatoes, and more in July and August (don't miss the Pennsylvania peaches!) Celebrate all those apples, pumpkins, and mums in the gorgeous autumn months. December is all holiday pine-scented balsam décor and great shopping at Sunnycrest. Be sure to check their Web site for a complete schedule of annual events, including crafts shows, garlic festivals and antique tractor exhibits.

During the busy summer months, Sunnycrest offers ice cream and casual food, and lots of annuals, perennials, and hanging baskets. Their huge farm market shop includes country décor, gardening accessories, local farm products, and diverse giftware suitable for everyone.

The Shildes have built on their early Peace Corps traditions and still travel to developing countries to consult on agricultural programs. The next generation, Tom and Laurie Schilde Schmidt, still plant every seed and care for every plant sold at Sunnycrest.

The Shilde Family
7869 Route 10
Sharon Springs, NY 13459
518-284-2256
sunnycrestorchards.com

# Lush Container Garden
## Sunnycrest Orchard Farm Market and Greenhouses

Everyone can garden, even if you have limited or no ground. Container gardens enhance porches and patios and are soul-satisfying projects. Sunnycrest supplies all the ingredients for gardening success, except for your tender loving care.

### *Ingredients*

**Container** – Practically anything can work, provided it has a drainage hole; Look for classic terra cotta pots, galvanized buckets, rustic wooden boxes, etc. Look for opportunities to re-use something around the house.

**Sunshine** – Decide the container placement and then determine how much sunshine and how much shade the location gets. Plants generally prefer full sun, partial sun or full shade, so knowing the amount of sunshine will help choose which plants will thrive in a chosen location.

**Plants** – Choose from Sunnycrest's thousands of gorgeous plants. All variety of colors, heights, blooming and non-blooming, herbs, and more are available.

**Soil** – The plants you choose will determine the soil they need. Most soils come with a fertilizer within the mix.

**Fertilizer** – Even with a well-chosen soil, you'll need to apply a liquid fertilizer once a week to ensure optimal plant growth and beauty.

**Water** – It's essential, of course. Water deeply in the cool morning hours and check again at the end of the day, especially during the summer dog days. Water again if necessary, and always keep the water near the roots, not applied to the flowers themselves.

Choose the container plants based on height, color, scent, and use. Place taller plants in the rear or center and place shorter, or trailing, plants accordingly. Herbs in containers are great for the kitchen and pots with marigolds deter mosquitoes. Herbs and flowers can be mixed. All foliage containers need no "dead heading" (removing spent blooms to encourage more flowers) and are easy care.

Be creative, have fun, and enjoy your efforts! The friendly Sunnycrest family can answer any questions.

# The American Hotel

*T*here are those who pass by once grand and regal buildings that have fallen on hard times, shake their heads and say, "Isn't that too bad?" And there are those who pass the same shabby building and say, "I can save that!"

Doug Plummer and Garth Roberts, to the greater glory of Sharon Springs, travelers, and fanciers of fine food, are mercifully the latter. Not only did they save Nicholas LaRue's 1847 American Hotel, their passion, even obsession, for its restoration has garnered them multiple historic preservation awards, rave reviews, and a visit from Rachael Ray.

The American Hotel's food is simply extraordinary. Lighter fare complements cocktails in the cozy bar; fresh and innovative multicourse dinners and brunches, featuring local and regional bounty, invite you to the dining room. American Hotel repasts are one of the first things you'll recall when someone asks, "How was your trip?" True to its designation, The American Hotel also offers nine comfortable rooms, all with en suite baths and a fine breakfast included.

Just sitting on the American Hotel's two-story front porch, enjoying a glass of sherry or a cup of tea, conjures idyllic pictures of the nineteenth century past. Ulysses Grant and Oscar Wilde trod the hardwood floors of this magnificent structure and Roosevelts and Rockefellers traversed the same areas as American Hotel guests do today. That palpable connection to our heritage was undeniably worth saving and Doug Plummer's and Garth Robert's admirable legacy.

Doug Plummer and Garth Roberts
192 Main Street
Sharon Springs, NY 13459
518-284-2105
americanhotelny.com

# Corn Cake Breakfast Stacks with Maple Butter
## The American Hotel

Rachael Ray featured this scrumptious breakfast on her popular $40 *a Day* travel series.

### Corn Cakes

4 large eggs

3 tablespoons butter, melted

1 cup yellow cornmeal

1 cup all-purpose flour

1½ to 2 teaspoons salt

1½ cups buttermilk

1 cup fresh sweet corn
   kernels (2 medium ears)

2 tablespoons sugar

1 teaspoon baking powder

### Maple Butter

1 cup (two sticks) butter, softened

½ cup dark amber maple syrup

### Apples and Bacon

8 strips thick-cut smoked bacon

Cinnamon

Salt

2 Granny Smith apples,
   cored and sliced

Mix eggs, buttermilk and butter together in a medium bowl. Stir in corn kernels. In a separate bowl stir dry ingredients together. Fold wet and dry ingredients together. Let stand for 20 minutes. In a third bowl, blend butter and syrup together and set aside.

Preheat oven to 250 degrees. Fry bacon and drain on paper towels. Transfer strips to a baking sheet. Sprinkle apple slices with cinnamon and salt, and sear in bacon fat until golden. Transfer to baking sheet with bacon strips. Keep warm.

*To prepare:* Drain bacon fat from frying pan, turn heat to medium, then coat bottom of pan with butter. Ladle a ¼ cup of corn batter into pan. Cook pancakes until edges begin to brown and bubbles appear on surface, about two minutes per side. Transfer cooked pancakes to baking sheet with bacon and apples to keep warm. Repeat until you have a dozen corn cakes. Place serving plates in oven to warm.

*To serve:* Place one corn cake on warm plate and top with two strips of bacon. Put another corn cake on top of the bacon, and two apple slices on top it. Place a final corn cake on top of the apples. Top with maple butter and warm maple syrup. Garnish with fresh mint sprigs, fresh blueberries or confectioner's sugar if desired.

# Worcester
## An Introduction

*T*his pretty little town of about 2000 folks is just off Interstate 88, on the way to Howe Caverns and Albany, between Cooperstown and Oneonta.

Worcester, NY, fits the idyllic definition of the American "home town." It has a broad Main Street, a stately school that seems to breathe knowledge, and most everyone knows each other. It's not too fast, it's not too loud; it just quaintly goes about its business. The Worcester White House Inn, in the center of Main Street, offers pleasant lodging and dining. A couple of doors away is Hornung's Worcester Market, the village grocery store that sells terrific shop-made sausages from their old-fashioned meat case. Across Main are years of artifacts preserved at the Historical Society. Down the street is the Wieting Memorial, Worcester's gem of a village movie theater.

A walk through The Worcester Historical Society Museum chronicles the evolution of this peaceful town. Stories of Worcester's past include the biography of Lewis Waterman, the inventor of the modern fountain pen, and his Waterman Pen Company. Abram Garfield, the father of President James Garfield was a Worcester native. Known to every Worcester elementary student is the name Seth Flint. He was Ulysses Grant's bugler and a witness to Robert E. Lee's surrender at Appomattox. The Worcester Historical Society has a terrific photo of the Civil War veteran blowing his bugle at a Memorial Day commemoration in 1939. The 20th century boasted Worcester's pride of the big leagues, baseball great and 1950 National League MVP Jim Konstanty.

To get to Worcester and the neighboring Schenevus, travel I-88 east from Oneonta. Take Exit 18 to Route 7. Turn right to go to Worcester. A left turn goes to Schenevus, Willys Farm and Cider Mill, Smokey Hollow Maple products, and the historic Twentieth Century Steam Riding Gallery No. 409, aka the Schenevus Fireman's Carousel.

# The Wieting Memorial Association

*T*his is how we should all get to (and once did) enjoy the movies. The Wieting Memorial Association maintains a beautiful, traditional theater. They show one quality film at a time on a big screen, over a stage that once hosted vaudevillians. You can even get a seat in the balcony. Located right on Main Street, the Wieting is an easy walk from anywhere in Worcester.

Hellen Wilder Wieting built The Wieting Memorial in 1910 (for $15,000) to honor her husband Philip, the third president of the Bank of Worcester. She intended that the stately colonial building be a community center. The building originally housed a gymnasium and bowling alley in the cavernous basement, along with the theater and auditorium on street level. Upon completion, the building was deeded to The Wieting Memorial Association. The Wieting Memorial is held in trust for the people of Worcester and managed by the Association.

In 1922, the East Wing was added to house the Iroquois Chapter of the D.A.R. and to enlarge the Worcester Free Library.

Take a stroll through Worcester. Embrace this classic American small town and treat yourself to what "going to the movies" once meant. Movies are shown on weekends from mid-June to mid-September, as well as the last weekend of school vacations. The theater boasts a new screen, projector and sound system. A family of four can enjoy the film, popcorn and drinks for about $25.

Worcester is an easy stop off of Interstate 88, between Albany and Oneonta. To find the Wieting Memorial, take Exit 18, and then follow Route 7 to Worcester.

168 Main Street
Worcester, NY 12197
607-397-7309

# Worcester Popcorn Balls
## The Wieting Memorial Association

*T*he Wieting Memorial means movies, and movies mean popcorn. Popcorn means popcorn balls and popcorn balls mean classic Halloween party treats. This recipe also pays tribute to the antique popcorn cart at the Worcester Historical Society.

*A candy thermometer is helpful when making this recipe.*

2 cups sugar
⅔ cup apple cider
⅔ cup pure New York maple syrup
½ cup butter
1 teaspoons salt
1 teaspoon vanilla
4 quarts warm popped popcorn
1 cup peanuts (any type)
1½ cups small dried fruit – cherries, blueberries, cranberries, etc.

Spread popcorn in a large pan, either buttered or coated with cooking spray. Stir in peanuts and dried fruit.

In a large, heavy saucepan, combine sugar, apple cider, maple syrup, butter, and salt. Bring to a boil, stirring occasionally. Brush down the sugar from the sides of the pan, using a wet brush. Now cook, without stirring, until mixture reaches 270 degrees on a candy thermometer, or the soft crack stage. Stir in vanilla.

Pour mixture over popcorn mixture and stir well. Butter or wet hands and shape into balls.

*Two tablespoons of unpopped kernels makes approximately 1 quart of popped popcorn.*

*New York maple syrup is available at Smokey Hollow Maple in the neighboring community of Schenevus.*

# Willys Farm and Cider Mill

Willys is an old-fashioned cider mill. The family-run operation offers apples, mazes, local artwork, fun, food, and cider during the fall foliage season only.

A fun place to take the family on an autumn day, Willys offers beautiful views, fall activities and open fields suitable for active children. Free corn and grass mazes keep the young ones busy, as will the corn teepee and weaving wall. Meet the Pumpkin People, Louie the Donkey and Pia the Goat. Wagon rides, hot cider and sing-a-longs in the barn complete the idyllic scene.

Set on a hill in Schenevus, NY, Willys grows and sells pumpkins and other autumn favorites. Their delicious apple pies and cider doughnuts are made from scratch. The big barn shop offers homemade jams, and locally produced farm products including syrup, honey, cheese, and soaps. Local artists and family members create the photography, paintings, jewelry, tin ware, woodcrafts, and fiber arts for sale in the retail area.

Willys is a long-time favorite tradition in this area. It is located about four miles from Schenevus on Badeau Hill Road. Take Exit 18 off I-88 and follow the red and white signs.

Call for hours and for group tour information. Custom apple pressing is available.

The Gartung Family
Badeau Hill Road
Schenevus, NY
607-638-9449
607-547-2186

# Classic Apple Pie
## Willy's Farm and Cider Mill

*I*t could hardly be a New York cookbook without an apple pie recipe, and there's no better source that Willys Cider Mill.

Preheat oven to 425 degrees.

*Crust for a double crust 8" pie*
  **2 cups flour**
  **1 teaspoon salt**
  **⅔ cup, plus 2 tablespoons shortening**
  **4 to 5 tablespoons cold water**

Mix flour and salt in large mixing bowl. Cut in shortening thoroughly. Sprinkle in water, one tablespoon at a time, until flour is moistened and a ball forms "cleaning" the sides of the bowl. You may need another spoon or two of water. Divide dough in half. On a floured board, roll each half into a circle two inches larger than pie pan. Line pie pan with bottom crust and fill.

*Apple Filling*
  **½ cup sugar**
  **3 tablespoons flour (a bit more if you use a juicier apple, such as an Empire)**
  **¼ teaspoon cinnamon**
  **A dash of salt**
  **5 cups thinly sliced apples (Paula Reds preferred, but use your own favorite)**
  **1 tablespoon butter**

Mix sugar, flour, cinnamon, and salt with apple slices. Pour into pastry lined pie pan. Dot with butter. Cover with top crust. Cut slits to allow steam to escape. Seal and flute.

Bake for 15 minutes at 425 degrees. Reduce oven temperature to 350 degrees and bake another 40 to 50 minutes until crust is golden brown, the pie bubbles and the apples feel tender when poked with a fork. You may need to bake a bit longer if using a firmer apple.

# Howe Caverns
## An Attraction Nearby

*While in the area, plan on visiting Howe Caverns, near Cobleskill. Follow Interstate 88 east to Exit 22.*

To create a spectacular cave, take massive amounts of limestone, let the underground River Styx flow through it for several million years, and decorate it with amazing speleothems (stalactites and other "pretties"). Serve to more than 200,000 visitors every year.

The Howe Caverns welcoming compound invites you to descend 156 feet to Lester Howe's 1842 discovery. On a hot summer day Farmer Howe noticed his obviously bright cow, Millicent, standing in an area of his field perceptibly cooler than the rest. Following Millicent, Lester discovered what the Native Americans called "blowing rock" – a stony ledge where cool air surfaced – and the opening to the cave.

Howe Caverns has been opened to the public ever since. It is one of the most visited natural sites in New York State, second only to Niagara Falls. Groups of fascinated guests take the 80-minute cave tour, walking lighted brick walkways and boating to Lake Venus, and discover geological works of art with every bend of the path. The Howe guides offer a wealth of information about the awe-inspiring formations of this natural wonder. If you happen to be startled by a drop of falling moisture, you've just been "kissed."

The Howe Caverns restaurant features the best local products and a terrific seasonal dining series. Accommodations, bike paths, and a wonderful view are also part of the Howe Caverns complex. Visit the Howe Caverns website for a schedule of special dinners and events, such as Halloween at Howe Caverns.

Adventure excursions for the serious explorer, private tours, cave weddings, and more are available by arrangement.

255 Discovery Drive
Howes Cave, NY 12092
518-296-8900
howecaverns.com

# Pecan Crusted Chicken Breasts with Spicy Apple Butter
## Howe Caverns

My, this is good. Savor New York thanks Howe Cavern's chef, JoAnne Cloughly, who also contributed Bear Pond Winery's Blueberry Sorbet recipe in the first edition of *Home Plate*.

### Chicken Breasts

4 chicken breast halves, boneless and skinless

3 tablespoons cornmeal

Freshly ground black pepper

2 tablespoons vegetable oil

⅓ cup rolled oats

⅔ cup pecan pieces

¼ teaspoon coarse salt

2 egg whites

1 tablespoon unsalted butter

Rinse and dry the chicken breasts. Blend or process oats to a coarse meal. Add pecans and pulse until nuts are uniformly chopped, no larger than small grains of rice. Add cornmeal, salt, and a couple of grindings of pepper. Pulse to combine. Spread out on a flat plate or clean cutting board.

Beat egg whites until foamy and pour them onto a plate. Dip both sides of chicken in egg, then coat with oat-nut mixture, pressing lightly. Shake off any excess crumbs.

Put butter and oil in a large skillet over medium-high heat. When hot, add chicken and sauté 2 to 3 minutes on each side, until nicely browned and cooked through. Serve with Spicy Apple Butter.

### Spicy Apple Butter

1 cup dried apple rings

1⅓ cups apple cider or juice

½ teaspoon cinnamon

1 tablespoon Calvados or apple brandy

1 small dried chipotle pepper, seedless and broken in large pieces

¼ teaspoon allspice

Combine all ingredients in a small saucepan and bring to a boil. Cover and reduce heat. Simmer about 20 minutes, until apples are tender. Pour contents into a food processor or blender and puree until smooth.

Serve at room temperature.

# *Worth the Trip*

## Great Swing Outs from Cooperstown
### Herkimer, Norwich, Gilbertsville

# Herkimer
## An Introduction

**P**rior to the Revolutionary War, Herkimer was known as the Palatine village, referring to the German immigrants who settled in the region and established it as a cheese district. The village, the town that surrounds the village, and the county that encompasses them both, were renamed to honor General Nicholas Herkimer, who succumbed to his wounds after the spectacularly bloody Battle of Oriskany. This battle proved a key link of the Saratoga campaign that ultimately determined the outcome of the Revolutionary War. General Herkimer's courage, strategic thinking, and a most convenient thunderstorm weave a compelling story, well worth further investigation.

Herkimer, and its neighbors Ilion and Little Falls, entice visitors with exceptional food, firearm history, and diamonds. Well, maybe not *real* diamonds at the *Herkimer Diamond Mines,* but amazing double-terminated quartz crystals. "Prospecting" is a fun family adventure and worth the trip from Cooperstown. On the way to the Mines, stop at the *Heidelberg Bakery and Café,* or go there simply because you appreciate breads the way they are supposed to be baked. The short and scenic drive to Little Falls rewards you with the marvelous fare of the *Canal Side Inn.* Find *Remington Arms* in Ilion, just two miles west of Herkimer. In the heart of Herkimer is *Herb Philipson's Army Navy Store,* where practically every local shops.

Herkimer is easily accessible, located at Exit 30 off the New York State Thruway. From Cooperstown, simply follow Route 28/80 north, about 45 minutes.

*Herkimer County is the site of Big Moose Lake, the backdrop for Theodore Dreiser's <u>An American Tragedy</u> and the Oscar-winning film <u>A Place in the Sun</u>. Dreiser's tragic character Clyde Griffiths (George Eastman in the film) is based on Chester Gillette. Gillette was convicted of the 1906 murder of his pregnant girlfriend, Grace Brown, by drowning her in Big Moose Lake. Find Craig Brandon's <u>Murder in the Adirondacks</u> in area bookstores.*

# Canal Side Inn

Take the time. Make the time. Go to this unpretentious and thoroughly authentic French restaurant. The Canal Side Inn is located in charming Little Falls, just a few minutes from Herkimer and well worth the trip from Cooperstown. Located in Canal Place, an area enticingly restored with art galleries, antiques shops and this stellar restaurant, the Canal Side Inn is within a few steps of the historic Erie Canal. Skip a meal or two, bank some calories and head to this culinary gift. (A lighter grill menu is available in the lounge).

Dinner begins in the lounge with a skillfully mixed cocktail or a selection from the Canal Side's wine cellar. Move to the main dining room and let the feasting begin. The only question is "What to choose?" Smoked trout, or duck pate, or the soup du jour? Chef James Aufmuth clearly respects and honors food, and his passion is your pleasure. The ingredients are fresh and glorious and near the earth; Chef James nurtures and coaxes them to their utmost potential. Choose any entrée; you won't err. Rest assured that whatever you fancy will be brilliantly prepared and served professionally. The Canal Side's waitstaff is superior.

Take your time and enjoy every succulent course; there is no rush at the Canal Side. Linger over coffee and whatever indulgent dessert calls you. Gift certificates are available and make a memorable present.

At the Canal Side Inn, even the butter is better.

*The Canal Side also offers overnight accommodations. Call for availability of their suites.*

James Aufmuth
395 South Ann Street
Little Falls, NY 13365
315-823-1170
canalsideinn.com

# Chicken Fly Creek
## Canal Side Inn

From renowned area chef James Aufmuth, this delectable dish recalls the country recipes of the apple orchard regions of Northern France. It is wonderfully rich, delicious and oh-so magnificently French – just like the Canal Side Inn. "Beurre manie" is French for "kneaded butter" and is simply equal parts soft butter and flour combined. It is used, in small quantities, to thicken sauces and soups and is a staple in French kitchens. Refrigerate any unused amounts for up to two weeks.

You will need a pan that can go from stovetop to oven.

Preheat oven to 350 degrees.

> **4-6 chicken breasts (8 ounces each)**
> **2 tablespoons clarified butter**
> **1 quart New York apple cider**
> **16 ounces heavy cream**
> **2 ounces (4 tablespoons) beurre manie**
> **1 teaspoon lemon juice**
> **½ teaspoon salt**
> **¼ teaspoon white pepper**

Lightly sauté the chicken breasts in clarified butter. Remove chicken and discard butter. Deglaze (stir the residual bits from the bottom) the pan with apple cider and reduce liquid by half. Return chicken to pan and bake for 25 minutes.

Remove chicken from pan and keep warm. Return pan to stovetop and reduce cooking liquid to two ounces. Add the cream and bring to a medium boil. Reduce slightly and whisk in the beurre manie. Let thicken and season with salt, pepper and lemon juice. Pour sauce over warm chicken breasts.

> *"Clarified butter" or "drawn butter" is the golden liquid that rises to the top when butter is melted. The white milk solids sink to the bottom. Clarified butter can withstand temperatures higher than regular butter without burning.*

# Gems Along the Mohawk
## *The Waterfront Grille*

Playing on the title of Upstate New Yorker Walter D. Edmonds 1936 bestseller *Drums Along the Mohawk,* Gems Along the Mohawk is a jewel of a stop to or from Cooperstown. Beautifully located at the Herkimer Marina, just off of Interstate 90 at exit 30, it is a terrific place for dining, shopping, information and canal cruises.

Have lunch or dinner at Rocky and Barbie Fiato's Waterfront Grille. Their spacious restaurant maintains an intimate ambience with its waterfront views, comfortable, casual food and steady stream of locals who frequent this community favorite. Barbie's homemade soups are famous in the area and Rocky's genial personality make the Waterfront a reliable stop. The service is friendly and a full bar is available for leisurely dining.

Next door is the exceptional shopping of Gems Along the Mohawk. Over sixty vendors, including many represented in *Home Plate,* sell the best of New York wares at this diverse and friendly marketplace. Find everything from cheese to soap to *Wizard of Oz* collectibles (author L. Frank Baum was from Chittenango, NY.) Gifts, foods, mementoes and items from several area museums are available.

While there, take a cruise on the Lil' Diamond line and experience the Erie Canal. Enjoy the calm waters and pleasant tour through the canal locks, and learn about the important role the Erie Canal played in the development of New York and the country.

Rocky and Barbie Fiato
800 Mohawk Street
Herkimer, NY 13350
315-717-0077 or 1-866-716-GEMS (4367)
gemsalongmohawk.com

# Steak Au Poivre
## The Waterfront Grille

*A* heavy bottomed frying pan (12-inch) and experience in the kitchen is essential for this striking steak preparation. The brandy, which gives the sauce its distinctive flavor, ignites briefly.

**Two 8-ounce New York strip steaks**
**1 teaspoon Dijon-style mustard**
**1 ¼ teaspoon kosher salt**
**¼ cup black peppercorns, coarsely cracked**
**2 tablespoons, plus 1 teaspoon vegetable oil**
**¼ cup minced shallots**
**¼ cup good quality brandy**

**1 tablespoon chopped garlic**
**2 cups veal or beef stock**
**½ cup heavy cream**
**3 tablespoons butter**
**Chopped fresh parsley**

Brush steaks on both sides with mustard and season each side with a ¼ teaspoon of salt. Place cracked peppercorns in a pie plate. Press steaks into pepper, coating each side with about a tablespoon.

Using the heavy-bottomed pan, heat two tablespoons of the oil to the smoking point. (Turn on a fan, or the smoke detector may go off!) Cook steaks three minutes per side. Transfer to a serving plate.

Add remaining teaspoon of oil to pan and sauté shallots about a minute. Remove pan from heat and add brandy. Return pan to fire and be prepared for the brandy to flame. When the alcohol has burned off, add garlic and stock. Bring to a boil and then turn heat down to a simmer, until stock is reduced by half. Stir in heavy cream and simmer about another two minutes, until sauce is again reduced by half. Stir in the remaining salt.

Pour sauce over steaks and garnish with parsley.

# Herkimer Diamond Mines
## *Crystal Chandelier Restaurant*

*A* full service recreational resort on the banks of beautiful West Canada Creek, Herkimer Diamond Mines offers unique and entertaining prospecting for the entire family. A KOA President's Award Winner, the compound includes a range of comfortable family accommodations, from tents to cabins. Enjoy the Scialdo's fascinating geological museum, gorgeous gem and jewelry shopping, water activities such as fishing and kayaking, and dining and banquet facilities.

Spend a few hours swinging a hammer, exploring over 200 acres of dolomite in search of the famous "Herkimer Diamonds." These double-terminated quartz crystals emerge from their drab encasement as clear and sparkling as frozen raindrops. They make stunning jewelry and one-of-a-kind souvenirs. Estimated at about a half a billion years old, they certainly qualify as antiques.

After working up an appetite, head to Rudy Scialdo's Crystal Chandelier for sumptuous Italian-inspired meals. Dinner favorites include steaks, chops, and chicken, veal and pasta specialties. The full bar and banquet facilities make the Crystal Chandelier a favorite for weddings, showers, brunches and parties.

The Scialdo family's enterprises are as multi-faceted as their crystals, and Rudy also provides the Adonis-Avanti Limousine Service for transportation service throughout the area.

The Scialdo Family
4606 Route 28 North
Herkimer, NY 13350
315-891-7355
herkimerdiamond.com

*Be sure to visit "Randy" the prehistoric skull of a Majungatholus, a dinosaur similar to a Tyrannosaurus Rex, unearthed in Madagascar and now at home in the Herkimer Diamond Mines Museum.*

# Grilled Rosemary Pork Tenderloin
## The Crystal Chandelier

An outdoor grill and a meat thermometer is all you need to make this tasty tenderloin perfectly. It makes the simplest and most elegant of meals when accompanied by a salad, good bread and good wine.

1 pound pork tenderloin

*Marinade*
1 cup balsamic vinegar
1 teaspoon dried rosemary
1 teaspoon dried thyme
¼ cup olive oil
1 teaspoon black pepper
1 teaspoon crushed red pepper
1 teaspoon kosher salt

Combine marinade ingredients together in a large bowl. Add tenderloin and cover entirely. Let marinate in the refrigerator for an hour.

Heat grill on medium high heat. Cook tenderloin for 20 minutes, turning several times until pork is slightly pink in the center, or the internal temperature on the meat thermometer reads 155°.

Let pork rest five minutes before cutting into slices. Serve over rice pilaf and with steamed vegetables of your choice.

# Remington Arms

Remington Arms was the result of Eliphalet Remington following one of the oldest tenets of commerce: In 1816 he built "a better mousetrap" in the form of a superior rifle and the shooting world did, indeed, beat a path to his door. By 1828 his gunsmithing company moved to Ilion, NY (next door to Herkimer) near the newly constructed Erie Canal, where the Remington Arms' largest factory still stands. It is the oldest continuously operating manufacturer in North America.

The Remington Arms Museum is open to the public free of charge, and they offer a fascinating tour of the manufacturing facility (call for schedule). The displays include artwork portraying their role in American history, and examples of their various sport and hand guns (which the company no longer produces) from almost two centuries of its history. George Armstrong Custer, Annie Oakley and Gary Cooper are but a few of the famous owners of Remington firearms. Annie Oakley's husband, Frank Butler, was once a company employee, showcasing Remington guns at Wild West shows.

The Remington Company has ventured into other enterprises over the years, including bicycles, sewing machines, cutlery, agricultural implements, cash registers and, most famously, typewriters in 1873. Among the first owners of the table model was Mark Twain. It is disputed whether or not he actually typed his classic Tom Sawyer on it; it may have been Life on the Mississippi on a Remington #2 model. Remington Arms sold their typewriter branch in 1886. The division became Remington Rand, and then Sperry Rand.

Visit the Remington Arms Museum and Country Store in Ilion, NY. From Route 28, turn west onto Route 5-S for about three miles to Ilion.

14 Hoefler Avenue
Ilion, NY 13357
315-895-3200
remington.com

# Venison Stroganoff
## Remington Arms

Upstate New York entices hunters every deer season, and Remington produces a variety of superior game rifles. Venison is a lean meat, much lower in fat than beef or even chicken, and long and gentle cooking is key to a tender outcome. Other game, such as elk, also work well in this rib-sticking recipe. This is a simple approach to classic stroganoff and an easy success, even if you are a better hunter than cook.

1 pound of venison, cubed
Salt and pepper to taste
Garlic powder to taste
Olive or vegetable oil
1 onion, chopped
2 cans cream of mushroom soup
One 1-pound bag egg noodles
One 8-ounce container sour cream

Season venison cubes with salt, pepper and garlic salt. Heat a tablespoon or two of oil in a large skillet over medium heat and sauté onion until softened. Add venison and brown until no longer pink. Stir in both cans of soup. Reduce heat and simmer, partially covered, until meat is tender. Stir occasionally and add water, broth or white wine if more liquid is needed.

Bring a large pot of salted water to a boil. Cook noodles al dente, or to desired softness. When noodles are nearly done, stir sour cream into venison mixture. Ladle meat and sauce over hot noodles. Serve with good bread and green vegetables.

# Turning Stone Resort Casino
## An Attraction Nearby

*While in the area, plan on visiting this destination. Turning Stone is just a half hour west of Herkimer on Interstate 90 at Exit 33.*

Offering a bevy of compelling diversions, Turning Stone is a sophisticated and gleaming playland, easily accessible (and visible) from Interstate 90, and just an hour and a quarter from Cooperstown. The sleek, neon-illuminated buildings stand out in beguiling contrast to their rural settings on lands of the Oneida Indian Nation, between Utica and Syracuse.

Turning Stone is constantly active; open every day of the year and every hour of the day. The Resort offers a wonderful array of excellent accommodations, golf, entertainment, gaming, and more, designed to suit every budget. Thousands of Turning Stone staff members are at the service of Resort guests, tending to every detail to make your stay relaxed and enjoyable. Talented chefs prepare fabulous fare at Turning Stone's many top restaurants, including American, Italian, pan-Asian, and organic cuisines; professional aestheticians care for body and spirit in their stellar spas; horticulturalists constantly tend the seasonal flowers adorning the lobby, grounds and golf courses.

Shop for compelling Native American art at Oneida Sky; retreat to the unique Ska: na: Spa at Turning Stone's Condé Nast Johansen Award winning accommodation, The Lodge; arrange your next business conference or exhibit at Turning Stone's excellent facilities; attend a headline concert; try your skill on the PGA course, Atunyote, or anytime at a blackjack table.

Whether your pleasure is exceptional dining, spectacular golfing, extraordinary spa services, marquee concerts, or any manner of gaming, Turning Stone Resort is a premier destination of Central New York.

5218 Patrick Road
Verona, NY 13478
800-771-7711
turningstone.com

# Oneida Indian Fry Bread
## Ka:ye:ke watnatalu: takwe'
## Turning Stone Resort Casino

*T*his simple, traditional bread has a plethora of uses. Hot out of the skillet, it can be dipped in sugar (maple sugar is fabulous) and enjoyed with coffee, similar to a New Orleans beignet. Sliced open, they can be stuffed with numerous savory ingredients for sandwiches. Raisins, or other dried fruit, and/or nuts may be stirred into the dough before frying, making it richer still.

1¾ **cups flour**
1 **teaspoon baking powder**
¼ **teaspoon salt**
½ **teaspoon sugar**
¾ **cup water**
1 **cup vegetable oil, for frying**

Stir 1½ cups of flour and remaining dry ingredients together in a medium bowl. Make a well in the center of the flour mixture and add water. Mix thoroughly, making a soft dough. Take a generous spoonful of dough and flatten with floured hands, using the remaining ¼ cup of flour to keep dough from sticking. Make size according to your preference and use.

Heat oil in a skillet (cast iron is best) to 350 degrees (hot, but not smoking). Fry dough rounds one at a time (or, if rounds are small, be careful not to crowd pan – this will lower the oil temperature), watching them rise beautifully and turn golden brown. Use metal tongs and turn rounds over to brown on the other side. Drain on paper towels.

*The Oneidas are a matrilineal society, divided into three Clans: The Bear, that teaches gentleness and strength; The Turtle, that teaches patience and to never give up; and The Wolf, that teaches to be watchful and instills a strong sense of family.*

*To learn more about the fascinating rich history and proud culture of the Oneida Nation, visit www.oneida-nation.net, or tour their Shako: wi Cultural Center near Verona.*

# Norwich
## An Introduction

If Hollywood were to remake the classic *It's A Wonderful Life*, movie moguls need look no farther than Norwich, NY to recreate the fictional Bedford Falls.

Broad Street is Norwich's main thoroughfare. It boasts an emporium in the McLaughlin Department Store, and a treasured movie house in the historic Colonia cinema. The community parks, dignified churches, maintained Victorian homes, and diversified shops and restaurants paint a picture of a classic American hometown. Norwich (population 7,000+) is the county seat of neighboring Chenango County, and its stately court house underscores the point. *Home Plate* can neither confirm or deny a Mr. Potter equivalent.

Norwich was named for Norwich, CT, and formed as a village in 1816. Nearly a century later, in 1914, it was incorporated as a city. The term is the only commonality with a metropolis. This clean place, with its flowing waterways, rolling green vistas, surrounding dairy farms, and low crime rate is the antonym of every city stereotype.

The Northeast Classic Car Museum, Ives Cream, and the Evans Farmhouse Creamery make Norwich worth the trip from Cooperstown. In August, look for the Chenango Blues Festival and the Colorscape Chenango Arts Festival in September.

### *Suggested Route to and from Norwich:*

An easy and pretty drive, take Route 28 south from Cooperstown about 2 miles to the Hartwick turn onto County Route 11. Follow it about 6 miles to the Hartwick four corners. Turn left onto County Route 205 and stay on it nearly to Oneonta. Turn right onto County Route 23. This will take you directly to Norwich. Stop along the way in West Laurens at the **Fox Hollow Nursery** farm stand. Just outside of Norwich on Route 23 is the **Evans Farm House Creamery Shop. The Northeast Classic Car Museum** is on Route 23 and clearly marked. You'll find **Ives Cream** around the corner from the Museum, on Broad Street (Route 12).

Returning from Norwich, take Route 23 back past the Evans Farm House Creamery for about 8 miles. Turn left onto Route 8 and travel about 7 miles to New Berlin. Stop at **Remember When**, just beyond the intersection of Routes 8 and 80, on your right, for refreshments. Return to Route 80 and follow it back to Route 28. Turn right and travel through Fly Creek, back to Cooperstown.

# Evans Farmhouse Creamery

The idea of the family farm is sometimes considered, by those with little rural connection, a quaint notion, replete with cows and gingham, barn dances, and tidy gardens. As with most generalizations, it's a bit of fact and a whole lot of spin. In Upstate New York, the family farm is a day-to-day hardworking reality, marked with long hours of (usually) rewarding labor, and the elusive satisfaction born of self-reliance. The Evans family exemplifies the values and kinship between man and the planet that have sustained humankind since agriculture evolved 10,000 years ago.

Dave and Sue Evans and their five children have created an organic dairy farm that respects their land, their animals, their consumers, and themselves. Their Jersey cows (the mostly brown breed) eat an organic diet, providing the fresh-tasting milk that comes from grass-fed, conscientiously nourished dairy herd. The Evans' cows are never subjected to rbst (recombinant bovine somatotropine) or other chemical company creations of that type. To quote another area dairy farmer, "We wouldn't do that to our cows."

Available at better markets statewide, Evans Farmhouse Creamery top-quality milk and yogurt is for sale in Cooperstown at Cooperstown Natural Foods and the Cooperstown Cheese Company.

An easy and pleasant stop on the way to or from the Northeast Classic Car Museum, Evans Farmhouse Creamery and Farm Store is just outside of Norwich on Route 23. Stop by for *real* milk, and other area-made organic products.

Dave and Sue Evans
5037 State Highway 23
Norwich, NY 13815
607-334-5339
evansfarmhouse@hotmail.com

> *"The fight to save the family farm isn't just about farmers. It's about making sure that there is a safe and healthy food supply for all of us. It's about jobs, from Main Street to Wall Street. It's about a better America."*
> —Willie Nelson

# Rhubarb Cupcakes
## Evans Farmhouse Creamery

Emerging rhubarb is a delicious declaration of spring. Looking like red celery, it is perfect tangy companion to the ripe sweet strawberries that blush rosily about the same time in Upstate New York. Rhubarb is biologically a perennial vegetable, though it is used as a fruit in sauces and salsas, as well as in wonderful desserts. Use the stalk only; the leaves are inedible.

Preheat oven to 350 degrees

½ cup butter, melted
1 cup buttermilk
1 teaspoon baking soda
1 egg

2 cups flour
1½ cups sugar
1½ cups chopped rhubarb

2 tablespoons sugar
2 teaspoons cinnamon

Dissolve baking soda in buttermilk. Add mixture to melted butter, stirring well. (It's okay if cold milk added to warm butter makes butter flakes.) Beat egg and stir into milk mixture.

In a mixing bowl, stir flour and sugar together. Add liquid ingredients and beat well. Fold in rhubarb until combined. Line a 12-cup muffin tin with paper liners and evenly spoon batter into them. An ice cream scoop makes this step much cleaner and more accurate. Stir sugar and cinnamon together and sprinkle on cupcakes, if desired. Bake for about 20 minutes, or until a toothpick inserted comes out clean.

The cupcakes may also be frosted or glazed after cooling, if desired.

*Regular listeners of Garrison Keillor's A Prairie Home Companion are familiar with rhubarb from one of the program's fictional sponsors, Bebop-a-reebop Rhubarb Pie and Bebop-a-reebop Frozen Rhubarb Pie Filling.*

# Northeast Classic Car Museum

*T*ake a breathtaking country drive to neighboring Chenango County and reap the reward of visiting the Northeast Classic Car Museum. Their astonishing collection of unforgettable automobiles numbers nearly 125, all meticulously restored and maintained. Included are vintage Cadillacs, Packards, Duesenbergs, Nashes, Stutz Roadsters, Rolls-Royces, even a DeLorean. Housed within the Museum's immaculate buildings is the largest assembly of New York State-made Franklin automobiles, manufactured in Syracuse from 1902-1934.

Either through personal memories of your grandparents' LaSalle, or references from black and white films, this motorized assortment cuts a broad swath of American history. Evoking the eras of Teddy Roosevelt, flappers, gangsters with gats, and Glenn Miller; carhops and seeing the USA in a Chevrolet, this prize of a museum kindles recollections with each different exhibit. Accenting the spellbinding vehicles are female mannequins dressed in period-appropriate attire.

A team of thoroughly-informed volunteers are on hand to answer questions regarding the business, history, production, engineering, and mechanics of the automobile. Hood ornaments, those exquisite little works of art that emerged from the humble radiator cap, is a fascinating narrative in its own right.

The Northeast Classic Car Museum is the stunning accomplishment of local collector George Staley, a former WWII airplane engine mechanic who worked on the fuel system of the Enola Gay. His non-profit Classic Car Museum imparts a fascinating view into America's past, through one of its defining and enduring loves — the automobile.

24 Rexford Street
Norwich, NY 13815
607-334-2886
classiccarmuseum.org

*Ask the man who owns one.*
—Slogan for Packard Motor Cars, 1901

# Classic Coleslaw
## Northeast Classic Car Museum

Coleslaw has been enjoyed practically since there has been cabbage and vinaigrette. The more familiar style, so popular at barbeques and potlucks, arose with the invention of mayonnaise in 1756. The word "coleslaw" derives from the Dutch word "koosla", meaning "cabbage salad".

This coleslaw is served at all Classic Car Museum events. The recipe is almost always requested.

> **One 16-ounce package coleslaw mix**
> **2 tablespoons minced onion**
> **⅓ cup white sugar**
> **½ teaspoon salt**
> **⅛ teaspoon ground black pepper**
> **¼ cup milk**
> **½ cup mayonnaise**
> **¼ cup buttermilk**
> **1½ tablespoons white wine vinegar**
> **2½ tablespoons lemon juice**

In a large bowl, combine the coleslaw mix and minced onion.

In a separate bowl, combine the sugar, salt, pepper, milk, mayonnaise, buttermilk, vinegar and lemon juice; mix until smooth. Pour mixture over the coleslaw and onion; stir well. Chill for 1-2 hours.

# Remember When
## Café, Antique Shop and Guest House

The charm of historic Upstate towns is largely due to the conscientious reinvention of wonderful old buildings. The people who undertake the often daunting renovations are a priceless breed. Kathi and Tom Enstrom applied their industrious talents and vision to New Berlin's former Chase Memorial Hospital and created the congenial Remember When Café, Antique Shop and Guest House.

The 15-room historic building has been beautifully redone in rich and soothing shades of purple and lavender, accented with verdant green and gorgeous Tiffany-style lamps. The guest rooms are comfortably cozy and the antiques are warmly nostalgic; the wines are varied, the food is satisfying, and the desserts are worth every calorie.

Kathi began her restaurant as a dessert café, but, if you do a thing well, it's inevitable that the public will demand more. Breakfast and lunch are now available Wednesday through Sunday, as well as a dinner special. Each night features a single entrée; there may not be a choice of main dish, but be sure that whatever Kathi prepares is *choice*. Friday Fish Nights are favorites, and Wednesdays feature the Upstate favorite, Chicken and Biscuits. Dinner begins with warm breads, wines are available, and an extensive dessert menu sweetly completes your meal. Their always fresh coffee is terrific.

Remember When is a half-hour drive from Cooperstown and the perfect stop between the National Baseball Hall of Fame and the Northeast Classic Car Museum.

Kathi and Tom Engstrom
34 North Main Street
New Berlin, NY 13411
607-847-9799
rememberwhenguesthouse.com

# Butterscotch Mudslide Pie
## Remember When

Sweet and easy and unapologetically indulgent, this is one of Remember When's most popular desserts.

1 graham cracker pie crust
¼ cup sweetened condensed milk
¼ cup semi-sweet chocolate chips
⅓ cup Cocoa Krispies cereal
2 packages instant butterscotch pudding
2 cups whole milk
1 carton Cool Whip, or whipped cream
Cocoa for dusting

Combine condensed milk and chocolate chips in a small saucepan and melt over low heat. Or, melt together in the microwave. Spread evenly on the bottom of the pie crust. Sprinkle the cereal over chocolate layer, pressing down firmly.

Beat pudding mix with milk. Layer half of the pudding over chocolate and cereal layer. Combine the remaining pudding with about the same amount of Cool Whip to make the mousse layer. Top with remaining whipped topping and dust with cocoa. Chill for at least two hours and – do we have to say this? – enjoy!

> "A mother is a person who seeing there are only four pieces of pie for five people, promptly announces she never did care for pie."
> —Tenneva Jordan

# Ives Cream

*I*ce cream parlors are a beloved tradition for good reason. They recall, as writer Heywood Broun characterizes, the "soul-stirring surprise" of sundaes and sodas and the events they helped celebrate. The mouth-watering combination of quality cream, sugar, and endless choices of enhancements, produce the simultaneously soothing and exhilarating experience that is ice cream.

The Ives Cream ice cream parlor is a charming presence on Broad Street, so appropriate to the charming city of Norwich. The street level parlor, with its milk can décor, beckons you with fabulous flavors, including chocolate peanut butter, mocha, and classic vanilla. Look for seasonal specialties, such as gingerbread, eggnog, or peppermint stick to add to holiday celebrations. Venture downstairs and watch the magic happen in the ice cream making viewing room. Their upstairs party room is available for your special events and gatherings. Ives Cream is the perfect stop when visiting the Northeast Classic Car Museum or taking in a movie at the Colonia, Norwich's *real* downtown movie theater.

Alex and Katie Ives represent six generations of dairy farming. Beginning with Alfred Ives in 1850, the Ives family has lived the rich experience of family farming, carefully tending the land and the dairy cows of their nearby Greenview Farms. The care they show their land, their animals and their traditions is obvious in the superior ice cream they produce.

Alex and Katie Ives
10 Broad Street
Norwich, NY 13815
607-336-9393
ivescream.biz

> *I doubt whether the world holds for anyone a more soul-stirring surprise than the first adventure with ice cream.*
> —Heywood Broun

# Apple Ice Cream Pie
## Ives Cream

Extremely easy to make and hands-down delicious, this showy dessert makes a memorable impression for any occasion. Keep one in the freezer for dinner party desserts, if you can resist diving into to it! Make it anytime, but especially when cool autumn nights bring New York State apples to their peak, and warm autumn afternoons make ice cream alluring.

> One 9-inch graham cracker crust, homemade or store-bought
> 2 tablespoons butter
> 3 NYS cooking apples, peeled, cored and cut into chunks
>
> ½ teaspoon cinnamon (optional)
> ¼ cup powdered sugar
> 1½ tablespoons lemon juice
> 1 jar caramel topping
> 1 quart Ives Cream vanilla ice cream
> ½ cup toasted nuts (pecans, walnuts, hazelnuts, or your preference)

Prebake crust, if necessary, and let cool. Melt butter in a large frying pan and sauté apples until nearly tender, five minutes or so. Add powdered sugar, lemon juice and cinnamon, if using. Cook for another minute or two. Remove from heat and place in a shallow dish to cool.

Spread cool apples evenly over crust. Drizzle some caramel topping over apples. Cover with foil and place in freezer for about a half-hour. When you put the apples and crust in the freezer, put the ice cream in the refrigerator to soften.

Spoon softened ice cream over apples and spread evenly. An offset knife, the type used by cake decorators, is useful for this, but the back of a fork works, too. Drizzle with more caramel, in a design if you feel creative. Top with nuts and place back in the freezer for at least an hour.

# Gilbertsville
## An Introduction

Abija Gilbert was so fond of his canine companions that he considered calling the village that would eventually bear his name, "Bulldog." This Revolutionary War-era dog lover could not have envisioned the bulldogged determination that would eventually save his community from engineered flooding, many generations hence.

Located in the beautiful Butternut Valley, about an hour from Cooperstown, Gilbertsville is a worthy stop for the art fancier, quilter, fisherman, or architecture buff. The entire village is listed on the National Register of Historic Places, due to the tenacity of Gilbertsville residents. Prior to World War I, the Army Corps of Engineers proposed a watershed project which would have made this area a three mile lake. Always opposed by residents, the project was resurrected time and again, following timely reprieves provided by World War I, the Depression and World War II. Like the hydra monster eventually vanquished by Herculean efforts, Gilbertsville residents permanently quelled the Army Corps of Engineers in 1983. This historic village of architecture and indefatigable spirit was listed on the National Register of Historic Places in May, 1983.

Take a scenic trek to this friendly and determined village, just a pleasant veer on the way to Norwich. Discover the *Majors Inn*, the stately site of concerts and a perfect venue for weddings and special events. Housed in the Tudor-style Gilbert Building across Commercial Street, you'll find the *Gilbert Block Quilt Shop*, the *Value-Way* country market, the *Gilbert Block Ice Cream Shop,* and a number of Gilbertsville's artist's studios. *Hilton Bloom Art Studio* and *Lake Clear Wabblers* fishing lures, art studios, and tucked-away treasures of this tucked-away community, are all nearby.

A picturesque drive, take Route 28 south from Cooperstown about two miles to the Hartwick turn. Turn onto County Route 11 and follow it about six miles to the Hartwick four corners. Turn left onto County Route 205 and stay on it nearly to Oneonta. Turn right onto County Route 23, and stop along the way in West Laurens at the *Fox Hollow Nursery* farm stand. Stay on Route 23 to Morris, turning south (left) onto Route 51. Route 51 leads to Gilbertsville.

# Gilbertsville Artists

Surely the Muses reside in the Butternut Valley, or at least visit there regularly. Gilbertsville, in the heart of this breathtaking hills-and-dales country, is home to a collection of artists of nearly every ilk. Amazing works of painting, sculpting, quilting, collages, and more are born in these tucked away glens.

Jane Evelyn Higgin's Hilton Bloom Art Studio is a clearinghouse for the talent that flows through Gilbertsville. Displays of her incredible collages and carefully selected antiques fill her studio, along with exhibits from more than a dozen of her fellow artists. Nona Slaughter's Gilbert Block Quilt Shop is another source of local art, including pottery, handmade jewelry, and fine quilted pieces by Nona and other fiber artists. More artist studios are upstairs in the Gilbert Block Building and in and around the Gilbertsville area. Ask about the art classes and workshops offered, and about the occasional artist's open house weekends when many studios are open and displaying wares.

Jane Evelyn Higgins
Hilton Bloom Art Studio
24 Bloom Street
Gilbertsville, NY 13776
607-783-2779
gilbertsville.com

*Greek Muses*
*Euterpe – lyric song*
*Melpomene – tragedy*
*Polyhymnia – sacred song*
*Terpsichore – dance*
*Thalia – comedy and bucolic poetry*
*Erato – erotic poetry*
*Urania – astronomy*
*Clio – history*

*Calliope – Lead Muse and*
*muse of epic poetry*

# Feed the Birds Cupcakes
## Gilbertsville Artists

These cakes are easy to make and more economical than commercial suet squares. They contain the rich fats and essential nutrients birds need to survive a challenging winter. Making the bird cakes is a fun family project and a great use for any odd bits of grain, dried fruits, and seeds lying about the kitchen. Also, save your eggshells! They can be ground and added to the mixture to help replenish the calcium birds use to make eggs.

February is federally recognized as National Bird Feeding Month, but don't wait that long to start feeding them. Any bird with courage enough to winter in Upstate New York deserves a few meals on us!

1 cup peanut butter
1 cup shortening, lard, or suet*
1 cup mixed nuts, seeds, and dried fruit; peanuts, sunflower
    seeds, raisins, and dried cranberries are all favorites, but
    the list is lengthy. Check your pantry and be creative.
1 cup mixed cornmeal, birdseed, oatmeal, or cracked corn.

In a saucepan, melt the shortening and peanut butter over a low heat. Add the remaining ingredients until mixture is stiff, but pliable. Put into paper lined muffin tins, or other containers, and store in freezer. Place cakes in wire suet feeders, or in mesh bags (the kind that oranges or onions come in) and hang in trees or shrubs. The birds will appreciate you, and you them.

To use eggshells in suet cakes, place empty shells in a 250 degree oven until dry and more brittle. Whir in a food processor, or place in a large freezer bag and crush finely with a rolling pin.

*Animal fats tend to go rancid quickly. If the food will be out more than a day or two, or if the temperature is warming, use the shortening.*

> *Use the talents you possess — for the woods would be a very silent place if no birds sang except for the best.*
> —Henry Van Dyke

# Gilbert Block Quilt Shop

The century old Tudor-style Gilbert Block is in the heart of Gilbertsville, and the heart of this signature building is Nona Slaughter's quilt shop. She caters to the quilter, but there's more than thread and batting to Nona and her store. Located on Commercial Street, across from The Major's Inn, her spacious location with its high ceiling and wooden floors, is fabric-filled, art-filled, and antique-filled. This is a terrific place to poke around, unearthing the unexpected. Much of Nona's inventory comes from Gilbertsville's artists and crafters, so even she can't predict exactly what will be on the shelves. Look for pottery, paintings, jewelry, local antiques, handmade doll clothes, or whatever caught Nona's fancy. Don't miss her sister's expert calligraphy.

True to its name you'll find beautiful quilts, wall hangings, table runners and quilting supplies in the Gilbert Block Quilt Shop. Bolts and bolts of colorful fabrics line the walls and there is usually a quilt on a frame or a top being pieced in the working area at the back of the shop. Gilbert Block Quilt is a favorite stop on quilter's shop-hops and Nona frequently welcomes quilting clubs, as she does the Pennsylvania Quiltswappers. The clubs' signature color is lime green; hence Nona welcomes them to the Butternut Valley with her Key Lime Pie.

Nona is also impressively versed in local history and can tell you practically anything you'd want to know about the area. You're welcome anytime for a pleasant chat and a pleasant browse of this pleasant shop.

Nona Slaughter
9 Commercial Street
Gilbertsville, NY 13776
607-783-2872

# Key Lime Pie
## Gilbert Block Quilt Shop

*T*here are a lot of traditions and gentle points of contention associated with Key Lime Pie, including which limes are used (Key limes, if available), whether or not it should be baked (yes); if it should be colored green (no); and if it is topped with meringue (no) or whipped cream (yes). Two things are constant: Norwich, New York native Gail Borden's invention of sweetened condensed milk, and the blissful enjoyment of this dessert classic.

**3 eggs**
**One 14-ounce can sweetened condensed milk**
**¾ cup lime juice (from Key limes, or the more familiar Persian limes)**
**One 9-inch baked pie crust, pastry or graham cracker**

Preheat oven to 350 degrees.

Separate eggs; set whites aside and beat yolks with the condensed milk. Gradually beat in the lime juice. Green food coloring is not traditional, but add a couple of drops if you like. Spoon evenly into pie shell. Traditionally, this version of Key Lime Pie is not baked, but pop it in the oven for 12 minutes to set the yolks and kill any wayward salmonella. Let cool.

Meringue is not traditional, but the golden peaks are handsome and you have the egg whites, anyway. Beat the three whites until stiff, gradually adding 6 tablespoons of sugar, one at a time. Pile on top of pie and brown in a 425 degree oven for 3-4 minutes.

Whipped cream *is* traditional and also an attractive topping. Beat one cup heavy cream and spread on the cool pie, or pipe it on with a pastry bag.

# Lake Clear Wabblers

Fishing is by far the most popular sports diversion in America, outdistancing even golf. It's a natural pastime in New York, with its abundance of lakes and streams. The brook trout is the state fish for good reason, and it's a good bet that one of Tom Delaney's lures catches the biggest one every year. Tom makes it a personal quest. For over eighty years, Lake Clear Wabblers has made lures to catch trout, walleye, muskie, northern pike and other game fish. Their experience shows in the quality, success record and outright beauty of their product.

The Delaney's make the prettiest lures. Whether the fish appreciate their good looks is a question, but there's no doubt that they strike them. The Delaney's hand finished casting and trolling lures have a proven record of catching the big ones. The brass, chrome and copper wabblers, Geneva spoons, skinner spoon bait and spinning lures are as pretty as jewelry and would be right at home adorning a fisherman's Christmas tree. Their light absorbing glow spoons are as vivid as fruit sherbet and irresistible to sport fish. Whether it's spoons or spinners, flutter weights or fluted skinner blades, the Delaney's experience gives them an inside track on what fish strike.

For fast or slow water, clear or murky conditions, bright or cloudy days, Lake Clear Wabblers has just the lure or trolling rig you need to catch the whoppers. Please call to arrange a visit. Order a free catalog at the contacts below.

Tom Delaney
10 Spring Street
Gilbertsville, NY 13776
Phone: 607-783-2587
lakeclearwabbler.com

# Garlic Mushroom Trout
## Lake Clear Wabbler

Garlic, butter, and mushrooms — these three ingredients practically guarantee the success of any entrée. Using them as a base, you could probably even gather snails from the garden and make them delicious. Wait — that's been done already.

Escargot aside, this is a sumptuous preparation of the day's catch. Serve with a side of spaghetti or rice and enjoy the rich sauce.

Five trout (¾ to 1 pound each)
Fresh ground black pepper
One 10-ounce package
   fresh mushrooms sliced
5 cloves garlic, chopped
2 tablespoons minced parsley

½ cup olive oil
Salt
¼ to ½ cup butter
4 tablespoons fine dry breadcrumbs
4 green onions, sliced
3 fresh lemons

Preheat oven to 375 degrees.

Rinse trout and pat dry. Rub outsides with a little olive oil; salt and pepper inside and out.

Place half of mushrooms in the bottom of a shallow baking dish. Place fish on top of mushrooms.

Mix bread crumbs with garlic, green onions and parsley. Sprinkle mixture over fish, and squeeze the juice of one lemon over all.

Melt butter and combine with olive oil; add the juice of 2 lemons. Pour half of the butter over fish. Bake for 20-25 minutes, until the fish flakes and bread crumbs are light brown.

Near the end of cooking time, heat the remaining butter mixture in a sauté pan and cook the reserved mushrooms. Serve trout with sautéed mushroom spooned on top. Garnish with more lemon wedges and parsley, if desired. Serve with pasta and vegetables on the side.

The Savor New York original art print, by Alyssa Kosmer, celebrates New York's plenty. Art prints and other products are available at savorny.org.

ABOVE: The Sandlot Kid in Doubleday Court in.

LEFT: Snow sculpture at Lakefront Park during Cooperstown's annual Snowfest.

Photos by Richard S. Duncan, unless otherwise noted.

ABOVE: The stillness of winter in Otsego County.

RIGHT: Diane Howards's *Winter Fun*.

LEFT: Market Basket

CEMTER: Saturday at the Cooperstown Farmers' Market

BOTTOM: Autumn bounty

Alpacas, right, and sheep below. Future fleecy sweaters and welcomed residents.

Renowned folk artist Ed Johnson's "Open Up the Earth...Let It Grow." Reproduction prints available.

ABOVE: Dairy cows
are a familiar and
pleasing site in the
Cooperstown area.

LEFT: How do you
spell adorable?
C - a - l - f.

This vintage photograph of Alex Ives grandfather, Paris, epitomizes the character of New York farming. See the original at Ives Cream in Norwich, NY.

Photo from the Ives Family Photo Collection

# Farmers' Markets

## and Maple Syrup Producers

# Farmers' Markets
## An Introduction

*You don't have to cook fancy or complicated masterpieces – just good food from fresh ingredients. –Julia Child*

To put Julia Child's wise words into practice, your first stop is the local farmers' market. Farm markets are keystone locations for genuine food, the origins of which are completely known. The people who grew the tomatoes or made the cheese are usually standing right behind the table.

After generations of chemical and commercial farming, small agriculture purveyors are finally getting their long overdue respect. In ever increasing numbers, consumers are demanding safe, quality food for themselves and their children; hold the chlorpyrifos, please. As Joni Mitchell sang, *"give me spots on my apples, but save me the birds and the bees, please."* Not that there are too many spots; natural and organic biodynamic methods are generally effective.

A visit to a local farm market confirms that nature does a great job of providing an ample banquet, without any food lab tinkering. Under the barrage of so many manufactured, assembly line products, a good rule of thumb is: if your great-grandmother wouldn't recognize it, don't eat it. Farm market food is the real thing.

There are compelling reasons to frequent farmers' markets, not the least of which is great food. In an era when too many people have no idea how broccoli grows, or how milk gets to the table, a farmers' market outing is an education. They are a locavore's (someone who eats food produced within 100 miles of he lives) paradise. The 100-mile philosophy grew in reaction to wasteful commercial methods that are the equivalent of agricultural strip-mining. Produce in the grocery store has traveled, on average, about 1500 miles, wasting resources and polluting along the way. It may also come from areas of unregulated pesticide use. Also, hybrids that travel well are usually inferior in flavor and quality. Fruits and vegetables are *supposed* to be *perishable*. Local fare is generally higher quality, more flavorful, untainted, healthier for you, and kinder to the planet. Buying it also supports your neighbors.

Regularly shop your local farmers' market, join a Community Supported Agriculture program; know what you and your family are eating. Visit sustainabletable.org, localharvest.org and eatwellguide.org for a bounty of useful information.

*Know your food, Know your farmer.*

# Cooperstown Farmers' Market

The Cooperstown Farmers' Market is located in beautiful downtown Cooperstown, just off Main Street in Pioneer Alley. The Market operates rain or shine, May through December.

**Summer Saturday Hours:**
    May 13 - Sept. 2, 8 am - 2 pm
**Autumn Saturday Hours:**
    Sept. 9 - Nov. 11, 9 am - 2 pm
**Holiday Saturday Hours:**
    Nov. 18 - Dec. 16, 10 am - 2 pm

*Vendors & Products*

### PRODUCE

**Acrospire Farm:** eco-logical seasonal vegetables and fruit. Full-time. 607-965-5241

**ARK Floral:** potted plants, fresh flower bouquets. Full-time. 607-293-8128

**Blue Stone Farm:** potted plants & seasonal veggies. Full-time. bluestonefarm.org

**Heller's Farm:** fresh flowers, vegetables, fruit. Full-time. 607-967-8321

**Herb Cupboard:** dried and fresh herbs and flowers, perennial plants. Full-time. 518-993-2878

**Lapps Produce:** fresh seasonal vegetables and fruit. Full-time. 315-823-0866

**Middlefield Orchard:** seven varieties of apples. Seasonal. sleepyvalley@earthlink.net

**Shadbush Farm:** organic produce. Full-time. 607-547-1353

**Summers End Orchard:** seasonal veggies, fruit, garlic, chilies. Full-time. summersendorchard.com

## MEATS, CHEESE, & EGGS

**Acrospire Farm:** eco-logical eggs, pork, beef, chicken. Full-time. 607-965-5241

**Bittersweet Ranch:** quail, pheasant, cornish game hens, turkeys, eggs. Full-time. 607-293-8336

**Blue Stone Farm:** eggs. Full-time. bluestonefarm.org

**Sunset View Farm:** chicken, ducks, turkeys, pork , grass fed/grain finished beef. Full-time. 607-433-1626

## PREPARED FOODS

**Acrospire Farm:** eco-logical breads & baked desserts. Full-time. 607-965-5241

**Blue Stone Farm:** granola, granola cookies, muffins. Full-time. bluestonefarm.org

**Italian Cookie Home:** baked desserts, prepared and hot foods. Full-time. 607-397-8432

**Middlefield Orchard:** apple butter, applesauce, grains & flour. Seasonal. sleepvalley@earthlink.net

**Pumpkin Hollow Maple:** maple syrup, maple products. Full-time. 607-278-5025

**Shadbush Farm:** flours, pies. Full-time. 607-547-1353

**Summers End Orchard:** jams, jellies, marmalades, rubs, sauces. Full-time. summersendorchard.com

**The Taste of Britain:** British baked goods, yogurt, Creme Fraiche. Full-time. pvowen@cnyconnect.net

## CRAFTS

**Clyne Creations:** hand-sewn and machine-stitched baby items and gifts. Full-time. 607-993-5488

**Herb Cupboard:** dried herb and flower products, bath salts, wooden crafts. Full-time. 607-993-2878

**Mary Marx:** hand-knit sweaters. Part-time. 607-547-5241

**Pumpkin Hollow Maple:** leather goods, reed baskets. Full-time. 607-278-5025

**Sarah's Snapshots:** photo cards, matted and framed photos. Full-time. 607-547-8667

**Surprise in Store:** dried flowers, handbags, children's clothing, doll clothes. Full-time. 607-547-2115

**The Soap Peddler:** bar and liquid soaps, bath products. Full-time. 518-234-1452

# Oneonta Farmers' Market

**ONEONTA FARMERS' MARKET VENDORS**
Main Street Plaza
Oneonta, NY 13820
607-437-0158
cadefarms.org

Open Seasonally June through October

Saturday 9AM-2PM, rain or shine

Also Tuesday 2PM-6PM, July through September

## *Vendor List*

**BREEZIE MAPLES FARM**
Larry Roseboom
607-638-9317
Maple syrup, cream, maple nuts,
mustard, candy, and pepper.

**BOUTON EGG FARM**
607-432-5134
Cage-free eggs, including colored
Arucana and brown Golden
Comet. Handmade woodcrafts.

**EARTH'S HARVEST FARM**
Paul & Julie Koch
607-263-5536
Greens, vegetables and garlic
grown naturally, without
chemicals or pesticides.

**JAMAICA DREAM FARM**
Gwen & Ward McMillen
607-638-9785
Large assortment of produce, including
corn-on-the-cob and pumpkins.

**KENNEDY FAMILY FARMS**
Meg Kennedy
607-293-8128
Fresh cut flowers and
bouquets, houseplants, hanging
baskets, bedding plants.

## Man in the Moon Herbs

Gail Todd

607-433-1087

Handmade and herbal gifts, including soaps and toiletries, cleaning supplies, wreaths, frames, pillows and sachets, essential oils and incense, also natural dog biscuits and catnip toys.

## Naturally Speaking

Sue Powell

607-988-6537

Naturally grown vegetables and berries, locally grown garlic and garlic braids, bulbs, perennials and annuals.

## Stone & Thistle Farm
## and Kortright Creek Creamery

Tom & Denise Warren

607-278-5773

Meadow raised lamb, goat, pork, beef, chicken, turkey, rabbit, eggs, raw (on-farm only) and pasteurized goat milk and goat milk products, lambskins, wool blankets and other wool products.

## Sabine Bodeman

Delhi, NY 13753

Homemade Hearth Breads

## Jill Carey

607-433-5029

Handmade jewelry, note cards, t-shirts, painted furniture.

## Patricia Caporale

607-278-5199

Handmade clothing and jewelry.

## Carol and Jim Deming

607-431-9440

Vegetables, berries, cut flowers.

## Ron Wilcox

607-433-2985

Photography

wilcox@hartwick.edu

# Otsego County Maple Producers

Maple syrup is a wonderful little miracle of nature. It is created in only one corner of the world: the upper eastern quadrant of the North American continent. Maple trees are found elsewhere, but sugar maple sap only rises with the amazing freeze-thaw pattern that occurs in the Northeastern United States and Canada, as winter yields to spring.

Maple sap rises in the warming sunlight of March and stops again as nighttime temperatures fall. When the "sweet water" runs, the trees are gently tapped and their precious liquid collected. While driving the countryside, if you see miles of blue tubing connecting trees, like a group of children roped together at the waist with baling twine (think of the film, *O, Brother, Where Art Thou?*), you've happened upon a maple stand, or *sugarbush*. The sap runs through these tubes and, by vacuum or gravity, is pooled into collecting tanks.

The Otsego County Maple Producers handle maple sap with skill and care; just as New York wine masters handle their grape juice. Like wine, maple syrup varies each season, depending on soil condition, rainfall and temperature. Otsego Maple Producers employ methods far more advanced than simple boiling. They use reverse osmosis to separate sugar from water molecules, and evaporation to produce the best-quality syrup.

Maple syrup is divided into Grades A and B. Grade A syrup is subdivided into Light, Medium and Dark ambers, the intensity of flavor corresponding to the deeper color. It is a fabulous topping for nearly everything. Grade B syrup is darker with a more robust flavor, and is prized for baking.

Underappreciated by those who think sticky brown "pancake topping" is the same thing, genuine maple syrup is well worth the additional price. There is absolutely no comparison in flavor and quality. Fellow maple syrup makers in neighboring Quebec, the world's largest producer, call the fake stuff *sirop de poteau,* which translates to "pole syrup," and infers that the colored corn syrup was tapped from telephone poles.

# Breezie Maples Products

One of the largest maple operations in the country, Breezie Maples uses over 14,000 taps to collect sap from their 40-acre sugar bush. Inspired sugarmaker Rick Newman joined forces with Larry Roseboom, whose family has made syrup in this area for over 250 years. The nearby town of Roseboom is named for his ancestors. Larry's resume and Rick's passion have merged to win more blue ribbons for maple syrup and sugar than any other producer in Otsego County.

Take a tour of Breezie Maples state-of-art maple production facility, especially if you are here during the sugaring-off weeks of March and April. Using reverse osmosis and evaporation, they reduce sap to superior syrup of all grades, carefully sampling and classifying the daily results. Depending on viscosity, it can take up to 50 gallons of sap to make a single gallon of the prized maple syrup. Breezie Maples products are available throughout the Cooperstown area and online. Call for a tour and directions.

Rick Newman and Larry Roseboom
2269 County Highway 34
Westford, NY 13488
607-638-9317
800-950-9676
breeziemaples.com

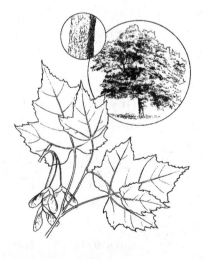

# New York Maple Brownie Sundae
## Otsego County Maple Producers

Genuine maple syrup and real butter make these brownies, or more accurately, "blondies," sumptuous in their own right. Used as a base for this New York State sundae they are incomparable.

*Brownies*

   1 cup butter
   ½ cup brown sugar
   1 cup pure maple syrup*
   2 eggs
   2 cups flour
   1 teaspoon baking powder
   1 cup walnuts, finely chopped

Preheat oven to 350 degrees

Cream together butter and brown sugar. Add eggs and beat until blended, then stir in maple syrup. Beat in flour and baking powder. Stir in walnuts.

Pour batter into a prepared (greased and floured) 9" x 13" baking pan. Bake about 30 minutes, or until a toothpick inserted into the center comes out clean. Cool and cut into squares.

*Now...* to make a dessert that is beyond decadent: Place a Maple Brownie square onto a dessert dish and top with vanilla or maple walnut ice cream. Drizzle with pure light amber maple syrup and sprinkle with toasted walnuts. Fresh or dried blueberries are a fine addition, too. Classy, delicious and affectionately New York.

*\*Dark syrup has a more robust flavor and is preferred for baking. Lighter syrups are generally used for toppings. Let your taste decide.*

> *"My advice is not to inquire why or whither, but just enjoy ice cream while it's on your plate, that's my philosophy."*
> – Thorton Wilder

# Dismal Inn Sugar Company

Ya gotta love that name. It's funny and perfectly reasonable; Bruce Phillips' first attempts at farming were, by his own admission, "dismal."

He and Lucia got better at it, of course, and now they dabble on a number of agricultural fronts, including making superior maple syrup and products. Using reverse osmosis technology, they produce fine grade syrup using less heat. Bruce and Lucia also do a bit of lumbering and growing natural produce, including garlic, pumpkins and heirloom vegetables.

Lucia Phillips paints country life in her primitive folk art, capturing a markedly different tempo from what she knew when working on Wall Street. Her paintings may be viewed by appointment.

The Phillips maple products, garlic, pumpkins, herbs, and other produce are available seasonally in regional shops. Call to place your order and the Phillips' will arrange a pick-up or delivery time.

Bruce and Lucia Phillips
Hartwick, NY 13348
607-293-6488
607-293-6164

# Maple Baked Beans
## Dismal Inn Sugar Company

*I*f you've never tried real baked beans (i.e. not out of a can) treat yourself to these rich, substantial favorites, so popular in neighboring New England. The long, slow baking time allows the maple syrup and other ingredients to deeply imbue the bland beans with flavor. Perfect on a winter day when the additional heat from the oven is most appreciated.

**2 pounds dried white beans**
**½ pound lean salt pork (optional)**
**½ teaspoon baking soda**
**1 teaspoon salt**
**1 teaspoon dry mustard**
**1 medium-sized onion, peeled**
**1½ cups pure New York maple syrup**

Start the night before you plan to serve beans. Rinse beans and pick over for stones. Place in a pot and cover with cold water. Add baking soda and soak overnight. The next morning, drain the beans. Cover with fresh water and boil gently until skins wrinkle. Drain cooking liquid and save. Preheat oven to 325 degrees.

Place whole, peeled onion in the bottom of a bean pot or covered casserole. Add all ingredients except pork, if using, and stir together. Score pork and place on top of beans. Cover beans with saved water. Place cover on pot and bake about 8 hours. Check occasionally, adding more reserved water as needed. Remove pot cover the last hour of cooking to brown top.

# Smokey Hollow Maple Products

For nearly twenty years, the family-run Smokey Hollow Maple Products have "tapped the mountain" on their 330 acre farm. A cat's cradle of bright blue sap tubing connects over 1700 sugar maple trees. Every March the trees convey their precious liquid by gravity and vacuum to George Loft's pump house on Sparrow Hawk Creek.

The sap is transported to the Smokey Hollow Sap House where it is transformed into premium quality syrup, maple cream, maple sugar and sprinkles. Their maple products are available for shipping and they count loyal customers nationwide and overseas. Give them a call before stopping by, to be sure that they are in; they might be anywhere on the mountain!

Smokey Hollow Maple Products is easy to find, between Cooperstown and Albany. From Interstate 88, take exit 18 to Route 7, Schenevus. Turn left onto Route 7 and right onto Smokey Avenue, just before Schenevus High School. Smokey Hollow is about two miles on the right.

George and Inga Loft
436 Smokey Avenue
Schenevus, NY 12155
607-638-9393

MAPLE SUGARING.

# Maple Bread
## Otsego Maple Producers

This dense, flavorful bread is delicious toasted and slathered with New York maple cream, spun honey, or butter for breakfast, tea, or after school snacks. The more robust flavor of dark maple syrup is preferred for baking. This bread machine adaptation does most of the work for you.

*Liquids*
- 1¼ cups skim milk
- ¾ cup pure maple syrup
- ⅓ cup cooking oil
- 2 eggs

*Dry Ingredients*
- 3 cups whole-wheat flour
- 1¾ cups all-purpose flour
- 2 packages active dry yeast
- 1 teaspoon salt
- 2 teaspoons cinnamon
- 1 cup raisins (optional)

Gently warm milk, syrup, and oil until very warm (120-130 degrees). Beat eggs and stir into syrup mixture. Place in bread machine bucket.

Stir dry ingredients, except yeast, together. Place on top of liquid ingredients. Make a well in flour mixture and place yeast in the center. Set bread machine on "Dough" cycle. Add raisins when the liquid and dry ingredients are combined.

When the cycle is complete, remove dough to a lightly floured board and divide in half for loaves, or up to 20 pieces for rolls. Place in lightly greased pans and put in a warm place to rise until doubled in size, 30-45 minutes.

Preheat oven to 375 degrees and bake 25-30 minutes for loaves, about 15 minutes for rolls. Remove when the bread is browned and sounds hollow when tapped on the bottom. Brush the tops with butter, if desired.

# *Celebrity Chefs*

# Home Run Recipes

*T*he Celebrity Chefs chapter is a favorite addition to every *Savor New York* book.

In *Home Plate*, many of our celebrities are, of course, baseball players, and many of them members of the National Baseball Hall of Fame. The celebrities chosen for *Home Plate* are held to the same criteria applied to every farm, business or attraction included in *Savor New York* publications. Establishments and celebrities are selected based on our standards of excellence, unique presence, and positive contributions to a given area. With our players, we weigh their role in baseball and the influence their performance, on and off the field, had on the game.

Not all players are invited, and not all accept our invitation. Space is a necessary consideration. But be sure, those who appear on these pages, without exception, exemplify what makes baseball the greatest game – diligence, fair play, generosity, and class.

Savor New York salutes our celebrities for their extraordinary careers and thanks them for being a part of our team.

# Harmon Killebrew

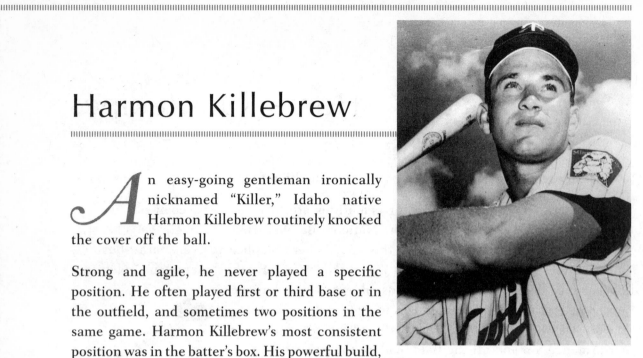

An easy-going gentleman ironically nicknamed "Killer," Idaho native Harmon Killebrew routinely knocked the cover off the ball.

Strong and agile, he never played a specific position. He often played first or third base or in the outfield, and sometimes two positions in the same game. Harmon Killebrew's most consistent position was in the batter's box. His powerful build, which he attributed to his mother Katie's "wonderful dinners of bear steak, wild pheasant and wild duck", translated into powerful hitting. After 22 seasons in the American League, he retired with more homeruns than any other right-handed batter in league history.

Signed at age 17 by the Washington Senators, Harmon Killebrew spent five years playing AA ball before moving to the majors in 1959. He hit 42 homers that year, the first of eight 40-plus homerun seasons. Harmon became a Minnesota Twin when the Senators moved to the Twin Cities in 1961.

Minneapolis' Metropolitan Stadium witnessed some of Harmon's greatest feats. In 1967 he blasted the longest homerun in the stadium's history, belting the ball into the second deck of the bleachers. In 1971, he hit the 500th of his 573 career homeruns at "The Met." Between those triumphs, Harmon Killebrew was named American League Most Valuable Player in 1969 after a dazzling season, hitting 49 homeruns, with 140 RBIs. It is widely believed that the Major League Baseball logo created in 1969 features Harmon Killebrew's swing in silhouette.

Harmon Killebrew was inducted into the National Baseball Hall of Fame in 1984, the first Minnesota Twin so honored. The Twins have retired his Number 3 jersey.

> *"The homers he hit against us would be homers in any park, including Yellowstone."*
> —Manager Paul Richards
> on Harmon Killebrew's hitting

# Killebrew Strobalaugh
## Harmon Killebrew

This generous recipe "feeds an army" as Harmon says. The dinner table at the Killebrew house seated 11, with Nita and Harmon and their nine children. These days Harmon Killebrew swings a golf club and stays active in charity causes and keeping up with his and wife Nita's numerous grandchildren.

| | |
|---|---|
| 2 large onions, chopped | 2 teaspoons salt |
| 2 large green peppers, chopped | 2 teaspoons pepper |
| 2 tablespoons butter | 2 tablespoons Worcestershire sauce |
| 4 pounds lean ground sirloin | 4 cups cooked rice |
| 2 28-ounce cans stewed tomatoes | One pound small shrimp (optional) |

Sauté onions and peppers in butter. Drain and set aside.

In a large pot, brown beef over high heat. Drain excess fat. Add onions and peppers and stewed tomatoes. Heat thoroughly.

Season to taste with salt, pepper and Worcestershire sauce. Add rice, cover and cook over low heat until heated through. Transfer to a large casserole dish and serve.

> *"My father used to play with my brother and me in the yard. Mother would come out and say, 'You're tearing up the grass.' 'We're not raising grass,' Dad would reply. 'We're raising boys.'"*
> — Harmon Killebrew

# Yogi Berra

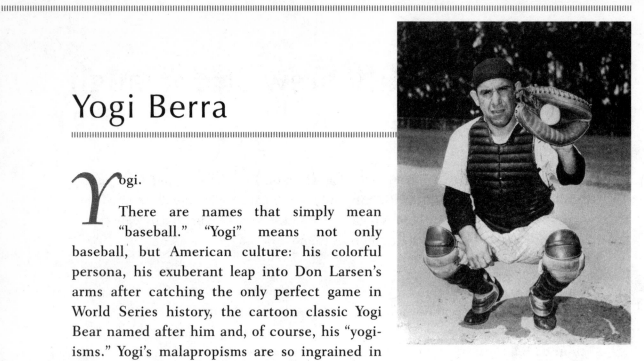

Yogi.

There are names that simply mean "baseball." "Yogi" means not only baseball, but American culture: his colorful persona, his exuberant leap into Don Larsen's arms after catching the only perfect game in World Series history, the cartoon classic Yogi Bear named after him and, of course, his "yogi-isms." Yogi's malapropisms are so ingrained in American vernacular that people who have no idea of the source often quote him. "It ain't over 'til it's over," "it's déjà vu all over again" and "when you come to the fork in the road, take it" all have the same sage source in Yogi.

A native of the "The Hill" Italian area of St. Louis, MO, Lawrence Peter "Lawdie" Berra was nicknamed "Yogi" because a childhood friend thought he resembled a yogi (a Hindu holy man) seen in a movie. His major league career began in 1946 after serving in the US Navy. During his 19-year career with the New York Yankees he was a 3-time Most Valuable Player and he appeared on 15 All-Star teams. He played in 14 World Series, hitting the first pinch-hit homer in Series history in 1947. As manager of the Yankees and the Mets, he led both American and National League teams to the World Series.

Yogi Berra was inducted into the National Baseball Hall of Fame in 1972, the same year the Yankee's retired his number 8. He is number 40 on The Sporting News' list of 100 Greatest Baseball Players and fans elected him to the Major League Baseball All Century-Team. Learn more about the national treasure that is Yogi Berra at his museum on the campus of Montclair State in Montclair, NJ.

Yogi. That's all you have to say.

> *"Williams was the most natural hitter, but Berra was the most natural ballplayer."*
> —Casey Stengal

# Yogi Berra's Tripe Dinner
## Yogi Berra

A handful of recipes from the first edition of *Home Plate* are special enough to also be included in *Home Plate: The Culinary Road Trip of Cooperstown*. Yogi's Tripe Dinner, like the man himself, is one of a kind. The recipe takes some time, but to tripe connoisseurs it's worth the wait. It gets better as it sits, so you may want to cook it one day and serve it the next.

**5 pounds fresh tripe (it will cook down considerably)**
**10 tablespoons salt**
**3-4 red potatoes**
**1-2 cups fresh or frozen lima beans**
**1-2 large carrots**
**2-3 celery ribs**
**1 large Empire Sweet onion**
**Basil and oregano**

Wash tripe in cold water. Cut in 1" pieces and place in good-sized pot. Cover with cold water and 5 tablespoons of salt. Bring to a boil and cook for two hours. After two hours, pour water off, cover with fresh cold water, another 5 tablespoons of salt and boil for another two hours. After two hours, take off heat and rinse in cold water. Return tripe to pot, cover with fresh cold water and cook for another hour, this time without salt.

Cook vegetables in a separate pot during the tripe's last cooking hour. The vegetables are versatile; use more or less to your taste. Cut potatoes and carrots into good-sized chunks. Dice celery and onion. Boil with a pinch of basil and oregano. When potatoes and carrots are al dente (cooked, but still firm), remove from heat. DO NOT DRAIN vegetables.

Drain cooking water from tripe. Add tripe to vegetables and vegetable broth. Stir in one teaspoon chicken stock granules. Salt and pepper to taste.

Serve with good bread and cold beer.

*Recipe courtesy of TJ's Place The Home Plate*

# Paul Blair

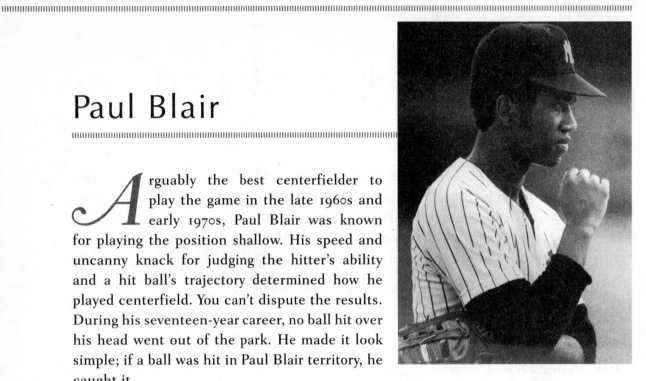

Arguably the best centerfielder to play the game in the late 1960s and early 1970s, Paul Blair was known for playing the position shallow. His speed and uncanny knack for judging the hitter's ability and a hit ball's trajectory determined how he played centerfield. You can't dispute the results. During his seventeen-year career, no ball hit over his head went out of the park. He made it look simple; if a ball was hit in Paul Blair territory, he caught it.

"If a ball went over my head, it was a souvenir." Paul Blair made no fielding errors during his entire career, posting a .988 fielding percentage.

Though his style may have been unorthodox, it worked, earning him eight Gold Gloves. He holds the American League record for the most Gold Gloves awarded to any centerfielder. He is the only Baltimore Orioles outfielder ever to win the honor.

His quickness, intuitive play and bunting ability extended his major league career to seventeen seasons, playing with the Baltimore Orioles, the New York Yankees and the Cincinnati Reds. Paul Blair appeared in six World Series, four with the Baltimore Orioles and two with the New York Yankees. His home run in Game 3 of the 1966 Series provided the only run in the Orioles 1-0 win over the Los Angeles Dodgers, in the Series the Orioles would go on to sweep.

Paul Blair was elected to the Baltimore Orioles Hall of Fame in 1984.

> *"I never saw Paul Blair's first step."*
> —Earl Weaver, on Paul Blair's remarkable fielding

# Chicken and Parsley Dumplings
## Paul Blair

This is a classic recipe and favorite of Mr. Blair. It takes some time, but it's a great standby in cold weather and it fills the house with inviting aroma. DO NOT lift the lid once the dumpling dough has been added to the broth.

*Chicken*

4 pounds cut-up stewing chicken
2 tablespoons oil
1 cup chopped celery
1 teaspoon dried thyme
Boiling water

Flour, seasoned with salt,
   pepper and paprika
1 cup chopped onion
2 teaspoons dried parsley
Salt

*Cornmeal Dumplings*

½ cup cornmeal
1 teaspoon baking powder
3 tablespoons butter
1 tablespoon chopped fresh parsley

½ cup flour
¼ teaspoon salt
½ cup milk

Rinse chicken and pat dry. Place flour mixture in a strong paper bag. Add chicken pieces a few at a time and shake to coat. Heat oil in a heavy Dutch oven or a deep skillet. Brown chicken on all sides. Add celery, onion, thyme and parsley and four cups boiling water. Reduce heat to low and simmer about three hours, until chicken is tender.

For dumplings, combine cornmeal, flour, baking powder, and salt; cut in butter with a pastry blender or a fork until mixture resembles coarse meal. Add milk and stir.

After chicken is done, salt and pepper to taste. Add enough boiling water to cover chicken. Bring to a gentle boil and drop dumpling batter by teaspoonfuls into broth. Cover and cook for 20 minutes. Do not remove cover during first 10 minutes.

# Bob Feller

Pitcher "Rapid Robert" Feller is the senior living member of the elite few elected to the National Baseball Hall of Fame. Elected in 1962, he spent his entire 18 year career with the Cleveland Indians, amassing 266 victories. His total wins may have been as much as 100 more, but for the four peak seasons he spent serving his country in the Navy during World War II. Enlisting after Pearl Harbor, he was decorated with five campaign ribbons and eight battle stars. He said of his time in uniform, "Baseball in the Navy always was much more fun than it had been in the major leagues."

A native of the farming region of Van Meter, Iowa, Bob Feller's father, in what must have inspired a famous scene from the film *The Natural*, built a backstop to encourage his son's gift and his strong arm. At the age of 17, Bob Feller made his major league debut with the Indians, striking out 15 batters. After that season, he returned to Van Meter to graduate from high school. The ceremony was covered on NBC Radio.

A dominating pitcher, Bob Feller has a bounty of awards and records to his credit, including three no-hitters. He is the only pitcher ever to throw a no-hitter on opening day (April 16, 1940 at Comiskey Park). He is the winningest pitcher in Cleveland Indians history. His number 19, retired in 1957, was the first they so honored. His statue stands at the entry to Cleveland's Jacob's Field.

Bob Feller explains the method behind his remarkable pitching ability like this:

"I just reared back and let them go."

You may visit the Bob Feller Museum in Van Meter, Iowa.

# Bob Feller Chili
## Bob Feller

s simple and straightforward as a Bob Feller fastball, everyone can make and enjoy this chili.

**1 tablespoon oil**
**½ cup chopped onion**
**¼ cup chopped green onion**
**1 pound lean ground beef**
**Two 8-ounce cans tomato sauce**
**One 16-ounce can of kidney beans**
**1 teaspoon salt**
**Chili powder**

Heat oil in a two-quart saucepan over medium heat. Cook onion, pepper and beef until lightly browned. Drain fat, if necessary. Add tomato sauce and cook over low heat for five minutes. Add the kidney beans and salt. Stir in one tablespoon chili powder, adding more to taste.

Serve topped with chopped onions, shredded New York cheese, diced tomatoes and sour cream, if desired.

*Recipe courtesy of TJ's Place: the Home Plate*

*"In his day, Bob Feller was the best pitcher living."*
      —Joe DiMaggio

# Carl Erskine

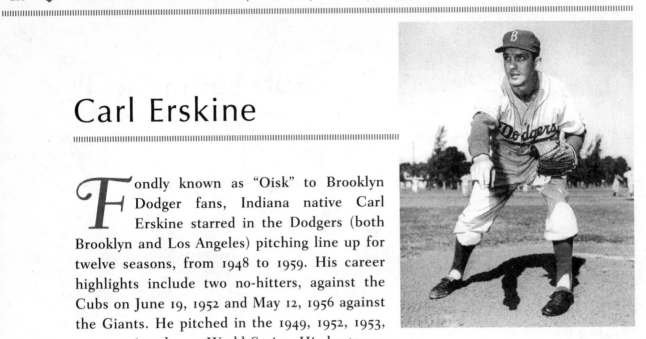

Fondly known as "Oisk" to Brooklyn Dodger fans, Indiana native Carl Erskine starred in the Dodgers (both Brooklyn and Los Angeles) pitching line up for twelve seasons, from 1948 to 1959. His career highlights include two no-hitters, against the Cubs on June 19, 1952 and May 12, 1956 against the Giants. He pitched in the 1949, 1952, 1953, 1955, 1956 and 1959 World Series. His best year was 1953 with 20 wins and six losses. It was in that year that he achieved the World Series record with 14 strikeouts (in Game 3), a record that stood for 14 years.

Carl Erskine was elected into the Indiana Baseball Hall of Fame in 1979.

He features the World Series Buttermilk Cake in his book, *Tales From the Dodger Dugout*.

*"During the 1955 season, the Dodgers were again the favorites to win the National League pennant. About mid-season, Frank Kellert, a rookie outfielder, received a package from his family in Oklahoma. It was a buttermilk cake. He shared it with the team before a game, and we won. The cake lasted long enough for us to win a couple more games. Sometime after that, the team went into a minor slump. Kellert was asked to contact his family for another buttermilk cake. The cakes kept coming, and we kept winning and clinched the pennant.*

*During the World Series, we had a supply of buttermilk cakes. We beat the Yankees in seven games for the first and only world championship in the 75-year history of the Brooklyn Dodgers.'*

# Carl Erskine's Series Winning Buttermilk Cake
## Carl Erskine

One of the few recipes featured in two volumes of *Home Plate*, this buttermilk cake is a favorite at book signing events. It freezes beautifully, and it's terrific sliced, toasted and buttered for breakfast or tea. Different frostings can be added to enhance this cake, including vanilla, chocolate, caramel, maple, even peanut butter. *Home Plate* thanks baseball's consummate gentleman, Carl Erskine, for sharing it with us.

That really is four <u>tablespoons</u> of vanilla. Use real vanilla for the best flavor. Butter can be used in place of shortening.

**Preheat oven to 350 degrees.**
**1 cup shortening**
**2 cups sugar**
**4 whole eggs**
**Dash of salt**
**1 cup buttermilk**
**½ teaspoon baking soda, dissolved in buttermilk**
**4 tablespoons vanilla**
**3 cups all purpose flour**
**1 cup finely chopped pecans**

Cream shortening and sugar together. Beat in eggs one at a time. Add flour and buttermilk, alternately. Add vanilla, stir well and fold in pecans.

Bake in a greased and floured tube pan for about 50 minutes, or until toothpick inserted in center comes out clean. Win World Series.

> *I've had a pretty good success facing Stan (Musial) by throwing him my best pitch and backing up third base.*
> –Carl Erskine

# Gaylord Perry

A colorful and controversial pitcher, Gaylord Jackson Perry played for eight different teams from 1962-1983. When he makes personal appearances he wears a jersey that sports all eight team logos. However, when he was inducted into the National Baseball Hall of Fame in 1991, he wore the San Francisco Giants cap. The Giants retired his number, 36, in 2005.

Gaylord Perry was the first pitcher to win the Cy Young Award in both leagues, the first in 1972 while playing for the Cleveland Indians and again in 1978 for the San Diego Padres, at age 39. He had five seasons winning 20 or more games.

The controversy surrounding Gaylord Perry centered on throwing spitballs. Whether he did or he didn't, or how often, he entitled his biography, *Me and the Spitter*.

Like most pitchers, Gaylord Perry's strengths shone on the mound, not at the plate. In 1963, he was quoted as saying "They'll put a man on the moon before I hit a homerun." On July 20, 1969, just hours after Neil Armstrong stepped on the moon, Gaylord Perry hit his first homerun.

In his 22 year career, he never appeared in a World Series. Gaylord Perry is listed among The Sporting News 100 Greatest Baseball Players.

> *"I reckon I tried everything on the old apple, but salt and pepper and chocolate sauce topping."*
>
> —Gaylord Perry

# Brook Trout Stuffed with Crabmeat
## Gaylord Perry

**G**aylord Perry is an avid fly fisherman. New York's state fish is the brook trout. Sometimes it's just karma.

**Four 12" trout, split and boned. Do not separate halves.**
**3 or 4 slices of good quality stale bread or dinner rolls**
**1 cup milk**
**1 egg**
**⅓ cup chopped onion**
**⅓ cup chopped raw bacon**
**8 ounces crabmeat**
**Pinch of oregano**
**Juice of ½ lemon**
**Salt & Pepper**
**Dashes Worcestershire sauce**
**Melted butter**
**Paprika**

Preheat oven to 400 degrees

### Trout Stuffing
Tear bread in pieces and soak in milk. When most of milk is absorbed, squeeze or press bread nearly dry and stir in egg.

Sauté bacon and onion, until onions are limp but not brown. Add the crabmeat and sauté another five minutes. Add crab mixture to bread mixture and combine. Stir in the oregano, lemon juice, salt and pepper.

### Trout
Spread stuffing mix evenly among the four trout. Place on bottom and fold the other half on top. Brush top of trout with melted butter and sprinkle with paprika. Bake 15 - 20 minutes, until skin is crisp and fish flakes.

# Ferguson Jenkins

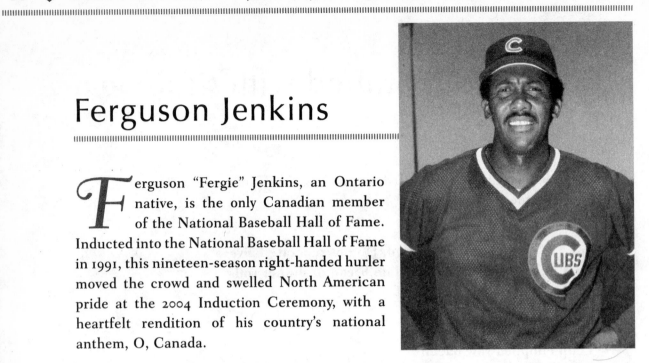

Ferguson "Fergie" Jenkins, an Ontario native, is the only Canadian member of the National Baseball Hall of Fame. Inducted into the National Baseball Hall of Fame in 1991, this nineteen-season right-handed hurler moved the crowd and swelled North American pride at the 2004 Induction Ceremony, with a heartfelt rendition of his country's national anthem, O, Canada.

His stellar career began with the Philadelphia Phillies in 1963. After a single season, the Phils traded him to the Chicago Cubs where he became one of the best pitchers in the major leagues. Incredibly, the Phillies made the same trading move in 1982 when, after a single season, they also sent Ryne Sandberg to the Cubs. Ryne Sandberg joined Ferguson Jenkins in the Hall of Fame in 2005.

Ferguson Jenkins was a three-time All Star, and a Cy Young Award winner in 1971. He had an incredible six consecutive seasons of 20+ wins and is one of only two pitchers to record more than 3000 strikeouts with fewer than 1000 walks (Greg Maddux is the other). Ferguson Jenkins retired with 267 complete games and 49 shutouts. He also holds the 9th-highest strikeout total in history with 3,192.

Since 1999, the Ferguson Jenkins Foundation has supported dozens of humanitarian efforts in North America "through the love of sport." Contact them to see how Fergie's altruism can benefit your good cause. Visit www.fergiejenkinsfoundation.org or write them at: PO Box 664 Lewiston, NY 14092-0664

*For more Ferguson Jenkins stats, rent the DVD This is Spinal Tap. Contained in the extra scenes is an amusing (and accurate) account of Ferguson Jenkins' shutout record as told by the unlikeliest of fans.*

# Baked Duck with Wine
## Ferguson Jenkins

His *Quail in Wine* was a favorite in our first volume of *Home Plate*, and avid sportsman Ferguson Jenkins returns with another game recipe, given to him by his father many years ago. Outside of Manhattan, New York State is mostly rural and offers great hunting and fishing. Duck is also widely available in markets and groceries.

**2 whole ducks, with skin**
**Salt and pepper to taste**
**2 apples**
**½ cup butter**
**1 cup sherry***

Preheat oven to 450 degrees.

Rub the ducks inside and out with salt and pepper.

Peel, core and quarter the apples and place inside duck cavities. Close openings with string. Sauté ducks in butter until light brown.

Place ducks in baking pan, add sherry and cover. Bake for 45 minutes.

Use the flavorful drippings to make gravy or stock, if desired.

Serve the baked ducks with the best farmers' market jam or jelly.

*Be sure to use a good sherry from the spirits shop, not cooking sherry from the grocery shelves which is inferior in flavor.

> *Mental attitude and concentration*
> *are the keys to pitching.*
> —Ferguson Jenkins

# Wade Boggs

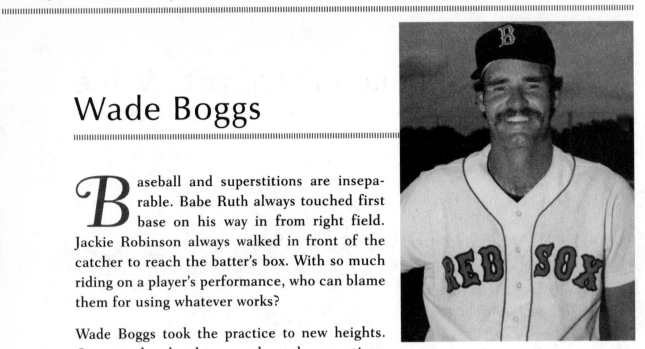

**B**aseball and superstitions are inseparable. Babe Ruth always touched first base on his way in from right field. Jackie Robinson always walked in front of the catcher to reach the batter's box. With so much riding on a player's performance, who can blame them for using whatever works?

Wade Boggs took the practice to new heights. On game days he always awoke at the same time. Before night games, he took batting practice at exactly 5:17PM and ran sprints at exactly 7:17PM. He took precisely 150 ground balls. Before every at bat he drew the Hebrew sign of life, n-chai, in the batter's box. He famously ate chicken before every game, accumulating some great recipes.

A Nebraska native, third baseman Wade Boggs spent most of his career in Boston, playing also as a Yankee and finishing his career as a Tampa Bay Devil Ray, hitting the first home run in the expansion team's history. An amazing hitter, he is the only player to reach the 3000 hit mark with a homerun. He is the only 20th century player to have seven consecutive 200-hit seasons. In his 18-year career he reached base safely an astounding 80% of his games.

Wade Boggs is listed on The Sporting News' list of the 100 Greatest Players. The Tampa Bay Devil Rays retired his number 12 and he was inducted into the Boston Red Sox Hall of Fame in 2004.

Wade Boggs was inducted into the National Baseball Hall of Fame in 2005.

> *Boggs may have the best hand-eye coordination of anyone I've ever seen.*
> —Ted Williams

# Chicken Tetrazzini
## Wade Boggs

**W**ade Boggs returns to *Home Plate* with another of his fabulous chicken dishes. This is his version of the classic cream sauce and spaghetti recipe, named for the early twentieth century opera star Luisa Tetrazzini, and generally thought to be created either in San Francisco or at the Knickerbocker Hotel in New York City.

**One 5-pound hen**
**1 medium white onion, peeled and halved**
**1 stalk of celery, cut in sticks**
**Dashes of salt, pepper, and parsley flakes**

Place hen in large, deep pot. Add onion and celery; sprinkle with salt, pepper and parsley to taste. Cover with water and bring to a boil. Reduce heat and simmer 1½ to 2 hours.

**2 teaspoon oil**
**1 cup chopped celery**
**2 medium white onions, chopped**
**3 cloves garlic, chopped**
**3 medium bell peppers, chopped**
**1 cup slivered almonds**
**4 cans cream of mushroom soup, undiluted**
**1 pound thin spaghetti**
**½ cup grated Parmesan cheese**

Heat oil in a large skillet and sauté celery, onions, garlic, peppers, and almonds. Set aside. Remove chicken from pot and reserve cooking liquid. Remove chicken from bones and cut meat in small pieces. Place chicken in large bowl and mix with mushroom soup. Combine with sautéed vegetables and almonds.

Preheat oven to 350 degrees. Cook spaghetti in reserved chicken broth until tender. Fold spaghetti into chicken mixture, adding 1-2 cups of the cooking broth. Place all into a large baking dish and sprinkle with Parmesan. Bake for 25-30 minutes, until hot and bubbly.

*Look for more of Wade Boggs' favorite chicken recipes in his book, <u>Fowl Tips.</u>*

# Jim Konstanty

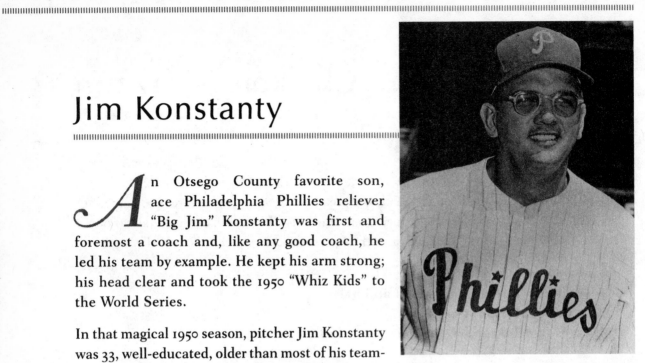

An Otsego County favorite son, ace Philadelphia Phillies reliever "Big Jim" Konstanty was first and foremost a coach and, like any good coach, he led his team by example. He kept his arm strong; his head clear and took the 1950 "Whiz Kids" to the World Series.

In that magical 1950 season, pitcher Jim Konstanty was 33, well-educated, older than most of his teammates and the adoring husband of his wife, Mary, and their two children, Jim and Helen.

In 1950 Jim Konstanty was also called the "Fireman" for his reliability on the relief mound, pulling the Phillies out of the flames and saving 22 games. He appeared in a then-record 74 games, putting 16 in the win column.

An unlikely hero, Jim Konstanty's palm ball, a confounding change-up pitch, was inspired by his friend Andy Skinner, a Worcester, NY, mortician who just happened to like to play pool and bowl. Andy and Jim worked together to translate the spin on billiard and bowling balls into a baseball pitch.

Their efforts were rewarded, with Jim heralding the emerging relief pitcher specialty. That year Jim was named the National League's Most Valuable Player, the first reliever to be so honored, the Associated Press' Athlete of the Year and The Sporting News' Pitcher of the Year.

After retiring from a major league career spanning 1944-1956, Jim Konstanty returned to Otsego County. He was instrumental in expanding the Athletic Department at Hartwick College, serving as its director from 1968-1972. The Konstanty Sporting Goods store was a fixture on Oneonta's Main Street for nearly 40 years.

> *"I felt about hitting the way Konstanty felt about pitching. He never thought a hitter should get a hit off of him. If a hitter ever got a hit, he didn't credit the hitter, he blamed himself."*
> —Hall of Famer and fellow Philadelphia "Whiz Kid" Richie Ashburn

# Jim Konstanty's Family Favorite Kapusta

*J*ohn and Appolonia Konstanty reared their six children, including future MVP pitcher, Jim, in modest circumstances in western New York. This classic Polish peasant meal was a familiar dish in their immigrant household during the first part of the 20th century. Kapusta's inexpensive ingredients of cabbage, sauerkraut, and kidney beans, coupled with its "stick-to-your-ribs" goodness made it a dinner staple. Kapusta's robust flavors and the warm memories they imparted continue to make it a favorite of Jim Konstanty's descendents to this day.

One medium head of cabbage
One large can sauerkraut
One can red kidney beans, drained and rinsed
One stick oleomargarine*
½ cup flour
1 teaspoon salt, or to taste
Pepper to taste
Optional: Sautéed bite-sized pieces of ham, polish sausage, or salt pork.

Bring a large pot of salted water to a boil. Coarsely chop cabbage and add to boiling water.

Drain sauerkraut in a colander and rinse three times in cold water, to reduce the strong tang. Drain and rinse kidney beans. Add both to cooked cabbage and stir together.

In a medium frying pan, melt butter (or oleo) over medium heat. Slowly stir in flour, making a roux. Stir constantly until roux is a deep golden brown. Gradually add browned flour to hot cabbage, stirring with a large wooden spoon and combining thoroughly. Add pepper to taste and simmer on low about a half hour, occasionally stirring up from the bottom of the pot.

*Butter is more flavorful, but the original recipe as told to Jim's wife Mary by his father John in 1948, calls for margarine.*

# Rollie Fingers

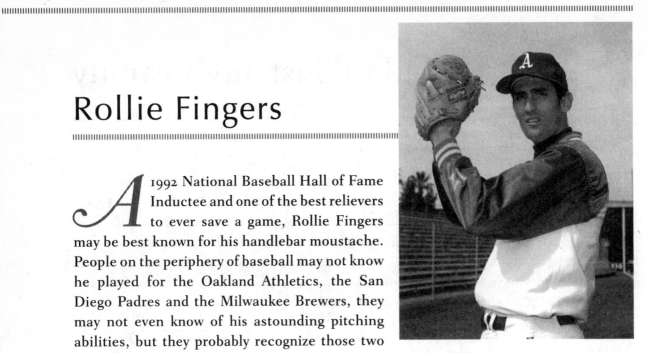

*An early photo of
Rollie Fingers without his signature
handlebar moustache.*

A 1992 National Baseball Hall of Fame Inductee and one of the best relievers to ever save a game, Rollie Fingers may be best known for his handlebar moustache. People on the periphery of baseball may not know he played for the Oakland Athletics, the San Diego Padres and the Milwaukee Brewers, they may not even know of his astounding pitching abilities, but they probably recognize those two perfect curls above his lip.

Growing the moustache was a Charlie Finlay marketing ploy, paying each of the Oakland A's $300 for the addition. Rollie Fingers accepted the bonus and, like his pitching, he did his a little better and more flawlessly than everyone else. His control, his durability and his moustache became his trademarks, on and off the field.

Baseball commentators are hard-pressed to identify any shortcomings in Finger's play. He retired as the greatest relief artist in baseball history after a 17 year career, highlighted with a host of honors, including both the American League Most Valuable Player and the Cy Young Awards while playing with the Brewers in 1981. When he hung up his cleats in 1985 he held the major league record for the most career saves (341) and World Series saves (7). He is among The Sporting News 100 Greatest Baseball Players.

Rollie Fingers is a familiar face, in Cooperstown and at many baseball venues. You can't miss the moustache.

> *A fellow has to have faith in
> God above and Rollie Fingers
> in the bullpen.*
> —Alvin Dark

# Honey Mustard Fingerlings
## Rollie Fingers

Fingerling potatoes are roughly finger-shaped, low in starch, and great for roasting, pureeing, or in potato salads. They are small, cook more quickly than bigger counterparts, and require less preparation – usually no peeling or cutting. There are numerous varieties, often sold in bags of mixed colors.

This flavorful recipe is easy and makes a terrific side dish for almost any entrée.

Preheat oven to 425 degrees

- **2 pounds fingerling potatoes**
- **2 tablespoons olive oil**
- **1 tablespoon coarse salt**
- **1 tablespoon ground black pepper**
- **1 tablespoon Dijon-style mustard**
- **1 tablespoon New York honey**
- **1 tablespoon fresh chopped chives**

Wash fingerlings and pat dry; set aside. In a large mixing bowl, whisk together the oil, salt, pepper, mustard and honey. Add potatoes, tossing well. Place in a 9"x13" baking pan. Bake uncovered, 20-30 minutes until potatoes pierce easily. Garnish with chopped chives and serve.

*Chives*

# Brooks Robinson

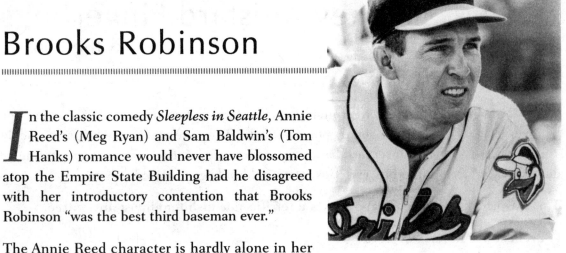

*I*n the classic comedy *Sleepless in Seattle,* Annie Reed's (Meg Ryan) and Sam Baldwin's (Tom Hanks) romance would never have blossomed atop the Empire State Building had he disagreed with her introductory contention that Brooks Robinson "was the best third baseman ever."

The Annie Reed character is hardly alone in her opinion. Not only is Brooks Robinson generally acclaimed as the greatest defensive third-baseman of all time, the Arkansas native is also recognized as one of the most decent, generous players ever to don a uniform.

Brooks Robinson played his entire 23-season career (1955-1977), at third base, with the Baltimore Orioles. On a team known for their superior defensive play (including the graceful and deadly center fielding of team mate Paul Blair), Brooks Robinson's incomparable style earned him a slew of records and the moniker "the human vacuum cleaner."

Despite his opinion that he was "an average player", Brooks Robinson's consistent and frequently spectacular plays won him 16 consecutive Gold Gloves, a record only he and pitcher Jim Kaat hold. He was the starting third baseman on 15 consecutive All-Star teams and he holds the lifetime record for third baseman for most games (2,870), best fielding percentage (.971), most putouts (2,697), most assists (6,205), and most double plays (618). That's some definition of "average."

Brooks Calbert Robinson was inducted into the National Baseball Hall of Fame his first year of eligibility (1983) with a whopping 92% of the votes. He is on the Sporting News' list of the 100 Greatest Baseball Players, and was elected to the Major League Baseball All-Century Team. Fellow Hall of Famer George Brett chose his uniform number five in honor of Brooks Robinson.

> *"Whether you want to or not, you do serve as a role model. People will always put more faith in baseball players than anyone else."*
> —Brooks Robinson

# Susan Skiles' Sweet Potato Casserole
## Brooks Robinson

Get dual service from these sweet potatoes as a side dish or as a dessert. The sweet custard base and crunchy nut topping add contrasting balance to savory and spicy entrees. They are equally delicious finishing a meal as a sweet potato pudding.

*Potatoes*

4 cups cooked and mashed
  sweet potatoes

2 eggs, well beaten

1 teaspoon vanilla extract

1 cup sugar

½ cup melted butter

⅓ cup milk

*Topping*

1 cup brown sugar

2 cups chopped walnuts

½ cup flour

5 tablespoons butter, melted

Preheat oven to 350 degrees

Combine potatoes, sugar, vanilla, butter, and milk and mix well.

Spread mixture in a 9" x 13" baking dish.

Mix topping ingredients except butter, stirring thoroughly. Cover sweet potato mixture with topping, and drizzle the 5 tablespoons melted butter evenly over all. Bake for 30 minutes.

*Recipe courtesy of Susan Skiles, Brooks Robinson's friend and self-proclaimed "biggest fan".*

*Though frequently confused, sweet potatoes and yams are not in the same plant family, and yams are not as readily available in the United States. The deeply orange-fleshed sweet potatoes are highly nutritious and remarkably high in vitamin A. They are in the same family as morning glories.*

# Earl Weaver

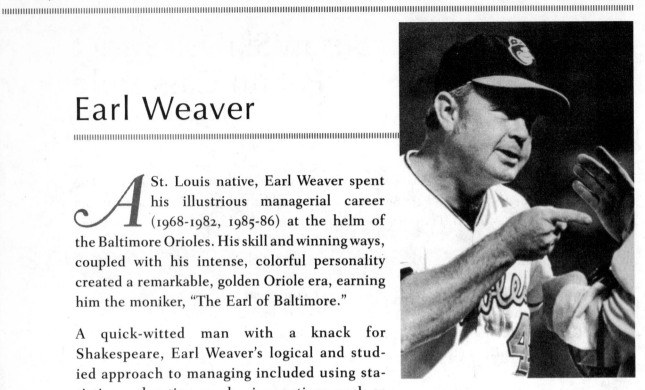

A St. Louis native, Earl Weaver spent his illustrious managerial career (1968-1982, 1985-86) at the helm of the Baltimore Orioles. His skill and winning ways, coupled with his intense, colorful personality created a remarkable, golden Oriole era, earning him the moniker, "The Earl of Baltimore."

A quick-witted man with a knack for Shakespeare, Earl Weaver's logical and studied approach to managing included using statistics and patience, plus innovations such as radar guns to track the speed of pitches (a practice he pioneered in spring training in 1972). This scholarly tack was often incongruous with his lively behavior on the field. Earl Weaver's pugnacious style was the bane of American League umpires, leading to a record 96 ejections (many reports say 99,) a statistic he still holds in the American League. "The job of arguing with the umpire belongs to the manager, because it won't hurt the team if he gets thrown out of the game," he said.

Among Mr. Weaver's more flattering statistics are five 100+ win seasons (the only manager in the history of the club to accomplish the feat,) six Eastern Division titles, four American League pennants, and the World Series championship in 1970. Under Earl Weaver, the Orioles dismantled the "Big Red Machine" of Cincinnati in five games, clinching the Series with a stinging 9-3 defeat of the Reds.

The Orioles retired Earl Weaver's number 4 in 1982. He was inducted into the Baseball Hall of Fame in 1996.

> *"You can't sit on a lead and run a few plays into the line and just kill the clock. You've got to throw the ball over the damn plate and give the other man his chance. That's why baseball is the greatest game of them all."*
>
> *—Earl Weaver*

# Earl and Marianna's Chili Mac

## Earl Weaver

S ome recipes are deceptively easy and addictively good, like this version of Chili Mac. With its spaghetti and cumin, it's reminiscent of Cincinnati-style chili.

1½ to 2 pounds ground beef
1 large green pepper, coarsely chopped
1 small red pepper, coarsely chopped
1 large onion, coarsely chopped
2 large garlic cloves, chopped
One 28-ounce can crushed tomatoes
Two 8-ounce cans tomato sauce
3 tablespoons chili powder
3 tablespoons ground cumin
⅓ pound thin spaghetti
Crushed red pepper to taste

In a large pot or Dutch oven, brown ground beef along with peppers, onion and garlic. Drain excess fat.

Add tomatoes, sauce, chili powder, cumin, and crushed red pepper, if using. Cover pot and cook about 45 minutes. Break spaghetti into thirds and add to pot. Cook until spaghetti is *al dente*.

Serve topped with your favorite shredded cheese.

# Eddie Murray

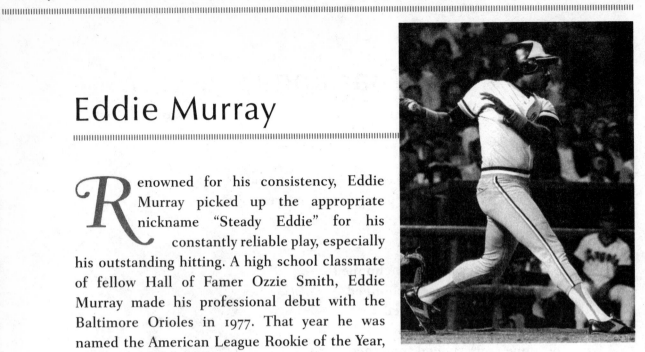

Renowned for his consistency, Eddie Murray picked up the appropriate nickname "Steady Eddie" for his constantly reliable play, especially his outstanding hitting. A high school classmate of fellow Hall of Famer Ozzie Smith, Eddie Murray made his professional debut with the Baltimore Orioles in 1977. That year he was named the American League Rookie of the Year, marking the beginning of a stellar career that spanned 20 seasons.

A member of one of baseball's most elite clubs, Eddie Murray is one of only four players in the history of the game to attain more than 500 homeruns and 3000 hits, and the only switch-hitter among them. He collected a number of impressive statistics on his way to Cooperstown, including three Gold Gloves, eight All-Star appearances, and he has the most RBIs of any switch-hitter with 1,917. He hit the most sacrifice flies of all time with 128, and hit 19 career grand slam homeruns, placing him third and in the fine company of Lou Gehrig and Manny Ramirez. He holds the all-time record for hitting homeruns from both sides of the plate in the same game. Mr. Murray accomplished that spine-tingling feat 11 times in his career.

Eddie Murray spent the most seasons with the Baltimore Orioles, playing also for the Los Angeles Dodgers, the New York Mets, the Anaheim Angels, and the Cleveland Indians. He wore the number 33 his entire career and, fittingly, hit his 500th homerun in an Orioles uniform. The Orioles retired his number in 1998. In 1999, the Sporting News ranked him 77th in their list of Baseball's Greatest Players.

Eddie Murray was inducted into the National Baseball Hall of Fame in 2003.

> *Eddie Murray's bronze bust in Cooperstown will chatter only slightly less than the man himself. The first line of text on the monument should read: He spoke rarely and carried a mighty bat.*
>
> —Sportswriter David Ginsburg

# Louisiana Gumbo
## Eddie Murray

This legendary gumbo is Louisiana through and through, a version of the Creole classic that is meaty, spicy and makes enough for the team. Gumbo can call for a variety of ingredients, but they all start with a dark *roux*, which gives it a distinctive, rich flavor.

### Roux*
2 cups flour
1½ gallons water

Cooking oil to generously
cover bottom of pan

### Meats
3 packages smoked pork
sausages, sliced
2 pounds shrimp, peeled and
deveined crab legs and claws

5 packages hot links, sliced
1 large, family-size package chicken
drumsticks or pieces, dredged in
flour, salt, and pepper for frying

### Vegetables
1 large onion, chopped fine
5 or 6 cloves garlic, chopped fine

1 small green bell pepper, chopped
8 stalks celery, chopped fine

### Seasonings
3 cans chicken broth
2 bay leaves
1 teaspoon black pepper
½ teaspoon cayenne pepper
½ bunch fresh parsley

1 teaspoon Nature's Seasons salt
1 teaspoon Season All seasoned salt
½ package dried shrimp
2 teaspoons Gumbo file powder
Lots of white rice

In large stock pot, heat oil over medium heat until hot, and gradually whisk in flour. Cook until roux is richly browned, but not burned. Add water and bring to a boil.

In a separate skillet, sauté onion, pepper, garlic, and celery in oil until soft and glassy looking. Drain and add to pot.

Brown sliced sausages lightly and add to pot. Add seasonings, except for parsley and file powder. Fry chicken, drain on paper towels and add to pot.

Skim any oil from surface. Lightly sauté shrimp until pink and add to pot, along with crab pieces. Add parsley and file powder just before serving. Serve over rice.

*The roux is key to any gumbo. If you burn it, toss it out and start again. You can play with the amounts of meat. If you are a beginner, consider omitting the more expensive seafood until you get the knack of this Murray family favorite.*

# Ozzie Smith

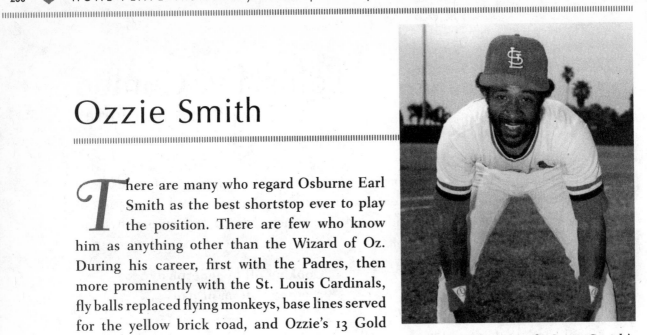

There are many who regard Osburne Earl Smith as the best shortstop ever to play the position. There are few who know him as anything other than the Wizard of Oz. During his career, first with the Padres, then more prominently with the St. Louis Cardinals, fly balls replaced flying monkeys, base lines served for the yellow brick road, and Ozzie's 13 Gold Gloves more than adequately made up for ruby slippers. Any player with Ozzie Smith's stunning defensive gifts needn't hide behind anything, least of all a flimsy curtain.

Ozzie Smith's play at the critical number six position was nothing short of jaw-dropping sensational. The same acrobatic skill that thrilled fans when he turned back flips, he applied to defense, completing the most double plays and assists of any shortstop. He was once quoted, "my fielding is just one of those things. I just do it." He played fleet of foot, stealing 580 bases in the course of his 19 professional seasons. Challenged at the plate early in his career, his hitting improved so that he retired with over 2,400 hits.

He was named the National League Most Valuable Player in 1985, but perhaps his best single season was in 1987 when he batted .303, stole 43 bases, had 75 RBIs, scored 104 runs, and hit 40 doubles. He appeared in 15 All-Star games.

Ozzie Smith was inducted into the National Baseball Hall of Fame in 2002, elected on the first ballot with nearly 92% of the vote. He is on the Sporting News' list of the 100 Greatest Baseball Players, and the St. Louis Cardinals retired his number 1 in 1996.

> *I think umpires have too much power, without any system of checks and balances and the more money a player makes, the more the umpire tries to show off that power to him. Unfortunately, since I signed my contract my strike zone has suddenly become a lot larger.*
>
> – Ozzie Smith

# Collard Greens
## Ozzie Smith

Collards, and other dark, remarkably nutritious greens, are far too unappreciated north of the Mason Dixon line. Greens cooked with "pot liquor" (or "likker"), their vitamin-rich cooking liquid enhanced with smoked meats, is a gift of Southern cuisine. Unlike tender spinach or chard, collards and the similar mustard greens, turnip greens, or kale benefit from long, slow cooking.

Try teaming these Collard Greens with Ozzie Smith's high school classmate, Eddie Murray's Louisiana Gumbo.

Two large bunches of collards, well washed
½ large onion, chopped
2 stalks celery, chopped
½ red or green bell pepper, chopped
1 ham hock or smoked wing or leg of turkey
2 tablespoons vinegar
Fresh chopped garlic, or granulated garlic
1 thin slice of habañero (orange) pepper
(Habañero is *the* hottest pepper, so handle with care. Wear
    rubber gloves and do not touch your eyes or nose.)

Coarsely chop clean collards, removing any thick stems. Place onion, celery, bell pepper, and smoked meat in soup pot; cover with water and place over medium heat. Bring to a boil; add collards, vinegar, garlic to taste, and habañero. Reduce heat, cover pot and cook about an hour, stirring occasionally, until collards are tender and liquid is reduced. (Some recipes call for literally hours of cooking.)

Collards, or a "mess o' greens" are traditionally served with savory cornbread. Good enough to make you want to do back flips on the infield.

*Want to try something really country Southern? Make collard sandwiches the next day, using ice-cold collards on light bread.*

# Ryne Sandberg

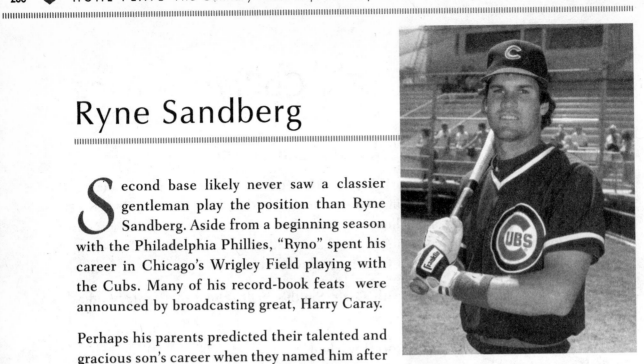

Second base likely never saw a classier gentleman play the position than Ryne Sandberg. Aside from a beginning season with the Philadelphia Phillies, "Ryno" spent his career in Chicago's Wrigley Field playing with the Cubs. Many of his record-book feats were announced by broadcasting great, Harry Caray.

Perhaps his parents predicted their talented and gracious son's career when they named him after Yankees relief pitcher Ryne Duren. (There is precedent for this in baseball: Mickey Mantle's father named him after Hall of Fame catcher Mickey Cochrane). Whether or not they could tell the future, their son did them and Spokane, Washington proud with his brilliant play that spanned 16 major league seasons.

Dramatic and consistent defensive play earned Ryne Sandberg nine consecutive Gold Gloves and 10 All-Star game appearances. He was the National League's Most Valuable Player in 1984, leading the Cubs to their first post-season appearance in almost 40 years. His streak of 122 errorless games is a National League record and he retired with a career fielding percentage of .989. No slouch in the batter's box, Mr. Sandberg hit 40 homeruns in the 1990 season, the first second baseman to do so since Rogers Hornsby in 1922. During the June 23, 1984 "Sandberg Game" he drove in seven runs against the St. Louis Cardinals, and hit back-to-back homeruns off fellow Hall of Famer Bruce Sutter, winning the game for the Cubs 12-11 in extra innings.

Since his retirement, Ryne and Margaret Sandberg established Ryne Sandberg Kid Care to assist in the lives of children with serious illnesses. Ryne Sandberg was inducted into the National Baseball Hall of Fame in 2005. The Chicago Cubs retired his number, 23, the same year.

> *I played it right because that's what you're supposed to do — play it right and with respect.*
> — Ryne Sandberg

# Pico de Gallo
## Ryne Sandberg

"Pico de gallo" translates literally to "rooster's beak," although the derivation and application to this favorite fresh Mexican condiment is muddled.

Simple, delicious, versatile, and perfect after a summer trip to the farmers' market, pico de gallo can be used on steaks, chicken, in salads, or on chips. *Home Plate* thanks Margaret and Ryne Sandberg with a hearty "gracias!"

Chop all ingredients well.

> **6 fresh, meaty tomatoes – Romas are good**
> **Half a bunch of cilantro**
> **1 yellow onion**
> **4-5 jalapeños, (seed to reduce heat, if you like)**
> **Squeeze fresh lemon juice to taste**
> **Salt to taste**

Mix all ingredients well, and refrigerate. Make early in the day so the flavors may blend.

*Chicago's Wrigley Building*

> *Every time I look at that flag flying, I'll think of the Cubs fans that were there for me every day. You have never let me down, and for that I will never forget you.*
> — Ryne Sandberg

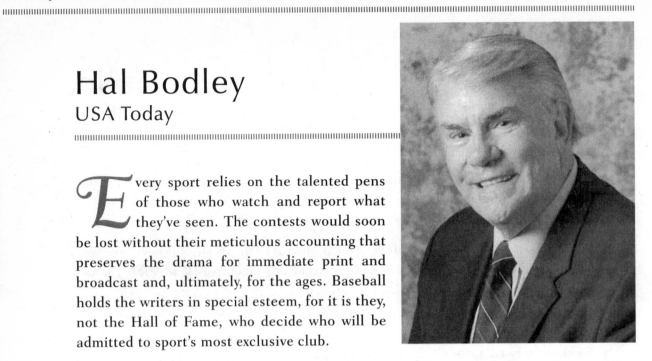

# Hal Bodley
## USA Today

**E**very sport relies on the talented pens of those who watch and report what they've seen. The contests would soon be lost without their meticulous accounting that preserves the drama for immediate print and broadcast and, ultimately, for the ages. Baseball holds the writers in special esteem, for it is they, not the Hall of Fame, who decide who will be admitted to sport's most exclusive club.

Hal Bodley is one of the writer's whose vote is counted for the Induction elite. His journalism career began in 1958 and he has been the baseball editor-columnist of USA Today since its first edition in 1982. Hal Bodley's column is read by millions of subscribers. He is also the bestselling author of *The Team That Wouldn't Die*, about the 1980 Philadelphia Phillies, and *Countdown to Cobb*, about Pete Rose's pursuit of Ty Cobb's all-time career hits record.

You could make the case that Hal Bodley has seen it all. He has reported history as it happened at dozens of World Series and All-Star games, numerous Super Bowls, Olympiads, and Triple Crown races. With a roster of awards and a lifetime of experience, Hal Bodley is widely respected as a leading authority on baseball. It is likely more accurate to state that he, surely and modestly, simply knows everything about the game.

For nearly half a century, Hal Bodley has served as our national chronicler. Reporting baseball and sporting events from the small to the sweeping, his deft pen has illuminated our memories.

# Strawberry Salad
## Hal Bodley

P at Bodley is a great source of stellar recipes on behalf of her husband, Hal. This refreshing summer salad is great for barbecues and dinner parties. Have copies of the recipe ready; Pat says guests are sure to ask for it! Make the dressing the night before for convenience, and to allow the flavors to blend.

### *Salad*
One head Romaine lettuce (may add some curly green lettuce)
1 pint fresh strawberries
½ cup walnuts, almonds, or pecans (toasted)
1 cup sharp white cheese or Monterey Jack, grated

### *Dressing*
Whisk together:

½ cup, plus 2 tablespoons sugar
½ cup red wine vinegar

Add:

1 cup vegetable oil
2 cloves garlic, chopped
½ teaspoon paprika
½ teaspoon salt
¼ teaspoon white pepper

Wash, spin and tear lettuce(s) into a large serving bowl. Slice or quarter cleaned and hulled strawberries and add, along with nuts and grated cheese, to the torn greens. Cover and refrigerate until ready to serve. Dress the salad immediately before serving. Refrigerate any leftover dressing.

# Bill Madden
## New York Daily News

Since the first election to the Hall of Fame in 1936, members of the Baseball Writers Association of America (BBWAA) have decided who in the game would have their image cast in bronze and hung in that honored hall in Cooperstown. They also decide Major League Baseball's Most Valuable Player Award, Rookie of the Year Award, the Cy Young Award, and Manager of the Year.

Bill Madden is one of the members of that influential club. He has written about and embraced the boys in pinstripes for over a quarter century. Covering the Yankee beat for the New York Daily News from 1978, he became their national baseball columnist in 1989. When Billy Joel croons longingly for *The Daily News* in his reflective favorite, *A New York State of Mind*, perhaps it's Bill Madden's baseball column that he's missing. Bill Madden's affection for the Yankees began in childhood, including witnessing Don Larsen's perfect game as a fifth-grader in 1956

Bill Madden's book, *Pride of October: What It Was to Be Young and a Yankee* profiles various Bronx players from across generations, eloquently crafting multi-layered and very human looks at Yogi Berra, Phil Rizzuto, Reggie Jackson, Don Mattingly, and other Yankees. He also penned Don Zimmer's bestselling autobiography *Zim – A Baseball Life* and co-authored *Damned Yankees* with Moss Klein.

Bill Madden is a supporter of the Baseball Assistance Team (B.A.T.), the non-profit organization that provides life assistance to members of the extended baseball family.

# Summer Salmon
## Bill Madden

Take a trip to the farmers' market for fresh tomatoes and make this light summer entrée. The tomatoes and pineapple marry with the lime juice to make a zingy enhancement for the heart-healthy salmon. Serve with Hal Bodley's Strawberry Salad.

Make the salsa early in the day to allow full flavor to develop.

### Salmon
4 salmon fillets, 6-8 ounces each
Olive oil
Lemon pepper

### Tomato-Pineapple Salsa
¼ cup fresh lime juice
¼ cup extra virgin olive oil
2 tablespoons soy sauce
3 tablespoons chopped red onion
1 teaspoon sugar
½ cup finely chopped pineapple
2 large garden tomatoes, diced
¼ cup chopped fresh basil
Salt and pepper

Whisk together lime juice, olive oil, soy sauce, shallots, and sugar. Stir in the pineapple, tomatoes, and basil. Salt and pepper to taste. Cover, and refrigerate.

Take the salsa out of the refrigerator prior to cooking salmon. It will take some of the chill off and the flavors will be heightened.

Brush salmon fillets with olive oil and sprinkle with lemon pepper. Grill over medium-high heat until fish flakes easily. The time will depend on the thickness of the fish. Start checking after about eight minutes for 1" fillets.

# Area Representatives
## State Senator James L. Seward and Assembly Members William Magee, Marc W. Butler, and Peter D. Lopez

*A*ll politics is local, or so goes the maxim often attributed to former Speaker of the House Thomas "Tip" O'Neill. That idea is nowhere truer than in small towns in rural regions, where accessibility to elected officials may be as simple as running into a member of the Assembly or Senate at the hardware store on a Sunday afternoon.

The *Home Plate* area is ably represented by State Senator James Seward, and three members of the New York State Assembly: Bill Magee, Marc Butler and Pete Lopez. Collectively they have served Upstate New York and their part of Otsego County for over 54 years, more than half of that contributed by Senator Jim Seward. Assemblyman Lopez, who represents some of *Home Plate's* outlying areas, was elected in 2006.

These public servants travel thousands of miles a year, sit through sometimes grueling legislative sessions, walk in their share of parades, cut ceremonial ribbons, and serve on copious committees. They bring their Upstate backgrounds to Albany, championing farmers, small businesses and rural concerns. It is, needless to say, a sometimes thankless job. Judging from their respective tenures, it must also be a rewarding one.

Savor New York acknowledges Senator Seward, and Assembly Members Magee and Butler for their involvement with our 2006 charitable edition of *Home Plate: The Traveler's Food Guide to Cooperstown and Otsego County, NY*, a joint project designed to benefit Cooperstown and Otsego County.

*Speechmaking – a political must*

# Autumn Pork Medallions
## Area Representatives

*A*s in most things in life, in politics it helps to have a sense of humor. *Home Plate* appreciates Assemblyman Marc Butler's completely tongue-in-cheek suggestion that a pork recipe be paired with the politician's page.

Pork, apples, and onions are natural partners in this quick and easy recipe. The pork tenderloin is available at one of Assemblyman Butler's constituents in Worcester, Hornung's Worcester Market. Dan, the owner, runs an old-fashioned meat counter and makes great sausage.

The flavor of these pork tenderloin medallions is heightened with sweet apples and spiked with pumpkin pie spice.

**1 whole pork tenderloin**
**½ teaspoon ground black pepper**
**1 teaspoon pumpkin pie spice**
**Vegetable oil**
**1 small onion, chopped**
**1 large apple, cored, coarsely chopped**
**½ cup apple cider**

Slice tenderloin into eight equal pieces, or ask the butcher to do it for you.

Season medallions on both sides with pepper and pumpkin pie spice. Put one or two tablespoons of oil in a large frying pan over medium-high heat. Brown pork on both sides. Tenderloin is a lean meat, so be careful not to overcook it. A couple of minutes per side should do it. Remove medallions from pan and reserve. Add onion and apples to skillet, and sauté until soft. Add apple cider to skillet and bring to a simmer. Return pork medallions to pan, cover and simmer for 5 minutes.

This simple dish can be paired with almost any side vegetable and starch. Risotto and butternut squash are good, as are wild rice and broccoli.

> *Ideas are great arrows, but there has to be a bow. And politics is the bow of idealism.*
> —Bill Moyers

# James Fenimore Cooper

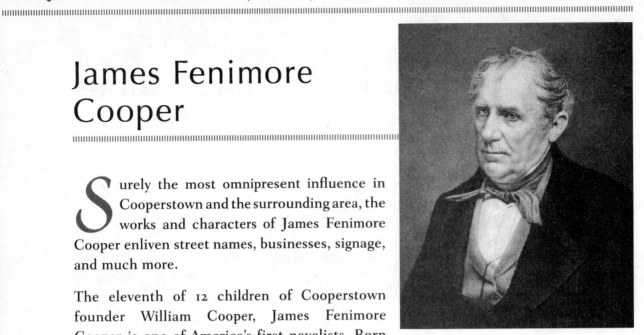

S urely the most omnipresent influence in Cooperstown and the surrounding area, the works and characters of James Fenimore Cooper enliven street names, businesses, signage, and much more.

The eleventh of 12 children of Cooperstown founder William Cooper, James Fenimore Cooper is one of America's first novelists. Born in New Jersey in 1789, he spent his formative years in the "western wilderness" that is now Otsego County. Cooper was educated by tutors and, for a time, at Yale. There he admittedly learned little and was eventually expelled for, among other practical jokes, teaching an ass to sit on his professor's chair. Cooper's early adulthood was spent at sea where he gained experiences that would later appear in his novels.

Still not of the literary life at age 30, he reportedly began writing at the urging of his wife, heiress Susan Augusta De Lancey. Supposedly upon reading a disappointing novel, he announced that he could write a better story. His wife challenged him to do so and thus *Precaution* was born. An unsuccessful first effort, it led to a prolific career nonetheless. His five Leatherstocking novels include *The Pioneers*, set in frontier Cooperstown and introducing his American hero, Natty Bumpo; *The Last of the Mohicans*, widely considered his best work, *The Prairie*, *The Pathfinder*, and *The Deerslayer*.

Although a successful writer, he was personally controversial and encountered much derision from contemporaries in Cooperstown and abroad. Writers Honore de Balzac and Victor Hugo admired him, but later in the nineteenth century, Mark Twain took Cooper's writing to task in his amusing *Fenimore Cooper's Literary Offences*.

James Fenimore Cooper's statue stands in Cooper Park, next to the National Baseball Hall of Fame and Museum. He is buried, with his family, in Cooperstown at Christ Episcopal Church.

# Pease Porridge
## Era of James Fenimore Cooper

*Pease porridge hot, pease porridge cold*
*Pease porridge in the pot, nine days old*
*Some like it hot, some like it cold*
*Some like it in the pot, nine days old*

A thick soup based on dried peas and other ingredients, such as potatoes, onions, dried herbs, and smoked pork (if you were flush) that could be stored over the winter. It could simmer in a fireplace cauldron for days, simply by replenishing peas, water or ale, and other ingredients as necessary. The driest, "woodiest" peas could be used in pease porridge, even, presumably, if they had to cook nine days. The nutritious, hearty, peasant fare kept many a Colonial body and soul together.

4 cups dried peas
6 peppercorns
1 or 2 onions, chopped
Smoked pork hock,
    if desired and available
Herbs, such as sage, thyme,
    lovage, summer savory, etc.

4 quarts water (part may be ale)
3 cloves garlic, chopped
3 potatoes, cubed
Maple syrup
Salt

Place peas and water or ale in a large pot with peppercorns, garlic, onions, pork if using, and herbs. Put the pot over a brisk fire and bring to a boil. Skim any foam that rises to the top. Simmer several hours, depending on age of the peas. Soaking the peas overnight will reduce cooking time.

When peas are nearly done, add potatoes and cook until they are soft. Add salt and more herbs to taste. Add more water or ale as the peas thicken, depending on your preference. Serve with maple syrup on top, for flavor. It is also much improved by the addition of a quart of good ale in place of a quart of water.

> *...no civilized society can long exist,*
> *with an active power in its bosom that*
> *is stronger than the law.*
> —James Fenimore Cooper

# *Special Orders*

## Pages for Particular Interests

# Financial Institutions with ATMs

"Where is the nearest ATM?" is a visitor's frequently asked question. Listed are some of the most convenient locations to refill coffers.

### COOPERSTOWN

Wilber National Bank
62 Main Street
607-547-9941
or
5378 State Highway 28
607-547-7222
(next to Haggerty Hardware)

Key Bank
103 Main Street
607-547-2551

NBT
62 Pioneer Street
Cooperstown, NY 13326
607-547-9971
or
Cooperstown Commons
Route 28 South
(next to Dreams Park)
607-547-8301

Leatherstocking Region Credit Union
24 Glen Avenue
607-547-5700

### EDMESTON
NBT
One West Main Street
607-965-8636
(between Cooperstown and Norwich)

### HERKIMER
NBT
399 East Albany Street
315-867-2133

### ONEONTA

Wilber National Bank
245 Main Street
607-432-1700 or
1-800-374-7980
or
2 FoxCare Drive (Route 7)
607-432-6910
(between Brooks BBQ and
downtown Oneonta)

NBT
One Wall Street
607-432-5800

Sidney Federal Credit Union
53 Market Street
877-642-7328

### NORWICH
Wilber National Bank
18 S. Broad Street
607-334-2277

NBT
52 South Broad Street
607-337-BANK

### RICHFIELD SPRINGS
NBT
194 Main Street
315-858-2800

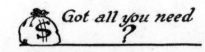
Got all you need?

# How to Preserve Children
## Banks and ATMs

"How to Preserve Children" was a favorite "recipe" from the first version of *Home Plate*. It is a gift from Janice Eichler, manager of the Wilber Bank Cooperstown branch. The bank is housed in a charming old brick building on Main Street, just across from the National Baseball Hall of Fame.

This heart-warming recipe invites creativity. Make it repeatedly.

*Ingredients*:
  One large, grassy field
  About a half-dozen children
  2 or 3 small dogs
  A pinch of brook
  Small amount of pebbles
  Add to your liking: Flowers, sun, and sky

Mix children and dogs together well and put them in the grassy field. Stir constantly.

Pour brook over pebbles. Sprinkle the field with flowers, spread under a deep blue sky and bake in hot sun. When children are thoroughly heated, remove and set to cool in a bathtub.

# Antiques
## Cooperstown to Oneonta on Route 28

Spend a few pleasant hours winding your way south on Route 28, shopping for antiques along the way. The shops are listed in geographical order, starting at the Cooperstown traffic light.

**ROBERT SCHNEIDER FINE ART**
20 Chestnut Street
Cooperstown, NY 13326
607-547-1884
*In Jordan Cottage, at the
traffic light in Cooperstown*

**HARMONY HOUSE**
6208 State Highway 28
Fly Creek, NY 13337
607-547-4071
*Just three miles north on Route 28/80,
at the Fly Creek flashing yellow light.*

**BROCKMAN ANTIQUES CENTER**
Rt. 28, RD1, Box 104
Milford, NY 13807
607-547-9192
Great smalls and more at this
multi-dealer shop. *Across Route
28 from the Dreams Park*

**WOOD BULL ANTIQUES**
Route 28
Milford, NY 13807
607-286-9021
A must-stop. Three floors of
antiques and more on the lawn.

**BROOKLYN BRIDGE ANTIQUES**
3975 State Highway 28
Milford, NY 13807
607-286-9288
Good selection of clean furniture

**GOODYEAR LAKE ANTIQUES**
Rt. 28, RD1, Box 205
Oneonta, NY 13820
607-432-9890
Architectural goods a specialty.
*From Route 28, turn right
onto Route 7. Follow it to the
flashing light and turn right.*

**COLLIERSVILLE COTTAGE ANTIQUES**
6129 State Highway 7
Colliersville, NY 13747
607-432-7427

**LETTIS AUCTIONS**
23 Reynolds Street
Oneonta, NY 13820
607-432-3935
Auction every Thursday at 5:30
PM. Turn left onto Reynolds from
Route 7, across from the cemetery
*Route 7 runs through Downtown
Oneonta as Main Street.*

**SARATOGA TRUNK**
195 Main Street
Oneonta, NY 13820
607-432-9208

# Quilting and Fibers

This is just a smattering of the fabrics and fibers available in the Cooperstown area, at easy stopping points on the way in or out of town. Most of the shops listed below offer classes. The friendly proprietors can give lots of advice about stores and sources of patterns, yarn, and fabric, as well as information about meetings and events.

**HEARTWORKS QUILTS & FABRICS**
6237 State Highway 28
Fly Creek, NY 13337
607-547-2501
heartworksquilts.com

**KNITTING IT ALL TOGETHER**
175 Main St
Oneonta, NY 13820
607-432-2154

**PIECEWORKS**
453 Chestnut St
Oneonta, NY 13820
607-431-9675

**COUNTRY FABRICS**
3200 Chestnut Street
Oneonta, NY 13820
607-432-9726

**HOLY MYRRHBEARERS MONASTERY**
Yarns, knitted goods, more
144 Bert Washburn Road
Otego, NY 13825-2265
607-432-3179
holymyrrhbearers.com

**GILBERT BLOCK QUILT SHOP**
9 Commercial Street
Gilbertsville, NY 13776
607-783-2872

**SEW NICE**
6142 State Highway 12, North Plaza
Norwich, NY 13815
607-334-2477
sewnicenorwich.com

**THE YARDSTICK**
115 Plaza Lane Suite 8
Cobleskill, NY 12043
518-234-2179
yardstickny.com

**THE QUILTBUG QUILT SHOP**
On Route 20, between
Cooperstown and Albany
169 Main Street
Esperance, NY 12066
888-817-6577
518-875-9400
quiltbug.com

# Historic Properties

Experience the Cooperstown area's compelling history tangibly with a tour of numerous preserved buildings. This is only a sample of the American history that stands in diligently tended bricks and mortar. Many of the homes, post offices and churches are maintained through the vigorous efforts of dedicated volunteers. Most listed here are on the National Register of Historic Places. Some entire areas, including Otsego Lake, Gilbertsville and much of Cooperstown are also listed. Check with the Cooperstown Chamber of Commerce or Otsego Tourism for more information and directions.

### COOPERSTOWN

Hyde Hall and Hyde
Hall Covered Bridge
*Adjacent to
Glimmerglass State Park*
hydepark.org
607-547-5098

Otsego County
Courthouse
193 Main Street
Cooperstown, NY 13326
607-547-4321

Old Middlefield
Schoolhouse
District No. 1 School
County Route 35
Cooperstown, NY 13326
607-547-9515
middlefieldmuseum.org

Fly Creek Historical
Society and Museum
208 Cemetery Road
Fly Creek, NY 13337
fcahs.org

### ONEONTA

Swart-Wilcox House
*The oldest house
in Oneonta*
Junction of Wilcox
Avenue and Henry
Street (next to
Riverside School)
Oneonta, NY 13820
607-433-2795

Fairchild Mansion
(Masonic Temple)
Queen Anne style
318 Main Street
Oneonta, NY 13820

Old City Hall
Municipal Building
238-242 Main Street
Oneonta, NY 13820
607-432-6450

George Wilber Mansion
11 Ford Avenue
Oneonta, NY 13820
607-432-2070

### MILFORD

David Sayre House
and Store
7 North Main Street
Milford, NY 13807
davidsayrehouse.com
607-286-7038

### GILBERTSVILLE

Major's Inn and
Gilbert Block
Commercial Street
Gilbertsville, NY 13776
artmakers.com
607-783-2967

### SCHENEVUS

Twentieth Century Steam
Riding Gallery No. 409
aka Schenevus Carousel
Schenevus Fireman's
Carnival (third
weekend of July)
Schenevus, NY 12155

# New York State Apple Muffin
## Swart-Wilcox House

*T*he last two residents of the Swart-Wilcox House were bachelor brothers, Fred and Mert Wilcox. As they grew older and less agile, they "rented" the trees in their orchard to local families who worked on the railroad. Most were recent immigrants, living in crowded apartments. The nearby supply of fresh apples was very popular.

This apple muffin recipe was featured at the Phoebe's Fall Applefest in 2004.

### Muffin Topping
½ cup chopped walnuts
½ cup brown sugar
¼ cup flour

1 teaspoon cinnamon
1 teaspoon grated lemon peel
1 to 2 tablespoons melted butter

### Muffin Base – Dry Ingredients
2 cups flour
½ cup granulated sugar
1 ½ teaspoons cinnamon
⅛ teaspoon nutmeg
½ teaspoon salt

¾ cup brown sugar
2 teaspoons baking soda
½ teaspoon cloves
½ cup chopped walnuts

### Muffin Base – Wet Ingredients
2 cups NYS cooking apples, coarsely chopped
4 ounces cream cheese, cut in small cubes

½ cup raisins
3 eggs, slightly beaten
½ cup melted butter
½ teaspoon vanilla

Make muffin topping first and set aside. To make the base, combine dry ingredients in a large mixing bowl. In a separate bowl combine wet ingredients. Thoroughly stir wet and dry ingredients together, but do not over mix. Portion batter into greased or lined muffin pans, sprinkle with topping and bake 20-25 minutes at 375 degrees.

*Recipe courtesy of Helen Rees, President of the Friends of Swart-Wilcox House Museum.*

# Walking Tours

Walking tours are a great way to learn the intricacies of this richly historic area, with well-informed guides retelling the wonderful, human details that make every area's individuality come alive. They can answer those frequently asked questions, such as "Why is the Hall of Fame in Cooperstown?" and "What's Leatherstocking?" or even "How much snow do y'all get up here?" Learn the highly interesting backgrounds of many Cooperstown buildings, places, characters, even ghosts! The following guides add entertaining scope and narrative to your visit, from a local's perspective:

**COOPERSTOWN WALKS**
Chuck D'Imperio
cooperstownwalks.com

**CANDLELIGHT GHOST TOURS**
Bruce Markusen
cooperstownghost.com
607-547-8070

**GUIDED TOURS OF COOPERSTOWN**
Paul Kuhn
607-547-6181

# Golfing

*T*he Cooperstown area's rolling green topography makes gorgeous, and often challenging, golf courses. The links listed below can meet any player's demands, from the weekend warrior to the professional.

## COOPERSTOWN AREA

Leatherstocking Golf Course
at Otesaga Resort Hotel
*Championship Course*
60 Lake Street
Cooperstown, NY 13326
800-348-6222
otesaga.com

Otsego Golf Club
144 Pro Shop Drive ·
(Off of Highway 80)
Springfield Center, NY 13468
607-547-9290

Meadow Links Golf Course
476 County Route 27
Richfield Springs, NY 13439
315-858-1646
meadowlinks.com

## OUTSIDE COOPERSTOWN

Courses at Turning Stone
Resort and Casino
*Championship and PGA Courses*
5218 Patrick Road
Verona, NY 13478
800-771-7711
turningstone.com

Seven Oaks Golf Course
*A Robert Trent Jones course*
Colgate University
Hamilton, NY 13346
315-824-1432
sevenoaksclub.com

Stonegate Golf Course
500 County Highway 19
West Winfield, NY 13491
315-855-4389
stonegategc.com

# Water Activities

O f all the resources richly endowed to this beautiful area, the abundant waterways are the most precious. All have names, from the gorgeous lakes (fortuitously left by convenient glaciers), to the merest trickle of streams, and their importance is never underestimated. Come and enjoy these glimmering treasures and honor them; take photographs and memories; leave good will and respect.

### COOPERSTOWN VICINITY LAKES

Otsego Lake
*Headwaters of the Susquehanna River and "Glimmerglass" to James Fenimore Cooper.*

Canadarago Lake
*On Route 28 North, near Richfield Springs.*

Gilbert Lake
*Five miles north of Laurens*

Goodyear Lake
*On Route 28 South, near Oneonta*

### RECREATION

Glimmerglass Queen Excursions
  10 Fair Street
  Cooperstown, NY 13326
  607-547-9511
  lakefrontmotel.com

C.P.'s Charter Service
Full and half-day fishing
  574 County Route 29
  Richfield Springs, NY 13439
  315-858-3922
  biggamehuntingny.com

Paddle Shack
River Kayak Rentals
  2882 State Route 28
  Portlandville, NY
  607-434-6666
  thepaddleshack.com

Sam Smith's Boatyard
Otsego Lake Rentals
  6098 State Highway 80
  Cooperstown, NY 13326
  607-547-2543
  samsmithsboatyard.com

Time Out Boat Rentals
  6714 State Highway 80
  Cooperstown, NY 13326
  607-287-7737
  cooperstowndreams.com

Dave Rees Marine
  Boat Rentals
  2385 Route 28 South,
  at Goodyear Lake
  Oneonta, NY 13820
  607-431-9978

Cooperstown Bass Guides
  Allan Green
  113 Pioneer Street
  Cooperstown, Ny 13326
  607-434-3871
  cooperstownbassguides.com

### PARKS AND BEACHES

Fairy Spring Park
  Located on County Route 31
  Cooperstown, NY 13326
  cooperstownny.org

Gilbert Lake State Park
  18 CCC Road
  Laurens, NY 13796
  607-432-2114
  nyparks.state.ny.us

Glimmerglass State Park
  1527 County Route 31
  Cooperstown, NY 13326
  607-547-8662
  nyparks.state.ny.us

Three Mile Point
  Located 3 miles east on
  State Route 80
  Cooperstown, NY 13326
  cooperstownny.org

# The Non-Baseball Shopper's Guide to Cooperstown

Cooperstown hosts much more than baseball memorabilia shops, though walking Main Street is a heady adventure for the fan. Baseball motifs are applied to everything from bats and bobbleheads, to baby rompers and earrings. Cooperstown commerce is far more diverse, of course. Starting at the National Baseball Hall of Fame, follow this guide and find the varied, intriguing merchandise of Cooperstown.

### MAIN STREET TO PIONEER STREET (VILLAGE FLAG POLE)

Cooperstown General Store
*Practically everything*

Cooperstown Book Nook
*Books and gifts*

Davidson's Jewelry and Augur's Books
*Books, gifts, jewelry*

Straws and Sweets
*Gifts, candies, fine chocolate*

Where to eat on this block:
*Triple Play Café*

### PIONEER STREET
*Shops on either side of the Village flag pole*

Purple Star Boutique
*Contemporary ladies fashions*

Cooperstown Wine and Spirits
*Wine and spirits*

Stone House Gifts
*Home accents and gifts*

Christmas Around the Corner
*Holiday ornaments and decorations*

Where to eat on this block:
*Foo Kin John Chinese*
*Village Bagels*
*Red Nugget Ice Cream*
*Cooley's Stonehouse Tavern*

## MAIN STREET BETWEEN PIONEER AND CHESTNUT

Riverwood
*Eclectic gifts and toys*

CVS Pharmacy
*General merchandise and drugs*

LadyBug
*Gifts, home accents, ladies fashions*

Tin Bin Alley
*Gifts, fudge, artware*

Ellsworth and Sill
*Classic ladies fashions*

Muskrat Hill
*Life is Good products*

Willis Monie Books
*Antiquarian books and ephemera*

Metro Fashions
*Ladies fashions*

Where to eat on this block:
*Danny's Market*
*Doubleday Cafe*
*Nicoletta's*
*TJ's Place: The Home Plate*
*Alex and Ika*

## DOUBLEDAY COURT

Essential Elements
*Salon, fashions, jewelry*

Cooper Country Crafts
*Handmade by local talent*

Factory Outlet
*Clothing at great prices*

Dog Wild Canine Supply
*Goods for dog and cats*

Diastole
*Americana country ware*

Metro Cleaners
*Dry cleaning and laundry*

Where to eat:
*Double Dip*

## MAIN STREET TO RAILROAD AVENUE

Schneider's Antiques
*Antique smalls and furniture*

Main Street Video
*Video and DVD rental*

Clip Joint
*Hairstyling*

Little Bo' Tique
*Children's toys and clothing*

*Be sure to also visit the attractive gift shops at the Otesaga Hotel, Fenimore Art Museum, The Farmers' Museum Shop, and Todd's General Store at The Farmers' Museum.*

# The Shops Around the Corner
## Railroad Avenue in Cooperstown

Don't miss the storefronts on Upper Main and Railroad Avenue, just three blocks from the Cooperstown traffic light, west on Main Street. You'll find diverse shopping and personal service, neatly packaged in nostalgic charm.

### MOHICAN FLOWERS
Find beautiful plants and flowers beautifully arranged, to buy or send. Unique gifts, too.

### MAIN STREET BED AND BREAKFAST
A premium B&B, conveniently located on Main Street, central to all of the Upper Main and Railroad Avenue shops and just a short stroll to the National Baseball Hall of Fame.

### BRUCE HALL BUILDING SUPPLIES
Cooperstown thrives on this long-established shop. Find hardware, paints, plumbing supplies, tile, lumber, and much more.

### RADIO SHACK
Located just inside Bruce Hall, the convenient electronics store is another linchpin of daily village life. Great if you need batteries or a cell phone charger!

### THE COPY SHOP
Quick, efficient and friendly, Linda Flynn meets business demands for copies and more, and also shipping services, in case you buy more than you can pack!

### SPURBECK'S GROCERY
The last of the once many Mom-and-Pop Cooperstown grocery stores, the Smith's offer deli sandwiches, NY store cheddar, groceries, cold ones to go, and great history.

### AGWAY
Every small town in rural America needs a feed store. This one supplies nursery stock, gardening tools, clothing, pet needs, and house and garden gifts, too. Complete with in-store pet cats.

### THE SAGE CENTER
The shop is filled with wonderful herbs and natural mixtures for mind and body. Books, oils, and information about the harmony of natural plants.

### DEPOT DELI
Great sandwiches for breakfast and lunch, and coffee anytime, salads and the daily news, too. A local favorite.

# How Do You Say That?

The Otsego County area place names boast a rich Native American history and the influence of Dutch and other European settlers. Below is a phonetic guide to pronouncing a few of the sometimes-puzzling names bestowed on our geography.

Canadarago Lake – CANADA-RA-GO

Canajoharie – CAN-A-JO-HAIR-EE

Chenango – SHE-NANG-O

Delhi – DELL-HIGH

Norwich – NOR-WICH

NYSHA – KNEE-SHA

Oneida – OH-NY-DA

Oneonta – OH-KNEE-ON-TA

Otego – OH-TEE-GO

Otesaga – OH-TUH-SAGA

Otsego – OTT-SEE-GO

Schenevus – SKIN-KNEE-VUS

Schoharie – SKO-HAIR-EE

Schuyler Lake – SKY-LER Lake

Susquehanna – SUSS-KWE-HAN-NA

Unadilla – YOON-A-DILL-A

Worcester – WUSS-TER

An Iroquois Indian Village

# One Stop Shopping

*I*n the era of mass production, mass marketing and global economies, Savor New York believes in the fundamental good that results from buying the wares of our neighbors. Below are a number of area merchants who carry a significant variety of well-made, unique local products. Buy local; *it matters*.

## COOPERSTOWN/ FLY CREEK

Cooper Country Crafts
2 Doubleday Court
Cooperstown, NY 13326
607-547-9247

Cooperstown Cheese Company
Route 28 at Oxbow Road
Milford, NY 13807
607-286-7722
cooperstowncheesecompany.com

Cooperstown Farmers' Market
Pioneer Alley
Cooperstown, NY 13326
607-547-6195

Cooperstown Natural Foods
61 Linden Avenue
Cooperstown, NY 13326
607-547-8613

Fly Creek General Store
State Route 28
Fly Creek, NY 13337
607-547-7274

## GILBERTSVILLE

Gilbert Block Quilt Shop
9 Commercial Street
Gilbertsville, NY 13776
607-783-2872

## ONEONTA

Artisan' Guild
148 Main Street
Oneonta, NY 13820
607-432-1080

Da'Vida
179 Main Street
Oneonta, NY 13820
607-434-1962 Phone (00-1) 607-434-1962
davidafairtrade.org

Oneonta Farmers' Market
Main Street Plaza
Oneonta, NY 13820
607-437-0158

Regional Visitors Center
4 South Main Street
Oneonta, NY 13820
607-433-1453

## HERKIMER

Gems Along the Mohawk
800 Mohawk Street
Herkimer, NY 13350
315-717-0077 or
1-866-716-GEMS (4367)

# Food for Thought

## Area Artists and Authors

# Home Plate Artists

### ALYSSA KOSMER

A young artist whose future is strewn with stars, Alyssa returns with another stunning cover for Savor New York with *Home Plate: The Culinary Road Trip of Cooperstown.* She created the eye-catching cover for the first version of *Home Plate,* as well as the beautiful, bountiful art print, *Savor New York.* Alyssa may be contacted through savorny.org.

### RICHARD S. DUNCAN

An Upstate native, Richard is the Cooperstown area's premier photographer. His dramatic and sensitive work is featured in his coffee table books, *Otsego Lake… Past and Present,* and *Cooperstown.* His books and photography are available through NYSHA and in local shops. He returns to *Home Plate* with more heartfelt portrayals of our region's farming foundation. Contact Mr. Duncan at PO Box 616 Cooperstown, New York. 13326-0616

### ED JOHNSON

Renowned contemporary folk artist and Cooperstown resident Ed Johnson generously shares his work *Open Up the Earth…Let It Grow* in the *Home Plate Road Trip* book. A prolific artist since 1983, Mr. Johnson captures views of daily life in the country and in rural villages. His busy, colorful compositions are alive with joyful activity. Mr. Johnson's work is on display throughout the country and internationally. He may be contacted at: The Studio and Gallery of Lillyknoll in the Field, PO Box 1193, County Road 26, Fly Creek, NY 13337. 607-547-5695

### DIANE HOWARD

In the same spirit of another Upstate folk artist, Anna Mary Moses, local painter Diane Howard captures area rural life in her own style. She shares one of her many New York winterscapes with *Home Plate.* Diane is a Cooperstown native and the daughter of 1930's Major League pitching star Vernon "Whitey" Wilshere. Art and baseball are family traditions (Diane's mother painted and her brother is an artist) and both are apparent at her enterprise, TJ's Place: The Home Plate shop and restaurant on Main Street in Cooperstown. She may be contacted there, 607-547-4040.

# The Smithy-Pioneer Gallery

When William Cooper established Cooperstown in the late eighteenth century he needed, first and foremost, an apothecary and a blacksmith. The apothecary, George Pomeroy, married Mr. Cooper's daughter Anne; the blacksmith established himself on Pioneer Street. The apothecary shop* is long gone, but the blacksmith's shop is still where it has been since 1786.

Shadows of the former industry remain, but the forging and farrier's equipment have been replaced with area artists' fine creations. Three floors and a garden are the venues that serve the Cooperstown area's creative energy. The third floor hosts history exhibits; the second floor of the gallery celebrates their mission, which includes fostering community interest in art and encouraging cooperation of those engaged in artistic endeavors. The first floor, the site of the original blacksmithing, presents contemporary art and hosts special events. This gallery opens to the small, quiet oasis that is the Sculpture Garden.

Scores of artists of almost every type are a part of the Smithy-Pioneer Gallery. Landscape painting, grand metal sculpture, excellent pottery, watercolors and more are beautifully represented.

The Gallery was established, fittingly, by William Cooper's descendant, Dr. Henry S. F. Cooper in 1957 and is dedicated to him.

55 Pioneer Street
Cooperstown, New York 13326
607-547-8671
smithypioneer.com

*The apothecary is gone, but the Pomeroy House still stands, at the corner of Main and River Streets.*

# Tara's Garlic Hummus
## The Smithy-Pioneer Gallery

It's a wonderful thing to know how to make hummus. This easy, versatile puree of chickpeas (aka garbanzo beans and ceci beans) and tahini is inexpensive and can easily be whipped together at a moment's notice. The chickpea base is nutritious and eagerly accepts a variety of additions, such as red peppers, mushrooms, olives, cumin or cayenne, or whatever your imagination contributes. The ingredients can be kept on hand and a food processor makes this recipe a snap.

2 garlic cloves
1 can chickpeas
1 heaping tablespoon tahini
1 tablespoon soy sauce
1 tablespoon balsamic vinegar
½ teaspoon Tabasco
3 tablespoons lemon juice
½ teaspoon salt
¼ cup olive oil
½ cup vegetable oil

*Garlic*

Assemble all ingredients within easy reach of the food processor. Turn processor on and drop garlic cloves through feed tube. Add the remaining ingredients, except oil. Pulse until ingredients are blended, scraping sides of bowl with spatula, as necessary. With the processor running, slowly add oils in a steady stream, adding more oil if necessary. Adjust salt and lemon to taste.

Serve with raw vegetables, tortilla chips, pita wedges or French bread. Hummus can be used for sandwiches and for thickening soups. It will keep up to a week refrigerated and it can be frozen.

# Performing Arts in the Cooperstown Area

Commedia dell'arte arpeggio, soliloquy – all beautiful words that fall gracefully from the tongue and represent parts of performances that tug the human heartstrings. Afterall, what is art but our attempt to make tangible that which meager words define poorly at best? Music and stage have long been the venues used to identify, express and try to grasp what it means to be human. Listed here are the organizations of area talent which use their respective art to portray the human soul, with all of its humor, torments, joys, foibles and glories.

Check the company's respective websites or call the Cooperstown Chamber of Commerce, 607-547-9983, for more information.

## CATSKILL SYMPHONY ORCHESTRA

P.O. Box 14
Oneonta, NY 13820
607-436-2670
catskillsymphony.org
Performances take place on
the State University of New
York-Oneonta campus

## COOPERSTOWN CHAMBER MUSIC FESTIVAL, INC.

P.O. Box 230
Cooperstown, NY 13326
877-666-7421
cooperstownmusicfest.org
Performances take place at various
venues during June, July and August

## COOPERSTOWN CONCERT SERIES

PO Box 624
Cooperstown, NY 13326
607-547-1812
cooperstownconcertseries.org
Performances take place at various
venues during September-April

## FOOTHILLS PERFORMING ARTS CENTER

24 Market Street
Oneonta, NY 13820
foothillspac.org
Hosts a variety of shows, including
concerts, plays and musicals

## GLIMMERGLASS OPERA

P.O. Box 191
Location: 7300 State Highway 80
Cooperstown, NY 13326
607-547-2255
glimmerglass.org
The Opera's season runs during
July and August each summer

## LEATHERSTOCKING THEATRE COMPANY

189 Cemetery Road
Fly Creek, NY 13337
607-547-1363
leatherstockingtheatre.org
Performances are held during July
and August at historic Hyde Hall
in Glimmerglass State Park

## ONEONTA CONCERT ASSOCIATION

P.O. Box 244
Oneonta, NY 13807
607-432-0147
external.oneonta.edu/oca/
Performances are held at various
locations around Oneonta

## ORPHEUS THEATRE

P.O. Box 1014
31 Maple Street
Oneonta, NY 13820
607-432-1800
orpheustheatre.org
Broadway favorites performed
September through May, with Musical
Theatre workshops available year
round for adults and children.

# The Written Word

The fertile Cooperstown region produces prolific authors whose topics include: reflections on Upstate life, historical figures, baseball, fiction, gorgeous photo collections, travel, food, scandal, medicine, ghost stories, and more. There is no other perspective quite like primary source accounts from those who know an area's nuances and intriguing details. Look for the following publications in local shops and bookstores.

## COOPERSTOWN IN WORDS AND PICTURES

*Home Plate : The Culinary Road Trip of Cooperstown*
*Home Plate: The Traveler's Food Guide to Cooperstown and Otsego County, New York*
Brenda Berstler

*Cooperstown*
*Otsego Lake, Past and Present*
Richard S. Duncan photography

*The History of Cooperstown in Vintage Postcards*
*The History of Troy in Vintage Postcards*
Brian Nielsen and Becky Davidson-Nielsen

*From Fly Creek: Celebrating Life in Leatherstocking Country*
Jim Atwell

*Eva Coo, Murderess*
Niles Eggleston

*Cooperstown, Otsego and the World...*
*As Seen by the Badger*
Bob Seaver

*A Trip through Leatherstocking Country*
David A. Siegenthaler

*Dear Bert: Selected Letters Written by Grace Kull to her Sister-in-law*
Grace Kull

*Cranks from Cooperstown*
*Area bicycling routes*
Dennis Savoie

## BASEBALL

*Unhittable: Baseball's Greatest Pitching Seasons*
Gabriel Schechter

*The Kansas City A's & The Wrong Half of the Yankees*
Jeff Katz

*Hank Aaron: A Biography*
Charlie Vascellaro

*Line Drives: 100 Contemporary Baseball Poems*
Tim Wiles and Brooke Horvath, editors

*Roberto Clemente: The Great One*
*A Baseball Dynasty: Charlie Finley's Swingin' A's*
Bruce Markusen

## CEMETERIES AND GHOSTS

*Great Graves of Upstate New York*
Chuck D'Imperio

*Things That Go Bump in the Night*
Favorite ghost tales by Louis C. Jones

*Leatherstocking Ghosts:*
*Haunted Places in Central New York*
Lynda Lee Macken

*Classic Ghost Stories*
Bill Bowers, editor

*A Collection of Epitaphs, Family Plots*
*and Small Cemeteries in the Town of*
*Otsego*
Sherlee Rathbone and Cathy A. Rose

*Inscriptions from the Middlefield*
*Baptist Cemetery*
Dominick J. Reisen

## CHILDREN'S

*Winterfest with Abby & Cooper*
*Abby's Search for Cooper*
Paula Burns

*Police Cat*
Enid Hinkes

*Curse of the Raven Mocker*
Marly Youmans

*My Dad is a Freemason*
Richard Vang

## FICTION

*Eat the Document*
*Lightning Field*
Dana Spiotta

*Haunted House of the Vampire*
Bruce Markusen

*Cooperstown*
Eugena Pilek

## LOCAL COMMUNITIES

*Images of America: Oneonta, Oneonta*
*Then and Now, Reminiscing Across the*
*Valleys, Volumes 1-6 Images in Sports:*
*Soccer in Oneonta*
Mark Simonson

*Recollections of an Early Mill Town*
(Toddsville)
Lawrence W. Gardener

## OTHER INTERESTS

*The Clinton Comets* (hockey)
Jim Mancuso and Fred Zalatan

*Lymphedema: A Patient's Guide*
Patricia A. Lewis, MSN, FNP

*Oakhurst: The Birth & Re-birth of*
*America's First Golf Course*
Paula DiPerna and Vikki Keller

*Bring Me the Ocean* (nature)
Rebecca A. Reynolds

Books and more Books

# *Area Events and Local Reference*

# Cooperstown Area Annual Events

*L*isted here are only some of the special activities that draw people to the Cooperstown area. Sports, music, art, a wide variety of agri-tourism events, and more are celebrated. The Cooperstown Chamber of Commerce can provide more details about any of the festivities. Contact them at 607-547-9983 or visit cooperstownchamber.org.

### FEBRUARY

Winter Carnival (three day celebration)

SnowFest (three day celebration)

*These much welcomed winter break festivals take place on consecutive three-day holiday weekends; Martin Luther King Day and Presidents Day.*

### MARCH

Sugaring Off Sundays – The Farmers' Museum

Classic maple farm breakfasts served every Sunday
in March, celebrating the new tappings.

### APRIL

Epicurean Festival

*Yearly tasting party from the area's best restaurants and producers,
plus an auction to benefit the Catskill Area Hospice*

OH-Fest

*A rock concert and street fair in Neahwa Park, Oneonta,
the collaboration of SUNY-Oneonta, Hartwick College,
and the City of Oneonta officials and businesses.*

### MAY

Hall of Fame Game and Parade

*The annual meeting of two Major League Baseball teams
playing at legendary Doubleday Field in Cooperstown.*

General Clinton Canoe Regatta

*Canoeists compete for the best time in this 70-mile race down the
Susquehanna River every Memorial Day Weekend (since 1963).*

Annual Antique Auto Show & Flea Market – Chenango
County Fairgrounds, Norwich

*Featuring about 1200 antique cars, an annual event
on Memorial Weekend since 1965*

Earth Festival at Milford Central School

*Honoring, celebrating, and protecting the rural land we treasure.*

## JUNE

White Nights Ultimate Frisbee Tournament
*A co-ed Frisbee tournament on the beautiful grounds of the Brewery Ommegang*
Annual Benefit Horse Show
*Presented by The Farmers' Museum, Cooperstown*
Annual Antiquarian Book Fair
*A booklover's slice of Heaven; at the Clark Sports Center in Cooperstown*

## JULY

4th of July Parade, Barbecue and Concert – Springfield Center
*Norman Rockwell himself could not have painted a more American scene…*
Grand Old 4th Barbecue and Ice Cream Festival at The Farmers' Museum
*… unless he painted this one.*
Annual Otsego Lake Festival
*Honors the heritage and value of Otsego Lake. Cooperstown*
Belgium Comes to Cooperstown
*Brewery Ommegang celebrates its heritage with the
country's biggest Belgian-style beerfest.*
Hall of Fame Induction Weekend
*Cooperstown's biggest weekend, celebrating the National
Baseball Hall of Fame's newest members.*

## AUGUST

Dancing Veggie Farm Garlic Festival
*Garlic, garlic everywhere at the Ainslie Barn in Fly Creek*
Hop Picker's Picnic and Ball – The Farmers' Museum
*Recognizes and celebrates the role of hops in Cooperstown history*
Leatherstocking Sheep Dog Trials
*One of the best-loved events of the summer*
House Tour and Luncheon to benefit the Susquehanna SPCA
*A most delightful afternoon spent for the good of our canine and feline friends.*
Annual Glimmerglass Triathlon
*At Glimmerglass State Park, Otsego Lake*
National Soccer Hall of Fame Induction Ceremony Weekend
*Celebrating America's finest players of the world's game*
Chenango County Blues Festival – Fairgrounds in Norwich
*Featuring blues headliners from around the country, since 1992*

### SEPTEMBER

Labor Day Arts and Crafts Show
*Dozens of juried crafters at the Clark Sports Center Grounds, Cooperstown*

Susquehanna Garlic Festival
*The annual celebration of the wonderful, odiferous bulb*

Autumn Harvest Festival at The Farmers' Museum
*Great harvest displays, exhibits and food. A two-day event.*

OmmeFest at Brewery Ommegang
*Belgian food, beer and music*

### OCTOBER

PumpkinFest (some years the last days of September)
*The Pumpkin theme applied to everything from food to sailing. One of Cooperstown's biggest events.*

Waffles and Puppets
*Brewery Ommegang celebrates its birthday and all are invited!*

### NOVEMBER

Adorn-A-Door Wreath Festival – Cooperstown Art Association
*Silent auction of Holiday wreaths designed by local artists and businesses*

### DECEMBER

Candlelight Evening at The Farmers' Museum
*A beloved Cooperstown holiday tradition...*

Cooperstown Victorian Stroll
*...And another well-loved and well-attended tradition*

# Helpful Resources

For more information while you visit, or if you are relocating to this handsome, historic area, the organizations listed here are immensely helpful.

*Welcome*

**BASSETT HEALTHCARE**
One Atwell Road
Cooperstown, NY 13326
607.547.3456
1-800-BASSETT
bassett.org

**A.O. FOX HOSPITAL**
1 Norton Avenue
Oneonta, New York 13820
607-432-2000
aofoxhospital.com

**COOPERSTOWN CHAMBER OF COMMERCE**
31 Chestnut Street
Cooperstown, NY 13326
607-547-9983

**COOPERSTOWN/OTSEGO TOURISM**
242 Main Street
Oneonta, NY 13820
Phone: 800-843-3394
VisitCooperstown.com

**CHERRY VALLEY**
**CHAMBER OF COMMERCE**
Cherry Valley, NY 13320
607-264-3755
cherryvalleyny.com

**CHERRY VALLEY HISTORICAL SOCIETY**
49 Main Street
Cherry Valley, NY 13320
607-264-3303
cherryvalleymuseum.org

**OTSEGO COUNTY CHAMBER**
12 Carbon Street
Oneonta, NY 13820
607-432-4500
otsegocountychamber.com

**SHARON SPRINGS**
**CHAMBER OF COMMERCE**
Sharon Springs, NY 13459
518-284-2996
sharonspringchamber.com

**WORCESTER HISTORICAL SOCIETY**
144 Main Street
Worcester, NY 12197
607-397-1700
worcesterhistoricalsociety.org

**CORNELL COOPERATIVE EXTENSION**
123 Lake Street
Cooperstown, NY 13326
607-547-2536
cce.cornell.edu/otsego

**HARTWICK COLLEGE**
One Hartwick Drive
Oneonta, N.Y. 13820
607-431-4000
hartwick.edu

**SUNY-ONEONTA**
Ravine Parkway
Oneonta, NY 13820
607-
436-3500
oneonta.edu

# *Culinary Musings*

# Cooking 101

*T*he secret of good cooking is first, having a love of it... If you're convinced cooking is drudgery, you're never going to be good at it, and you might as well warm up something frozen. – James Beard

Cooking shouldn't be drudgery; nor should it be intimidating, frustrating, or a mystery. If it's any of those things, you're probably trying too hard. If you never don a toque (that crazy chef's hat) you can still be more than competent in your own kitchen. Relax and have a good time. What's more fun than playing with food?

There are two approaches to cooking. One is exact and scientific; the other is intuitive and freewheeling. Or, as Mimi Sheraton asked, "Are we going to measure, or are we going to cook?" (This underlying philosophy explains why I never took Home Economics; do we really need written instructions to make Cinnamon Toast?). There are those who never measure anything, and those who measure every ingredient, right down to a pinch of pepper. Neither method is superior to the other, and cooks usually fall somewhere along the spectrum.

If your pleasure is baked goods, veer to the more exacting side of the process. Baking takes a little more study and attention to the details that make cakes light, breads rise, pies and biscuits flaky, and cookies chewy. You can probably substitute fruits, nuts, and flavorings, but the ratio of fat to flour, sugar to eggs, and the correct use of leavening must be respected for successful results.

Cooking, on the other hand, allows much more latitude, creativity and interpretation. It is a running joke at *Savor New York* that the recipes we receive last invariably come from professional chefs. They are usually too busy creating their best dishes to think about exactly what they're using and in what amounts. We understand that to stop and write it all down is arduous, so we thank them once again.

In cooking, as with any skill, once fundamental techniques are learned, it's the infusion of your own imagination and resourcefulness that makes it fun. There's no right or wrong in your kitchen domain; just because it isn't written in a book doesn't mean your creation won't be spectacular. The world might never have known potato chips if a Saratoga diner had been less demanding for increasingly thinner fried potatoes, and the exasperated Saratoga chef had not responded with see-through slices, fried crisp and golden.

Buying quality ingredients is more than half of the recipe for culinary success. Get to know your local providers and farmers' markets. Good cheese and eggs, fine fruit, great bread, and colorful vegetables can practically stand alone, with no work at all. "Fast food" is a bogus term; it is generally neither fast, nor is it food, by any discerning definition. Grilled chicken or fish, steamed or sautéed vegetables, good bread and a glass of wine makes an elegant and nutritious meal in about 15 minutes, far less time than driving, idling, and waiting for the fatty, overly salted stuff.

If your kitchen has been little more than a coffee stop to this point, try seeing it from a new point of view. Pick up a copy of the classic, *The Joy of Cooking*, find a favorite cooking program, or ask your mother; cooking needn't be fancy or dramatic to be fabulous. Keep it simple, keep it fresh, and keep it enjoyable. BB

### Cinnamon Toast

Toast slices of good bread

Spread with butter while hot

Sprinkle with a mixture of sugar and a little cinnamon

# Kitchen Equipment

*W*ell begun is half done.
–Mary Poppins

No artist or craftsman can work without the right tools. What you need in your kitchen will depend on what you like to cook and your personal style. Aladdin's Cave of kitchen implements and gadgets is open to you and it's easy to clutter your kitchen with tools and machines you may rarely use. Keep in mind that much of the world cooks in a stone pot over an open fire. While you probably don't want to be that streamlined, avoid excess and, when it comes to what you truly need, get the best quality you can afford.

## GOOD KNIVES

Knives to a cook are like paint to an artist. They are absolutely essential. You'll need a paring knife, at least one chef's knife (preferably two, in different lengths), a carving knife and steak knives if you are a meat eater, and a long, serrated bread knife. Quality knives will last for decades, so splurge. Fifty or a hundred dollars, or more, may seem exorbitant, but it is not unreasonable for a good knife. The price per year of reliable service is great value. Take the time to hold the knife before you buy it and get a feel for the heft and balance.

No matter how expensive the knife, if it becomes dull it will be practically useless, if not dangerous. Learn to use a sharpening stone, invest in a good electric sharpener, or see if your local hardware store offers a sharpening service. NEVER put good knives in the dishwasher. The heat cycle can damage them to the extent that they literally "lose their temper" and can never again be properly sharpened.

## GOOD POTS

If knives are the paint, then pots are to the cook what the canvas is to the painter. Expensive pots aren't necessarily the best. Weight is a better guideline than price. For example, cast iron can be most reasonably priced and it is indispensable for some types of cooking, especially in the American South. (I've never seen my mother bake cornbread in anything other than a cast iron skillet).

Stainless steel pots and pans with copper bottoms make good workhorse cookware. The steel lasts for years, it cleans well, you can cook anything in it (unlike aluminum cookware that cannot be used for anything acidic, such as tomato sauce), and the copper bottoms ensure quick and even heat distribution. It is moderately priced new, and sets are frequently available at our local auction house at great prices.

### BAKING PANS

Ovenproof glass baking dishes – the 9" x 13" size is one of the most versatile baking dishes in the cupboard. An 8" or 9" square pan is handy, too.

*Muffin Tins* – a 12-cup tin is a great beginning. Get two if you make cupcakes. Consider using paper liners when making muffins. They are inexpensive, make washing the tins much easier and they keep muffins fresh longer.

*Cookie Sheets* – these are also indispensable in the kitchen. Even if you don't make cookies, you'll find multiple uses for one or two cookie sheets. Get heavy gauge ones so they will stand up to changes in heat and lots of use. Consider using parchment paper for the same reasons as paper muffin liners. Also, cookies do not stick to parchment, so you usually don't have to grease pans.

*Cake Pans* – this depends on how much you bake. Most cake recipes can be baked in muffin tins or the 9"x13" glass pan listed above. If you prefer layer cakes, you'll need 8" or 9" round pans. Again, get heavy gauge pans.

*Pie pans* – have pie pans on hand, even if you don't bake pies. They are handy for many uses, included marinating, breading cutlets and general baking.

### LIQUID AND DRY MEASURE CUPS

Do not make the mistake of using one for the other. Liquid and dry ingredients do not equally exchange. That is why there are graduated glass measuring cups for liquids and nested metal or plastic cups in increasing sizes for dry ingredients.

*Liquid* – Incredibly durable, microwave-safe glass graduated measuring cups come in a variety of sizes. The two-cup size is most useful, but get the one – cup and four-cup sizes as well.

*Dry* – Sets of four dry measure cups come in ¼, ⅓, ½ and one-cup units. If you do more than minimal baking, treat yourself and get a set of odd size cups and spoons, as well. They will save a lot of redundant measuring. Odd size cups include ⅛, , ¾, 1½ and two-cup volumes.

### MEASURING SPOONS

Many intuitive cooks never bother with measuring spoons, but if you bake or are just getting to know your way around the kitchen get a good set. If you bake, get the odd sized ones – two teaspoons, 1½ tablespoons and two tablespoons – as well.

### CUTTING BOARDS

Cutting surfaces are absolutely necessary unless you want to ruin your countertops. You'll need two types to keep meat and vegetables separate. Wood responds well to the knife blade, it absorbs heat and it's attractive. However, for poultry, meat or fish, plastic or glass is superior to wood because they can be thoroughly disinfected. Glass has its drawbacks because the knife blade slides a bit on contact and it is noisy.

### WOODEN SPOONS

Time-honored and historically proven, wooden spoons don't scratch or transfer heat. They're quiet, beautiful and immeasurably useful. If they have any downside, it's that they should be hand-washed. Fine cherry or maple spoons are available at Todd's General Store at the Farmers' Museum in Cooperstown. Make sure the handles are long enough to allow stirring without risking steam burns.

### HAND TOOLS

*Ladles* – perfect for getting soup out of the pot or pancake batter on the griddle.

*Flexible Spatulas* – these are practically indispensable. Make sure to get the type resistant to high heat, so you can use them either hot or cold.

*Can Opener* – a good manual kind is fine, unless you have a touch of arthritis.

*Corkscrew* – there is no other way to open a wine bottle.

*Vegetable Peeler* – economical and great for peeling carrots, cucumbers, zucchini, etc., it is perfect for shaving chocolate and hard cheeses.

*Bottle Opener* – most bottle tops these days twist off, but occasionally you'll still need the double-ended bottle opener, sometimes known as a "church-key." One end removes bottle caps, the other pierces cans of juice or evaporated milk.

*Box Grater* – the four-sided type will take care of most grating needs.

*Colander* – necessary for rinsing fruits and vegetables and draining pasta.

*Whisk* – indispensable for smooth sauces and gravies.

*Salad Spinner* – great for drying greens.

### MACHINES

*Electric Mixer* – not an absolute necessity, but if you've ever beaten egg whites into meringue by hand, you'll certainly appreciate one. Invest a bit on a heavy-duty electric mixer. Get one with enough power to meet the challenges of heavy batters and doughs.

*Toaster* – even the most basically equipped kitchen needs a toaster. Get one with slots wide enough to accommodate bagels and other thick breads.

*Food Processor* – whether or not you consider a food processor a necessity depends on how much you cook. They are wonderful work and time savers and do many laborious jobs in a matter of minutes or seconds. I frequently use mine for cutting butter or organic shortening (no trans fats) into flour for biscuits, scones, etc.

*Coffee Maker* – for many, the morning pot of coffee is akin to the sun rising. There are lots of ways to brew coffee, including stovetop percolators, French presses, and electric coffee makers ranging from a few dollars to hundreds.

If you are a regular at the local gourmet coffee shop, think about investing in a coffee grinder, as well, and brewing at home. It is much more economical, even using brand name beans, and you can enjoy your favorite roast in your pajamas.

*Microwave Oven* – not an absolute necessity, but it is very convenient, especially for reheating foods and melting butter or chocolate.

*Blender* – great for smoothies and pureeing soups.

### ALSO HANDY...

*Kitchen Organization* – save immeasurable frustration by keeping the most frequently used utensils in the same spot and within easy reach.

*Your Imagination* – it is absolutely your best asset in the kitchen.

# The Stocked Pantry

*I*f you cook for one or a crowd, or whether your kitchen is spacious or tiny, you need to keep essential ingredients on hand. You can make delicious and appealing meals surprisingly quickly when basic components are at the ready. Below is a list to help you create a variety of meals and avoid the frustration of finding yourself out of something critical in the middle of preparations. This is a good framework to get you started. Have fun tailoring it to fit your own tastes.

## ON THE SHELVES

Vegetable, poultry, beef stock (in cans, boxes, concentrated paste, or bouillon cubes or granules)

Onions, Potatoes, Garlic (These three root crops are indispensable for a bounty of dishes. They store well, if kept dark, cool, and apart from each other.)

Spaghetti, or other pasta shapes

Rice, brown or white

Dried and/or canned beans

Canned tomatoes and tomato sauce

Olive Oil

Vegetable Oil

Mustard (lots of local types to choose)

Ketchup

Peanut Butter

Canned Fruits and Vegetables (your preference)

New York State Maple Syrup

New York State Honey

Chili Powder

Italian Seasoning

Choice of Dried Herbs and Spices

Salt

Pepper

## IN THE REFRIGERATOR

Butter

Cheeses (i.e. New York Cheddar, mozzarella and blue)

Milk

Eggs

Apples

Spinach

Carrots

Celery

Seasonal Fresh Fruits, Vegetables and Herbs

## IN THE FREEZER

Ice

Vanilla Ice cream

Walnuts and/or pecans

Mixed vegetables

Spinach

## THE BAKING CORNER

All Purpose Flour

Granulated Sugar

Maple Sugar

Oatmeal

Brown Sugar

Chocolate Chips

Unsweetened Baking Chocolate

Cocoa

Baking Soda

Baking Powder

Cornstarch

Cornmeal

Cinnamon

# *Index*

# Index

# How to Order

*H*ome Plate: The Culinary Road Trip of Cooperstown is a great book to help plan your trip to Cooperstown. It is the essential handbook while visiting, and it makes a great reminder of all you enjoyed while there.

To order books before or after your visit, contact Savor New York at:

Savor NY Sales
6 Westridge Road
Cooperstown, NY 13326
Phone or Fax us at 607-547-1870
Order online at www.savorny.org

Wholesale orders are welcomed and discounts apply.

Look for all of Savor New York books and New York products at savorny.org.

# Author Biography

**B**renda Berstler is an Upstate New Yorker by choice, transplanted from her native Missouri. After graduating from the University of Missouri-Columbia, she traveled extensively, living in the United States and Europe before settling in picturesque Cooperstown, New York. Given her passions for art, music, literature, country living, and baseball, Cooperstown was the obvious choice.

Brenda, her husband John, and daughter Elizabeth bought an existing bed and breakfast and immersed themselves in redecorating and filling it with appropriate antiques, capturing much of house's original history. They renamed their architecturally significant home Bryn Brooke Manor. After welcoming and advising hundreds of guests, Brenda realized that while people enjoyed their stay in Cooperstown, they didn't always get to know the Cooperstown that she treasures.

There is an old chestnut that says writers should always write about what they know. Brenda knows food and travel, and a little bit about a lot of subjects. She's brings the same broad-based knowledge that made her a *Jeopardy!* champion to her fascinating *Savor New York* books. Her *Home Plate* culinary road trip guides deliciously illuminate the Cooperstown area, with its nuances, rich history, and compelling characters. She shines the same brilliant light on local farmers and small businesses as she does The National Baseball Hall of Fame and Glimmerglass Opera, giving area guests and newcomers a full grasp of this captivating area.

The Savor New York Company was established to welcome visitors and support New York family farming, small entrepreneurs, and unique visitor attractions. A portion of the profits from the sale of Savor New York books and products benefit area community programs.